EXPLOITING THE TROPICAL RAIN FOREST
An Account of Pulpwood Logging in Papua New Guinea

MAN AND THE BIOSPHERE SERIES

MAN AND THE BIOSPHERE SERIES

Series Editor: J.N.R. Jeffers

VOLUME 3

EXPLOITING THE TROPICAL RAIN FOREST

An Account of Pulpwood Logging
in Papua New Guinea

D. Lamb

*Botany Department, University of Queensland,
Australia*

PUBLISHED BY

PARIS

AND

The Parthenon Publishing Group

International Publishers in Science, Technology & Education

Published in 1990 by the United Nations Educational, Scientific and Cultural Organization,
7 Place de Fontenoy, 75700 Paris, France—Unesco ISBN 92-3-102646-1

and

The Parthenon Publishing Group Limited
Casterton Hall, Carnforth,
Lancs LA6 2LA, UK—ISBN 1-85070-266-7

and

The Parthenon Publishing Group Inc.
120 Mill Road,
Park Ridge
New Jersey, 07656, USA—ISBN 0-929858-20-4

© Copyright **Unesco 1990**

Printed and bound in Great Britain by
Butler and Tanner Ltd., Frome and London

British Library Cataloguing in Publication Data

Lamb, D.
 Exploiting the tropical rain forest : an account of pulpwood logging in Papua
New Guinea. – (Man and the biosphere series; v.3).
 1. Tropical rain forests. Environmental aspects
 I. Title II. Unesco III. Series
 333.75
 ISBN 1-85070-266-7

Library of Congress Cataloging-in-Publication Data

Lamb. D.
 Exploiting the tropical rain forest : an account of pulpwood logging in Papua
New Guinea / D. Lamb.
  p. cm. — (Man and the biosphere series: v. 3)
  Includes bibliographical references (p.).
  ISBN 0-929858-20-4 (Parthenon): $45.00 (U.S.)
 1. Gogol Timber Project (Papua New Guinea). 2. Clearcutting—Papua New
Guinea—Madang Province. 3. Rain forests—Papua New Guinea—Madang
Province—Management. 4. Pulpwood industry–Papua New Guinea–Madang
Province. 5. Wood chips industry–Papua New Guinea–Madang Province.
 I. Title. II. Series: MAB (Series) : 3.
 SD657.P26L36 1990   90-67′4
 333.75′15′099573–dc20   CIP

SERIES PREFACE

Unesco's Man and the Biosphere Programme

Improving scientific understanding of natural and social processes relating to man's interactions with his environment, providing information useful to decision-making on resource use, promoting the conservation of genetic diversity as an integral part of land management, enjoining the efforts of scientists, policymakers and local people in problem-solving ventures, mobilizing resources for field activities, strengthening of regional co-operative frameworks. These are some of the generic characteristics of Unesco's Man and the Biosphere Programme.

Unesco has a long history of concern with environmental matters, dating back to the fledgeling days of the organization. Its first Director General was biologist Julian Huxley, and among the earliest accomplishments was a collaborative venture with the French Government which led to the creation in 1948 of the International Union for the Conservation of Nature and Natural Resources. About the same time, the Arid Zone Research Programme was launched, and throughout the 1950s and 1960s this programme promoted an integrated approach to natural resources management in the arid and semi-arid regions of the world. There followed a number of other environmental science programmes in such fields as hydrology, marine sciences, earth sciences and the natural heritage, and these continue to provide a solid focus for Unesco's concern with the human environment and its natural resources.

The Man and the Biosphere (MAB) Programme was launched by Unesco in the early 1970s. It is a nationally based, international programme of research, training, demonstration and information diffusion. The overall aim is to contribute to efforts for providing the scientific basis and trained personnel needed to deal with problems of rational utilization and conservation of resources and resource systems, and problems of human settlements. MAB emphasizes research for solving problems: it thus involves research by interdisciplinary teams on the interactions between ecological and social systems; field training; and applying a systems approach to understanding the relationships between the natural and human components of development and environmental management.

MAB is a decentralized programme with field projects and training activities in all regions of the world. These are carried out by scientists and technicians from universities, academies of sciences, national research laboratories and other research and development institutions, under the auspices of more than a hundred MAB National Committees. Activities are undertaken in co-operation with a range of international governmental and non-governmental organizations.

Further information on the MAB Programme is contained in *A Practical Guide to MAB*, *Man Belongs to the Earth*, a biennial report, a twice-yearly newsletter *InfoMAB*, MAB technical notes, and various other publications. All are available from the MAB Secretariat in Paris.

Man and the Biosphere Book Series

The Man and the Biosphere Series has been launched with the aim of communicating some of the results generated by the MAB Programme to a wider audience than the existing Unesco series of technical notes and state-of-knowledge reports. The series is aimed primarily at upper level university students, scientists and resource managers, who are not necessarily specialists in ecology. The books will not normally be suitable for undergraduate text books but rather will provide additional resource material in the form of case studies based on primary data collection and written by the researchers involved; global and regional syntheses of comparative research conducted in several sites or countries; and state-of-the-art assessments of knowledge or methodological approaches based on scientific meetings, commissioned reports or panels of experts.

The series will span a range of environmental and natural resource issues. Currently available in press or in preparation are reviews on such topics as control of eutrophication in lakes and reservoirs, sustainable development and environmental management in small islands, reproductive ecology of tropical forest plants, the role of land/inland water ecotones in landscape management and restoration, ecological research and management in alpine regions, structure and function of a nutrient-stressed Amazonian ecosystem, assessment and control of non-point source pollution, research for improved land use in arid northern Kenya.

The Editor-in-Chief of the series is John Jeffers, until recently Director of the Institute of Terrestrial Ecology in the United Kingdom, who has been associated with MAB since its inception. He is supported by an Editorial Advisory Board of internationally-renowned scientists from different regions of the world and from different disciplinary backgrounds: E.G. Bonkoungou (Burkina Faso), Gonzalo Halffter (Mexico), Otto Lange (Federal Republic of Germany), Li Wenhau (China), Gilbert Long (France),

Ian Noble (Australia), P.S. Ramakrishnan (India), Vladimir Sokolov (USSR) and Anne Whyte (Canada). Bernd von Droste and Malcolm Hadley of Unesco's Division of Ecological Sciences are *ex officio* members of the board.

A publishing rhythm of three to four books per year is envisaged. Books in the series will be published initially in English, but special arrangements will be sought with different publishers for other language versions on a case-by-case basis.

To Margaret

CONTENTS

ACKNOWLEDGEMENTS

I would like to acknowledge the help I have received from many people in writing this book. I am especially grateful to Bob Bruce, former Regional Forest Officer, Madang, for many discussions over a number of years but I would also like to particularly thank Kevin White, Ian Whyte, Jack Noah, John Gardner, Alan Ross, Arenaso Masapuhafo, Don McIntosh, Jim Cavanaugh, K. Satoh, Scott Leslie, David Skelton, Peter Driscoll, Simon Saulei and many former colleagues in the Department of Forests for sharing their knowledge of the Gogol Timber Project with me. I am also grateful to Andrew Yavieb, former Director of the Department for allowing access to the Deparment's records.

The Gogol Timber Project formed part of Unesco's Man and Biosphere programme and I would like to thank Dr. Malcolm Hadley for his support and help in facilitating a return visit to Madang to complete the last chapter.

Drafts of the manuscript were read in whole or in part by Bob Bruce, Peter Driscoll, Jack Ewel, Ross Florence, Alan Ross, Simon Saulei, David Skelton, Len Webb and Kevin White. I am indebted to them for their comments; they may not agree with all that is in this final version and, needless to say, any errors are mine and not theirs.

Parts of the manuscript were written while visiting the Institute for Resource and Environmental Studies, Dalhousie University, Canada and the Botany Department, University of Florida, U.S.A. I am grateful to both for providing me with a temporary home. The manuscript was typed by Jocelyn Gamack, Sue Bertram and Missy Costantini while the maps and figures were drawn by Lyn Jessup. To all these I offer my sincere thanks.

My years in Papua New Guinea were memorable ones and I will always be grateful to the people of that marvellous country for my time there. This book represents, in part, an attempt to repay them, especially the people of the Gogol Valley. I hope that in some small way they may find it useful.

Finally, I would like to thank my wife Margaret, and my son, Andrew, for their support and understanding during my frequent mental absences over the several years it took to complete this book.

ABBREVIATIONS AND NOTES

BDU:	bone dry unit (BDU = 1.546 m³), a commonly used measure of woodchip volume.
CIF:	cost, insurance and freight
CSIRO:	Commonwealth Scientific and Industrial Research Organization – the Australian national research organization
Department of Forests:	Originally a separate Government Department but in 1978 it was reduced to a branch in the Department of Primary Industries and renamed the Office of Forests. In 1981 it was elevated once more to full departmental status. In the text it is always referred to as the Department of Forests. Note that in 1978 when Provincial Governments were formed throughout Papua New Guinea, each created its own Division of Forests to administer forestry matters leaving the national body with little but an essentially regulatory and research role. From that time administration of the Gogol Timber Project passed to the Madang Provincial Government.
FOB:	free on board
GTP:	Gogol Timber Project – includes forests in the Gogol, Naru, Gum and North Coast timber rights purchase areas.
GRC:	Gogol Reforestation Company – owned by Jant (51%) and the Papua New Guinea Government (49%).
JICA:	Japan International Co-operation Agency
K:	Kina – the Papua New Guinea currency In 1975 K1 = A$1 = US$1.26 = Yen 383 In 1981 K1 = A$1.30 = US$1.47 = Yen 323 In 1986 (December) K1 = A$1.54 = US$1.03 = Yen 166
MAI:	Mean annual increment

MTWG:	Madang Timber Working Group – formed in 1972 from representatives of the Departments of Forests, Agriculture Stock and Fisheries, Land Survey and Mines and the Department of the Chief Minister and Development Administration. It also had seven elected representatives of people of the timber area
PMV:	public motor vehicle – usually a truck with seats; a common form of public transport in rural areas
PNG:	Papua New Guinea
TRP:	Timber rights purchase — a method by which the government could purchase from landowners the rights to harvest the timber on their land; usually valid for 30 years. The Gogol Timber Project was made up of four TRP's.

PREFACE

The question underlying the whole of this book is — how might a society obtain the maximum benefit from its rain forests? In other words, what is an appropriate way to manage a tropical rain forest? The traditional objectives of foresters have been to develop a sustained yield of timber and other forest products and to use natural regeneration after harvesting wherever possible. Neither objective has been achieved in many rain forests. On the one hand, there have been a host of silvicultural difficulties such as high species diversity, poor ecological knowledge about many of these species, slow growth rates of most commercially desirable species and large amounts of damage to residual trees or seedlings in forests caused by logging. On the other hand there have been economic constraints such as a small proportion of the tree species being commercially acceptable, small volumes of such timber per hectare, long cutting cycles as a consequence of slow growth rates and a need for large areas of forest land to be set aside to sustain the whole enterprise (Leslie 1977).

There have been some successes, perhaps most notably in Malaysia, but, since the 1960's, there has been an overall decline in the number of tropical rain forests being managed according to a defined silvicultural prescription based on any real ecological knowledge.

Thus, Budowski (1982) has written,

'There is not a single example (in Central America or the Caribbean) of a large area of natural primary forest that has been, over an extended period of time, managed as part of what might be called a well-conceived management plan. The same forest may have been exploited several times over the years but not always for the same species and the result has always been degradation.'

In too many countries, it seems the insatiable demand for agricultural land and the apparently limited economic prospects of managed tropical rain forest have combined to ensure their gradual demise. At the same time, there has been increasing concern at an international level about the future of the world's rain forests. Some of those concerned believe much rain forest clearing is simply poor land use planning; rain forests are not being cleared because of a shortage of agricultural land but because it is politically easier to do this than increase the productivity of existing agricultural lands. Others argue that rain forest clearing is economically unwise since many of the benefits provided by rain forests to society have not been included in traditional economic analyses. Finally, there are those who express what might be best described as an ethical concern that a vital part of the world's Heritage is being eroded.

Papua New Guinea has large areas of tropical rain forest. On a simple area per capita basis, it is the best endowed country in the Asian–Pacific region. However, it has never been able to develop an appropriate way of managing its forests to help finance national development. For many years, it exploited these forests by selectively logging the few commercially saleable species. There was no real knowledge of the silvicultural consequences of much of this logging and the economic benefits were not especially high. Yet it seemed difficult to develop alternative approaches.

In the late 1960's, however, a change in paper making technology occurred that was to lead to a radical new approach to logging in Papua New Guinea. Paper chemists devised a way of using a mixture of tropical hardwood species woodchips to make paper pulp. This change in technology opened the way to overcome the problems of species diversity and commercial acceptability. Instead of selective logging, whole areas of forest could be clear-felled, giving a much higher wood yield. The cleared land could be replanted with fast-growing tree plantations as well as be used for various agricultural projects. The then Colonial Administration of Papua New Guinea seized upon the new approach, believing it would not only make more efficient use of the national forest resource, and diminish existing marketing problems, but would also lead to rural development in areas otherwise too isolated to benefit from the very gradual spread of Administration services. The Gogol Timber Project (GTP), as it came to be known, commenced in Papua New Guinea in 1973.

Not surprisingly, the GTP has attracted criticism on a variety of counts. Some have argued that the GTP is an ecologically disastrous form of forest exploitation and that such complete harvesting can have profoundly destructive effects on tropical forest ecosystems (Webb, 1977; Richardson, 1977). Others believe the effect of the logging on village people living within the forest has been harmful (De'Ath, 1980). Still others think the economic benefits of such large-scale operations to Papua New Guinea are outweighed by the costs, and that other less intensive forms of forest utilization are to be preferred (Jonas, 1976; Richardson, 1981). A concern implicit in all these criticisms is that pulpwood logging may become more widespread, both in Papua New Guinea and elsewhere in the tropical world, and that complex species-rich rain forest may be replaced by some degraded forms of forest or even grasslands.

My involvement with the Gogol Timber Project began in 1972 when I joined the Papua New Guinea Forestry Department. It continued, on and off, until 1977 when I left Papua New Guinea, although I have managed to visit the Project on several occasions since then. As part of an organization charged with administering such a project, it is all too easy to become less open to outside criticism than one should. Too often a 'we' versus 'they' atmosphere can develop. In fact, I believe that many of the critics have performed a useful service in highlighting some of the failures and difficulties associated with the Project. But, at the same time, I do not think many of these critics have been able to offer realistic or feasible alternative approaches to the fundamental dilemma facing a developing country forced to exploit its forests for export income. In many cases, the criticisms have been too superficial and simplistic for the complex intermix of biology, economics, sociology and politics that was involved at the time the project commenced.

It is important that projects such as the Gogol Timber Project do receive critical attention because only then might countries such as Papua New Guinea resolve the question I posed at the beginning of this Preface. But for this to occur it is necessary that the background to particular decisions and events be known and that the consequences be documented. My purpose in writing this book is to try to do this.

I am only too aware that my account has a number of gaps. Many were inevitable since the project was a commercial operation and not a grandiose experiment in tropical forestry. Ecologists, biologists and sociologists were not present to describe and interpret all the events that took place. I am especially conscious that my description of the effect of the project on villagers living in the area may be badly incomplete, though I hope it is not entirely wrong. De'Ath (1980) provides another view of the impact of the project on villagers. As will be clear later, I disagree with many of his conclusions, but his work complements my own.

The Gogol Timber Project was the first of its kind in Papua New Guinea, but it is not the only example of this radically new approach to timber harvesting. At about the time it started, a similar scheme commenced in the Pacific lowlands of Colombia at Bajo Calima (Carton de Colombia 1985; Frisk, 1978). It, too, is a clear-felling operation with the objective of producing wood pulp, but, unlike the Gogol Timber Project, the rain forest there is being allowed to regenerate to provide a second harvest at some time in the future and is not being replaced by plantations. Whether these two projects are to become useful management models for other tropical rain forests remains to be seen.

As the noted English writer, G.K. Chesterton, has said,'The disadvantage of men not knowing the past is that they do not know the present'[1]. For that reason, my account of pulpwood logging in the Gogol Valley begins with a brief account of the last years of the colonial era leading up to Papua New Guinea's independence in 1975. In this, I describe the economic and political context in which forest management decisions leading to the Gogol Timber Project were being made. My account then turns to a description of the Gogol Valley and, finally, to the project itself.

The Gogol Timber Project took place during an unusual time in Papua New Guinea's history. The disruptions and change taking place in the Gogol Valley were only a part of the much greater changes occurring elsewhere in the country. In ending this Preface, I can do no better than quote Sack (1974) who described the period as a

'....transitional period between colonialism and independence, when old problems appear in a new light and new problems begin to cast their shadows, when the old white administrators are not yet quite 'out' and the new black politicians are not yet quite 'in', when important decisions are imminent but have not yet been made, when the wheels of history turn with dazzling speed but history itself is suspended, when idealism and pragmatism, cynicism and naiveté, radicalism, conservatism mingle in the most amazing way and when almost everything seems possible and almost nothing real'.

Note

1. G.K. Chesterton (1933) 'On St. George Revivified', All that I Survey. Methuen, London.

CHAPTER 1

PAPUA NEW GUINEA — A BACKGROUND

INTRODUCTION

A traveller flying across Papua New Guina (PNG) cannot help being struck by the extent of the tall closed forests that cover most of the country. They dominate the lowlands and clothe much of the mountainous interior. There are areas of savanna and grassland, but it is the rain forests that characterize the landscape. They have always been one of the country's most important natural resources. Many Papua New Guineans live as shifting cultivators and depend on these forests for many of their day-to-day requirements. More recently, logging companies have also begun harvesting timber. Therein lies a dilemma. Can a local dependence and a national economic gain both be sustained in the same region? How should Papua New Guinea manage this valuable natural resource?

By most international standards, PNG is a young country. For many years it has been viewed by outsiders as an exotic out-of-the-way place, 'primitive' and somewhat mysterious. It was only late in the nineteenth century that different parts of the country were separately colonized by Britain and Germany[1]. Both colonies were later taken over by Australia. These events passed unnoticed by much of the population, many of whom remained hidden from outsiders until the 1930's. Then some of the last great exploration trips of the Twentieth Century took place into the mountainous interior. Since that time, many changes have occurred. Most people still live in rural villages and practice traditional forms of agriculture. But an increasing proportion of these villages are linked by an expanding road network. Further, the inhabitants produce various cash crops and sell these in the international market. Towns, airports, schools and hospitals are widespread and most parts of the country are connected by a sophisticated electronic communications system. Within the life times of many Papua New Guineans, a social and economic revolution has taken place.

This chapter gives a background description of PNG and its people as well as of the colonial administration in place before independence in 1975.

1

Its purpose is to provide the social and political context in which forest policy decisions were made that eventually led to the GTP and to explain something of the overall approach towards development that was taken in these early years in PNG.

A BRIEF GEOGRAPHY

Papua New Guinea occupies the eastern half of the island of New Guinea which, after Greenland, is the world's largest island. It stands on the Sahul Shelf, a submarine extension of the Australian continent and lies a few degrees south of the equator. Papua New Guinea is, in fact, made up of a mainland and nearly 600 other islands and archipelagoes which extend eastward to include the northern portion of the Solomon Islands. The mainland of New Guinea is dominated by a long central cordillera stretching from the Vogelkof Peninsula in the west to Milne Bay in the east, a distance of nearly 2400 km. This length, coupled with the general height of 2000–4000 m, makes it one of the great mountain systems of the world. Mountains cover much of the island and some 29 per cent of the topography is above 1000 m in altitude. Outwash from these mountains has helped form some of the large alluvial flood plains which occupy over 15 per cent of the land area. Many of these are flooded for several months of the year. Swamps and other poorly drained areas are common (Table 1.1).

New Guinea lies on a very mobile part of the earth's crust since it straddles the junction between the Papuan and Pacific tectonic plates. The relative movement of these and their associated boundary zone is complex but it appears that the Papuan plate is tending to rise over the Pacific plate. As a result of this, uplifting earth movements and volcanoes are common (Fig. 1.1, 1.2).

Although PNG lies wholly within the tropics, the climate varies because of the high mountain areas and the orientation of the land mass with respect to the regional wind pattern. Temperatures and humidities in the

Table 1.1 Topographic features of the PNG environment

Environment	Area (million ha)	Percentage
Coastal beach ridges and flats	0.2	0.5
Coastal and saline swamps	0.7	1.5
Freshwater swamps mainly 0–50 m	5.1	11.0
Alluvial plains and fans 0–500 m	6.9	15.0
Foothills and mountains below 1000 m	19.9	43.0
Mountains, including montane valleys 1000–3000 m	11.6	25.0
Mountains above 3000 m	1.9	4.0
Total land area	46.3	100

Source: after Paijmah (1976)

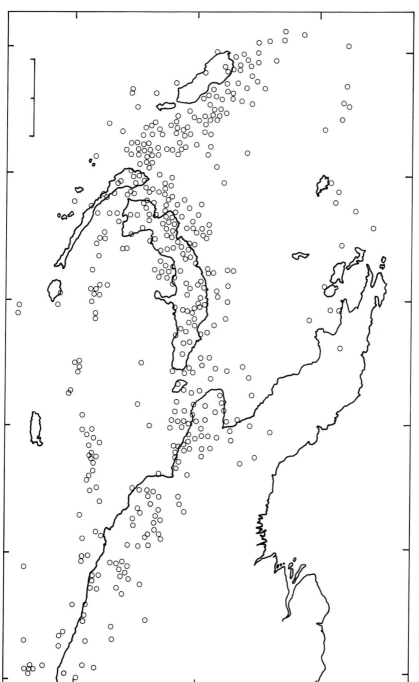

Fig. 1.1 Map showing earthquakes occurring between 1958 and 1968

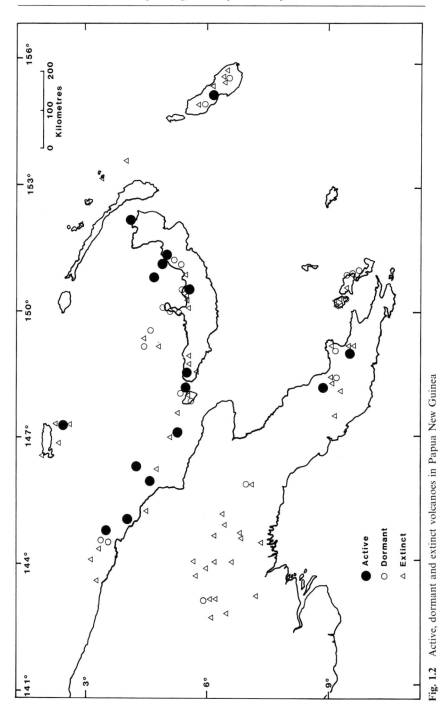

Fig. 1.2 Active, dormant and extinct volcanoes in Papua New Guinea

4

lowlands are typical of the humid tropics throughout the year, but the rainfall varies, being seasonal in some localities and more or less constant through the year in others. The average rainfall is generally high and amounts of 2000–3000 mm are common. In some places, averages of up to 7600 mm have been reached (e.g. the south coast of New Britain).

The vegetation of the country is primarily forest, although there are large areas of grassland and swamp (Table 1.2). Most of the lowlands are dominated by rain forest, with some smaller areas of savanna woodland occurring in drier zones. The lowland rain forests are extremely rich in species and have varying regional dominance of particular species. Above about 1000 m, the lowland forests give way to montane forest, and, in the higher areas above about 3900 m, an alpine flora of tussock grasses, tree ferns and shrubs occur (Paijman 1976).

Communications are limited. Some of the larger river systems are navigable for considerable distances, but the road network is still in its infancy. A good road runs from the coastal town of Lae, which is the second largest town in the country, into a network in the highlands. But this network is isolated from most of the other larger coastal towns, including the capital Port Moresby, because of the terrain. Road building in the lowlands is often difficult and expensive because of the many large rivers and their tendency to change course. As a result, many parts of the country, including those with the major forest resources, are extremely isolated.

Papua New Guinea's economy is essentially agricultural, and subsistence agriculture is the principal economic activity of most of the inhabitants. The money economy has diversified since the Second World War to include cash crops, mining, fisheries and forest products. Agriculture for cash has been dominated by copra, coffee, tea, cocoa and palm oil. The mining industry was initially based on gold mining but is now dominated by

Table 1.2 Types of plant communities in PNG

Community	Area (million ha)
Alpine	0.1
Montane forest	1.1
Lowland montane forest	9.1
Lowland forest	19.9
Grassland	3.0
Regrowth and gardens	2.4
Savanna	2.6
Swamp woodland	1.3
Swamps	2.2
Mangroves	4.5
	46.2

Source: McIntosh (1974)

5

several large copper mines. With the exception of agriculture, most of this economic activity is dominated by foreign investors.

PEOPLE OF PAPUA NEW GUINEA

The human population was estimated in 1971 to total 2.5 million and have an average annual growth rate of 2.6 per cent. Together, these people speak about 700 distinct languages. Prehistorians believe humans may have lived in PNG for as long as 25 000 years and to have practised shifting cultivation for 9000 years. This date for agricultural activity is quite early by world standards (Golson 1977). Perhaps because of this long history, the diversity of languages, and the formidable geographic barriers – mountains, rivers and swamps – there is a considerable social heterogeneity amongst Papua New Guineans. Social systems include patrilineal, matrilineal, and ambilineal descent systems. Social obligations amongst kinship groups are complex and members of a group generally have an obligation to assist and support others who might need help. This has carried over into the new urban communities where wantoks — a pidgin word describing members of one's clan — help mitigate the problem of new migrants, as well as assist in diffusing the earnings of those with employment.

In contrast to the diversity of languages and social systems, all Papua New Guineans share a common strong attachment to their land. The relationship is interwoven not only with agriculture and food gathering but also with kinship, political, economic and religious institutions. Burton-Bradley (1973) has described it thus:

'His land is the place where he was born, where he was subject to primary encultural, where he has lived the most important aspects of his life, where the values of his cultural-linguistic group have been constantly reinforced and where, in most instances, he may die. As he grows up, he learns it is the place where his ancestors preceded him, and to which they may return, thus giving the land a magico-religious sanction. It is the place where his children's children will follow. At the psychological level, it is clearly an extension of the concept of self.'

Land is commonly owned by a kin group rather than an individual, and an individual's use of land is a consequence of this membership of the group. Individuals are not permitted to alienate any part of the group estate. Harding (1972) notes that, in fact, it is more common for individuals to transfer themselves by affiliating themselves with a different kin group. As will be made clear later, this pattern of land ownership has played a significant role in the development of forestry in PNG.

The borders of land claimed by a clan may not be precisely defined but are generally known by reference to some natural feature such as river, rocks or groves of trees. A clan's land usually consists of a number of scattered and irregularly-shaped blocks varying considerably in size. These

Plate 1   Many people live in small communities of three or four houses

are interspersed amongst the land of other groups. The per capita land
holdings of each group can differ quite markedly in area. If the ratio of
people to land becomes too unfavourable, resources can be redistributed
in some communities by allowing a certain flexibility in the prevailing rules
of land tenure or by forcing other communities out of disputed areas
(Bulmer 1982).

Land and land ownership has been a constant source of dispute
throughout PNG. Some disputes are settled amicably but in many cases
war is the only answer. This means there is no permanent settlement, since
the defeated group will usually not accept its defeat but waits until it is
strong enough to renew the fighting. The gradual imposition of colonial
law reduced the extent of warfare but did nothing to resolve the problem.
Orken (1974) has summarised the arguments and counter arguments as
follows:

Group A: 'We are strong and defeated and dispersed the other side before
the Government came. We have controlled and used this land ever since
and were in control of it when the first white man came into the area. We
have established gardens on the land, planted trees there and have houses
there. Our burial and ceremonial grounds are situated there. In recent
years, we have planted coffee and peanuts on the land and we have disposed
of some of it to the Administration and we were the only ones to get paid
for it. It is ours and has been ours since the white man came.'

Group B: 'It is true that Group A dispersed us from this land before the
white man came. But we would have recovered the land if it had not been

7

for the patrol officers who came and stopped us from fighting and defeating our enemies. That is our traditional way. The other side has only been on this land since the Administration came. We have been on it for many years before that time. We also have burial grounds and ceremonial places on the land and we also planted many of the trees on it.'

Some of the implications and consequences for government land use policies of these patterns of land ownership will be discussed further in a later section.

The effect of colonisation on Papua New Guineans has been profound. For the first time, many have had the chance to travel beyond the valleys in which they and their fathers have always lived. The developing lingue franche — pidgin, and to a lesser extent Motu in the south — have allowed a much wider communication. For many, medical services have improved the quality of their lives. Road and cash crops have brought a new wealth to some and caused all to reappraise the value of their land and its natural resources. Education has benefited some and caused dissatisfaction with the old ways for others. Many younger people with some education have left the villages for the towns. In many places, old ways and old values have begun to change. And yet for the majority of people still living in villages much is probably as it always was. One's primary allegiance is to the clan and then to the village. The multiplicity of languages and cultures has, until recently, screened people from any self-recognition as a nation.

THE COLONIAL ADMINISTRATION

Following the First World War, the League of Nations appointed Australia to administer the old German colony under the name of the Mandated Territory of New Guinea while a separate Australian administration continued to control the old British colony then known as Papua. This dualism continued until the Second World War. In 1949, a joint administration of the Territory of Papua and New Guinea was approved by the United Nations, and this continued until independence in 1975.

Prior to the Second World War, the pace of development and change in PNG was relatively slow. Few roads were built and economic change was limited. Most people continued to live as they always had. Following the war, there was a sense of gratitude amongst Australians towards the help they had received during the fighting in New Guinea and a renewed recognition of the strategic importance of the country to Australia. In 1945, the Australian Minister for Territories, E. J. Ward, when moving in Parliament that the PNG Provisional Administration Bill be read a second time, said,'This Government is not satisfied that sufficient interest has been taken in the Territories prior to the Japanese invasion (during World War II), or that adequate funds had been provided for their development and the advancement of the native inhabitants. Apart from the debt of gratitude that the people of Australia owe...(my) Government regards it as its bounded duty to further...the advancement of the natives...(this) can be achieved only by providing facilities for better health, better education and for a greater participation by the natives in the wealth of their country and eventually in its government.'

In fact, development was slow to occur because of political changes and administrative indecision. The Australian Government changed in 1949 following an election and there were two new ministers responsible for PNG in the next 2 years. An Administrator was appointed in Port Moresby, the main town of PNG, but all major policy decisions were made in Canberra. (This continued to be the case until self-government[2] in 1973.) In the absence of government initiatives, expatriate entrepreneurs gradually took control of the economy. For the most part, this was dominated by copra production and gold mining.

In 1951 all this changed. A new Minister, P.M.C. Hasluck, was appointed and his time in office between 1951 and 1963 is characterized by his policy of gradualism and uniform development. Hasluck believed it was important that development should occur at a similar rate throughout the country even though some parts, having had a longer history of contact with Europeans, might have to mark time until others caught up. Government patrols started to move out into these areas still remaining unexplored, and a network of patrol posts and police stations was set up to establish administrative control. Economic development was sought via agricultural training in the villages and European settlers were encouraged to produce new export crops and to act as models for the people to emulate.

The World Bank report and economic development

In 1963, Hasluck was replaced as the Minister responsible for PNG in the Australian Government and the policy changed. Hasluck had commissioned a study by the World Bank (more formally, the International Bank for Reconstruction and Development) to recommend development strategies for PNG. A team visited in 1963, and its final report was delivered in 1964 and generally accepted by his successor, C.E. Barnes. The report had a major effect on economic planning, including forestry planning, in PNG. It suggested moving the emphasis away from gradualism and uniform development towards policies aimed at promoting rapid economic growth in those areas with the greatest potential. (International Bank for Reconstruction and Development 1965). The report pointed to the need to make PNG less dependent on Australian aid funds (then running at about A$50 million or 66 per cent of total Administration receipts). It suggested increased government spending on agriculture, forestry, transport and education. This was to be carried out at the expense, if necessary, of programmes such as health. Besides stressing the need for higher education and more responsibility for Papua New Guineans, it also gave emphasis to the importance of overseas investment and continued expatriate partici- pation in development strategies. It argued that Papua New Guinea would benefit ultimately from individuals taking advantage of expatriate initiatives and expatriate directed agricultural extension services. In a later review, the World Bank (1976) commented that the earlier policy under Hasluck of uniform development had had the effect of discouraging local political leadership and entrepreneurial talents and that this hampered the already difficult process of stimulating active local involvement in the developing modern society.

The changes initiated by the World Bank report were given added momentum by a 5-year plan published in 1968 entitled 'Programmes and Policies for the Economic Development of Papua New Guinea'. In the view of one later commentator, this called for nothing less than 'an economic revolution' in PNG that would disrupt the lives of people in order to give them better opportunities (Downs 1980). It was carried out almost in full, and, in the course of the programme, many nationals made money and became as profit conscious as expatriates. Others without the land assets or living in areas still remote from the main centres did not.

The main elements of the plan were a continuation of the policies recommended by the 1964 World Bank report, but with more stress placed on development by indigenous people. The plan aimed to obtain increased smallholder production in a variety of existing cash crops such as copra, cocoa, rubber, as well as establishing estates for crops such as tea and palm oil. The national beef cattle herd was to be nearly tripled and increased support was to be given to fisheries, mineral exploration and forestry.

The effect of these policies was a steady increase in the growth of the economy. Over the 10-year period between 1959/60 and 1969/70, export trade increased from $38 million to $94 million. However, most of these exports continued to be agricultural crops such as coffee, copra and cocoa which were dangerously subject to the vagaries of international prices. (Table 1.3). During the same period, imports also grew and the trade gap widened. In 1959/60, exports were 90 per cent of imports, but, by 1969/70, this had declined to 44 per cent (Fig. 1.3). Overall, therefore, PNG continued to depend on a substantial aid grant from Australia. This aid increased from around A$26 million in 1959/60 to over A$93 million in 1969/70, and then represented about a half of all Administrative receipts (Table 1.4). As will be seen later, the size of the trade deficit and aid grant had important consequences for the development of forest policy in PNG.

First pressures for self-government

Throughout this period, the Government and Opposition in the Australian Parliament had an essentially bipartisan approach towards PNG. Towards

Table 1.3   Major PNG exports during 1969–70

Item	$ millions
Coffee	20.1
Copra, copra oil	19.7
Cocoa	15.7
Timber	6.5
Rubber	2.9
Gold	0.8
Prawns, shells	0.7
Tea	0.6
Peanuts	0.6
Crocodile skin	0.5
Passionfruit extract	0.1
Other	2.9
Total Produce	71.1
Re-exports	22.6
Total Exports	93.7

Source: Department of External Territories (1971)

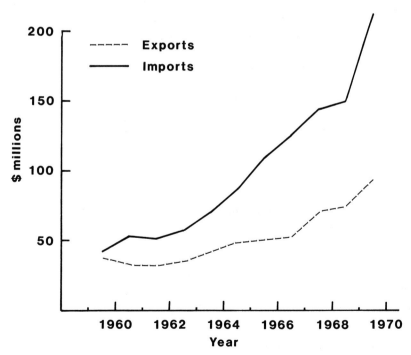

Fig. 1.3   Papua New Guinea imports and exports. Source: Department of External Territories (1971)

Table 1.4 Administration receipts between 1959/60 and 1969/70

Year	Grant from Australian Government		Internal Revenue		Loans		Total
	$ mill.	*Per cent*	*$ mill.*	*Per cent*	*$ mill.*	*Per cent*	*$ mill.*
1959–60	25.6	66	13.2	34	0.2	0.6	39.1
1960–61	29.6	65	14.9	33	0.9	2	45.4
1961–62	34.6	68	15.4	30	1.1	2	51.1
1962–63	40.0	67	18.0	30	1.9	3	60.0
1963–64	50.5	66	22.8	30	3.4	4	76.6
1964–65	56.0	62	28.0	31	6.3	7	90.2
1965–66	62.0	61	34.0	33	6.2	6	102.2
1966–67	69.8	59	42.5	36	6.2	5	118.5
1967–68	77.6	58	47.8	36	8.4	6	133.8
1968–69	87.3	58	55.1	37	7.2	5	149.6
1969–1970	99.3	49	72.4	35	32.5	16	204.2

Source: Denoon (1985)

the end of the decade, however, the Opposition Labor Party began to press for an indication that the Government had a target date for self-government in PNG. Earlier in 1960, Hasluck, as the responsible Minister, had told the United Nations that Papua would not be ready for self-government for 30 years (Webb 1960). In 1968, his replacement, Barnes, refused to set a target for even limited home rule. By this time, however, the Labor Party was in favour of granting independence as quickly as possible. The year 1968 saw elections in PNG for the second House of Assembly and the emergence of a strongly pro-independence group known as Pangu Party. This Party was led by Mr. Michael Somare who was later to become the first Prime Minister of PNG after Independence. Pangu Party in PNG and the Labor Party in Canberra were to force on the Australian Government and the PNG Administration a realization that time was running out, and that the colonial era was to end a lot sooner than had been expected only a few years earlier.

Social unrest

At the same time as these political developments were taking place, evidence of serious social unrest began to appear in several regions of PNG. Serious rioting occurred in 1969 on the island of Bougainville at the site of a major new copper mine. Even worse violence took place in the same year on the Gazelle Peninsula of New Britain, leading to the Army being placed on alert in case the police were unable to cope. These incidents led to local calls for secession and greater regional autonomy that were picked up elsewhere in PNG, especially in Papua.

It is worth briefly describing some of these events, not only because they occurred at the time that negotiations were underway that led to the GTP being established, but also because they exemplify the difficulty the Administration had in balancing national goals against local goals.

The main problem areas were as follows:

Bougainville

Copper was discovered in Bougainville in 1930, but it wasn't until the 1960's that serious exploration confirmed the existence of a massive ore body at Panguna. A decision to start mining was made in 1969, and the mine soon became the largest industrial enterprise in PNG, costing some A\$400–500 million to develop, and employing 4000 people. In a short time, the annual profits from the mine equalled half of the total revenue of PNG. Local villages looked upon the initial field work and testing on their land with suspicion. The mining legislation then in force allowed the company to go about its initial work without first obtaining the permission of the landowners. This constituted a trespass in the eyes of the villages and contributed a good deal to the friction and unrest that subsequently developed. Forceable resumption of land for the mine townsite in 1969 led to a serious confrontation between the village people and the Administration. Riot police were called in and forceable evictions followed. In the words of one senior Administration official, 'Things almost got out of control.' (Sinclair 1981).

Once the mine was built, the feeling of opposition was gradually replaced by one that Bougainvilleans should have all the royalties and taxes and not other Papua New Guineans. This attitude was promoted by a newly formed Bougainville nationalistic society known as Napidokoe Navita. The society had originally been formed to confront the Administration on land acquisition in 1969, but it now wanted to hold a referendum to ask Bougainvilleans whether they wished to remain with Papua New Guinea, or to secede and remain independent, or to secede and unite with some of the other PNG islands such as New Britain or with the nearby islands of the British Solomon Islands Protectorate. The Administration refused to hold such a referendum, so Napidokoe Navita held its own referendum in 1970 and found overwhelming support for secession. Not surprisingly, this support was ignored by the Administration. Pressure for secession continued, aided perhaps by increasing profits from the mine. At the very least, they led to rising economic expectations amongst the secessionists. The issue reached a climax in 1975 when Bougainville unilaterally declared its independence from PNG. This declaration too was ignored by the Administration and the matter was only finally resolved after PNG's independence in 1975, when a form of provincial government for Bougainville was agreed upon.

Gazelle Peninsula, New Britain

The second problem area in 1969 was on the Gazelle Peninsula and also involved land, but this time land that had already been alienated. During the period of the former German colony, the main town of the Gazelle Peninsula, Rabaul, had been the administrative centre. Nearly 40 per cent of the land in the area was acquired by the Germans, and most, but not all, converted to plantations. Natural population increases among the traditional owners, the Tolai people, led to acute land shortages at a time when the Administration was pushing for the adoption of cash crops by Papua New Guinea. The Tolais had always resented the extent to which foreigners controlled their land, and were especially upset that some of the alienated land remained unused.

In 1967, Tolai squatters occupied some of the unused land but were evicted by police. In 1969, a group formed the Mataungan Association to combat what they saw as foreign domination of their land and affairs. One immediate focal point was the newly proposed multiracial Local Government Council. The Councils were to have local people as well as expatriates, and were intended to be centres of grass roots political development. In other parts of PNG, the councils had led to racial harmony and less dependence on official advisors. The Mataungan Association decided it would oppose the Council and announced it would refuse to pay council taxes. It also organised a boycott of the first elections held in early 1969, claiming the Council was yet another device to enable Europeans to control Tolai land and affairs. A Council was elected despite the boycott, but trouble continued throughout the year. Eventually, the army was placed on alert in case the police were unable to maintain control. Scuffles and clashes between the Mataungan Association, supporters of the new Council, and the police were almost continuous after February 1971. The violence reached a climax later that year when the District Commissioner, the most senior official in the area, was murdered during a dispute involving land ownership and squatting. Such an action against so senior an administrator official was unprecedented.

The situation improved in 1972 after elections for the Third House of Assembly which led to the emergence of the *de facto* National Government led by Mr. Michael Somare. The resumption of some of the alienated land and the creation of strictly Tolai Local Government Councils eventually allowed the situation to calm.

Papua

A third group with a grievance and a strong sense of regional identity were the Papuans. Although PNG's capital, Port Moresby, was in what had been the old colony of Papua, most economic development had occurred in the former Territory of New Guinea, and many Papuans believed they had always been neglected. Since Papua had an apparently poorer agricultural potential and fewer natural resources than New Guinea, the effect of the 1964 World Bank report was to accentuate this difference. Like the Bougainvilleans, many Papuans came to believe that the Administration was more concerned with the success of foreign businessmen than with their own needs. In 1971, a group of Papuans in the House of Assembly formed a pressure group known as Papuan Action, and used the threat of secession to press for more economic development in Papua. Supporters of Papuan separation were also vocal in the third House of Assembly elected in 1972, and the Port Moresby City Council elections in 1974 resulted in a Council dominated by separatists. However, while support for greater economic development was widespread in Papua, support for separation was restricted to Port Moresby. The secessionists made a unilateral declaration of independence for Papua in early 1975, but the movement gradually lost support in later years.

Although each of these three cases had separate origins, they were all linked by a dissatisfaction with economic development at the grass roots level, and the extent to which the particular regions were seen as being disadvantaged by the economic and political policies of the Administration in Port Moresby. Two used the threat of secession to foster their objectives. All posed serious problems for an Administration increasingly aware of the possibility of self-government in the near future, and concerned with the need to maintain national unity in a society composed of groups having a prime allegiance to local communities rather than the nation. All increased pressure on the Administration to find ways of bringing economic development to the rural communities of PNG.

Land

Land ownership was at the heart of the Bougainville and Gazelle disputes, as it has been in so many situations before and since in PNG. Hasluck, when Minister in the 1950's, had been keen to change the system of land tenure from group ownership to individual ownership. The obvious advantages were that this would allow easier management and planning of larger scale land-uses, such as forestry, as well as avoiding inheritance problems when cash crops were introduced. However, little progress was made during his period in office. There were too many claims and counter claims, demarcation disputes and long delays in settlements. The Administration eventually sought overseas advice and engaged consultants having experience with similar land problems in Africa. Following the receipt of their report, and extensive debate within the Administration, four Bills were introduced into the House of Assembly in 1970. These Bills would have had the effect of individualizing customarily owned land and registering the resulting title. However, the Bills were widely condemned throughout the country and were rejected by the House. The Administration tried again in 1971, but they were rejected a second time. It was hardly surprising, given the events then going on on the Gazelle Peninsula of New Britain. The problems of land ownership and land-use planning continued to trouble the Administration after 1971, but were left for the new independent Government that was obviously soon to come.

Overseas investment

The 1964 World Bank report strongly recommended allowing overseas investment into PNG to help develop the economy. It claimed economic growth in key areas would eventually lead to an overall improvement in the welfare of all Papua New Guineans. This was essentially the trickle-down theory of development and was accepted by the Government in Australia since it more or less coincided with that Government's approach to overseas investment in Australia itself. For most of the 1960's, overseas investment in PNG was dominated by Australian companies. The emergence of political groups in PNG in favour of independence in the late 1960's, however, led some to believe that further investment by Australian or other companies could be threatened (Philips 1968). On the other hand, others believed that the Minister's refusal to announce a timetable for self-government was the primary cause of political and economic uncertainty by potential investors (Niall 1968).

In fact, it seems that a number of foreign nations were beginning to 'discover' PNG towards the end of the decade and were not too worried about the political changes. Chief amongst these were the Japanese. The initial Japanese interest was generated by groups of war veterans coming to the old battlefields and burial grounds to recover the bones of the dead and take them home. Then came individuals who the Administrator at time later described as being primarily interested in 'a fast yen.' (Johnson 1983).

Not all Japanese fell into this category, of course, and the Australian Embassy in Tokyo believed most Japanese were primarily interested in obtaining access to raw materials. In 1971, the Australian Department of External Territories reviewed the Japan–PNG relationship and concluded that 'it is clear that increased access to Japan's market will be crucial to the Territories' (of Papua and New Guinea) trading problems in the forseeable future' (Johnson 1983).

In 1972, elections for the Third House of Assembly were held which resulted in the Pangu Party, led by Michael Somare, forming a coalition with the smaller Peoples' Progress Party and winning office. The Administrator in a letter to his Minister in Canberra wrote that the Peoples' Progress Party had an orthodox capitalist approach to development and favoured a high level of overseas investment. On the other hand, he believed the Pangu

16

Party had a more socialist approach and took the view that 'economic growth *per se* has no merit, nor has foreign investment unless it can contribute to rural improvement. It is suspicious of foreign capital. There is an air of unreality in its expectation of being able to write its own terms for foreign investors and also for international aid.' (Johnson 1983).

In the event, the new Government in Port Moresby — for it was now clear that independence was only a matter of time and that the Third House of Assembly was the *de facto* Government — welcomed Japanese and other investment provided it was investment that would benefit PNG. In this, they were more bullish about relations with Japan than the Australian Government, and did not see the Japanese endangering their social and economic goals any more than Australia did. They were also prepared to renegotiate agreements entered into earlier which they believed were not entirely to PNG's benefit. The foremost of these agreements was that concerning Bougainville's copper mine. Profits from the mine had soared far beyond earlier expectations and it had become extraordinarily lucrative. Somare announced in 1972 that the Government would re-examine this agreement, a statement which Johnson believed 'did little to lower the temperature of major investors in PNG resources.' A new agreement was finally reached in 1974.

Overall, the change from the 1960's to the 1970's marked a change in the political climate and a change in attitudes towards investment. The gradualism of the 1960's and the apparent favouring of Australian invest-ment was replaced by a sense of excitement and urgency that welcomed investment from anywhere, but on particular terms. A chronology of some of these events is given in Appendix 1.

CONCLUSION

Several conclusions emerge from this overview. The first is that, when the Administration adopted the World Bank's recommended strategy for national development, it replaced its old policy of slow but uniform development by one which had the effect of leaving some people out of the development process and forcing others to shoulder a disproportionate share of the costs of achieving national growth.

The second is that, despite this new strategy, the rate of economic growth in PNG was unable to keep pace with the Administration's expenditure. Exports did increase, but the trade gap widened. Perhaps even more significantly, growth did not match the rising level of expectation among many people.

Third, the Administration began the 1960s with the belief that indepen-dence was many years away, but ended the decade with the certain knowledge that self-government, if not independence, was imminent. This meant that, towards the end of the period, political uncertainties increased and some major problems such as the matter of land tenure were left for some future national government to resolve.

All these matters affected the evolution of forest policy in PNG. Forest exploitation had always been viewed as a source of national export income and a vehicle for local rural development. The increasing pace of political change throughout the decade simply intensified the demands being placed on the country's forests. But, as the next Chapter will show, political developments were not the only factor affecting the development of forest policy.

Note 1: Papua New Guinea is on the eastern half of the island of New Guinea. The western half of the island originally formed part of the Dutch colonies of the East Indies but has subsequently become a province of Indonesia.

Note 2: With self-government, PNG became effectively independent from Australia in all matters except foreign affairs and defence. Full independence was achieved in 1975.

CHAPTER 2

THE FORESTS OF PAPUA NEW GUINEA

INTRODUCTION

Papua New Guinea lies within the region known to biogeographers as Malesia. This comprises the countries of Malaysia, Indonesia, the Philippines, PNG and the Solomon Islands to the east. The region is biologically diverse and environmentally heterogeneous. Though recognised as an entity, there are several gradients running through it. This is illustrated by the numbers of so-called demarcation lines drawn through the region. The most famous of these is'Wallace's Line' which separates western and eastern Indonesia. There is also a strong biogeographical boundary at Torres Strait between New Guinea and Australia (van Balgooy 1976). The supposed significance of these demarcation lines and the affinities of the plants and animals within Malesia have provoked much debate. The current view among plant geographers is that PNG belongs to the Indo-Malesian floral region while zoogeographers, mainly those basing their case on the distribution of animals and birds, place PNG in the Australian region (van Balgooy 1976).

From a forestry viewpoint the most interesting difference between PNG and the remainder of Malesia is the comparatively poor representation of the Dipterocarpaceae in PNG. Some genera are present (e.g. *Hopea*, *Anisoptera*) but this commercially valuable family is not as dominant as it is in the forests to the west and north. Otherwise, the forests of PNG are rich in species, with the families Combretaceae, Sapindaceae, Sterculiaceae and Anacadiaceae particularly well represented. The forests may have canopy heights over 30 m with even taller emergents over 50 m. Palms, vines and rattans are common. Above 1000–1400 m altitude, the lowland rain forest gives way to montane forest and this extends to about 3900 m. The canopy heights in these forests decrease to 15–25 m and emergents are usually absent, except in the case of *Araucaria* species. Above about 2000 m elevation, *Nothofagus* forest is common. The alpine flora above 3900 m is generally restricted to tree ferns, tussock grasses and shrubs.

AGENTS OF DISTURBANCE

The warm, humid climate of the tropical lowlands provides almost year-round growing conditions. As a consequence of this, many visitors perceive tropical lowland rain forests as being particularly stable plant communities and perhaps even primeval. But their stability is an illusion for there is mounting evidence from throughout the world that most tropical forests have been subject to numerous disturbances in the recent past and that these have greatly influenced their ecology and composition.

Evidence from PNG comes from two sources. First, palynological studies in the highlands have suggested the alpine tree line has fluctuated by several thousand meters over the last 30–38000 years due to climate changes. Between 8500 years and 12000 years ago, it was around 4000 m above sea level; i.e. 1100 m higher than at present. These movements have caused major changes to highland forests and are likely to have significantly altered lowland forests as well (Powell and Hope 1976).

Second, there are a number of current phenomena obviously influencing the forest environment. These include:

(i) Earthquakes and landslips: PNG is at the junction of the Papua and Pacific tectonic plates and has a high earthquake frequency (Fig. 1.1). Between 1958 and 1968, for example, there was an annual average of 500 earthquakes of a magnitude 4.5 to 5.5 on the Richter scale. These commonly cause widespread landslips and slumping.

(ii) Volcanoes: Volcanic activity has had a marked influence on the present environment of a large part of the country. Individual blast areas may be up to 300 km^2 and extensive areas can be affected by fumes. Pumice showers covering a radius of 24–32 km have been observed near Rabaul on the island of New Britain (K. White 1975).

(iii) Rivers: Changes in river courses, as well as alterations in drainage patterns caused by such changes, have affected large areas of forest. Stream braiding, ox bow lake formation and shingle banks are common along many lowland rivers.

(iv) Wind: PNG is not in the main cyclone area of the south west Pacific. However, cyclones such as Cyclone Hanna in 1972 which affected 42 500 ha of lowland forest on the north east coast of PNG are not uncommon and strong winds have caused local damage to forests elsewhere.

(v) Fire: There are poorly documented reports of widespread fires in lowland forest in various parts of the country, especially after severe drought periods. For example, fires are believed to have destroyed large areas of lowland rain forest near Madang (Cavanaugh 1975) and there are reports of extensive fires in the forests of east New Britain (Lane-Poole 1925).

(vi) Frost: Infrequent frost can cause substantial damage to natural

20

Plate 2 A landslip probably triggered by earthquakes in hill forest outside the southern boundary of the Gogol TRP

communities. In 1972, for example, frosts caused widespread plant death in large areas of the highlands. This included swamp forest and *Nothofagus* forest (Brown and Powell 1974).

These and other disturbances are described more fully in K. White (1975) and Johns (1986).

Such natural phenomena are, of course, not restricted to the forests of PNG. There are reports of wind damage to the rain forests of the Caribbean (Lugo *et al.* 1983), the Solomon Islands (Whitmore 1974), Sarawak (Anderson 1964), Sri Lanka (Dittus 1985) and Australia (Webb 1958); a wildfire in East Kalimantan was reported to have damaged 3.5 million ha of lowland rain forest (Wirawan 1984), and Salo *et al.* (1986) have suggested river dynamics account for much of the forest diversity in the western Amazonian basin.

Disturbances of these kinds can affect the composition of the forest and

21

if the disturbances recur frequently enough, secondary species representative of the earlier stages of successions are favoured over primary forest species more typical of late, more mature sucessional phases.

While there is no real evidence concerning the frequency of the natural phenomena described above, White (1975) noted that long-lived secondary species are a major component of many lowland forests in PNG. Some support for this suggestion, based on a number of large scale timber surveys in lowland forests, is given in Table 2.1. This shows that, of the total tree stocking, the percentages of commercially useful secondary species present in smaller diameter size classes are quite low, but that in the larger size classes, the proportions can rise to over 75 per cent. A similar case exists when the data are expressed in terms of timber volumes. In these lowland forests, between 20 and 68 per cent of the commercial volume is made up of secondary species (White 1976a). White concluded that physical and biological disturbances are sufficiently frequent and widespread to ensure that large areas of forest in PNG are maintained in an advanced secondary stage.

THE FOREST RESOURCE

The total area of closed forest in PNG is 34 million hectares. Of this area, 14 million hectares can be classed as accessible and potentially commercial forest. The remainder is either physically inaccessible or disturbed by shifting cultivation. Although this forest area is not as great as that of most neighbouring states in South East Asia, PNG has a comparatively large forest area per capita. Thus, PNG has 4.5 ha/capita while Indonesia has 0.5 ha/capita and Philippines only 0.1 ha/capita (Table 2.2). The gross volume per hectare of timber in undisturbed forest in PNG is low in comparison with the South East Asian States, but the timber resource per capita is again comparatively high. Thus, PNG has about 586 m^3/capita while Indonesia has 97 m^3/capita, Malaysia has 277 m^3/capita and the Philippines has 31 m^3/capita. the implication arising from these simplistic comparisons is that PNG is rich in forested land and timber. There should, therefore, be less pressure to clear large areas of forest land for agriculture and a greater chance for the creation of a permanent national forest estate.

Table 2.1 Commercially valuable secondary species as a percentage of total tree stocking

Forest area	Diameter size class (cm)								
	15–19	20–29	30–39	40–49	50–59	60–69	70–79	80–89	90+
Cape Rodney	4	5	8	19	32	43	51	64	61
Gogol	8	11	15	23	37	49	50	61	58
Vanimo	7	10	17	27	40	49	59	66	75
Open Bay	9	9	12	26	41	43	48	59	35

Source: White (1976a)

Table 2.2 Estimates of areas of closed forest (broadleaved and conifers) and standing volumes estimated for 1980 in Papua New Guinea and South-east Asia (includes logged and unlogged forest)

Country	Area closed forest			Volume from productive forest	
	Total 000 ha	Productive 000 ha	Productive ha/capita	millions m³	m³/capita
PNG	34 230	14 085	4.5	1817	586
Brunei	323	287	2.1	83	610
Indonesia	113 895	73 735	0.5	13 823	97
Malaysia	20 995	15 552	1.1	3735	277
Peninsula	(7578)	(5807)	(0.5)	1422	(125)
Sabah	(4997)	(3200)	(3.6)	801	(910)
Sarawak	(8420)	(6545)	(5.0)	1512	(1163)
Philippines	9510	6890	0.1	1543	31

Source: FAO/UNEP (1981)

TRADITIONAL USE OF THE FOREST

The creation of a commercially utilized national forest estate depends, however, on the acceptance of the idea by village people living within the forest and accustomed to a certain level of forest disturbance.

Most Papua New Guineans live in small villages or hamlets and practice various forms of subsistence agriculture. Agriculture is a major source of food, but the forest also provides a significant input to the food intake of many lowland people. Estimates of dietary sources for a number of New Guinea societies are given in Table 2.3 and suggest this forest input may be around 20–30 per cent. Besides food, the forest can provide miscellaneous raw materials for building purposes, tools and weapons, artefacts, clothing and personal ornamentation and materials for ritual and magical purposes. Powell (1976) has listed some 1035 plant species (representing 470 genera and 146 families) used for a variety of such purposes. Many genera and species are multipurpose and some, such as coconuts, bananas, sago and pandanus, provide both sustenance and material needs.

In many parts of PNG, particular forest trees are retained during shifting cultivation, or their growth is actually promoted in various ways because their fruit or timber is especially prized. Examples are the enriched *Pandanus* forests of the highlands, the *Terminalia* and *Gnetum* food tree management by the Koiari people and the widespread semi-cultivation in the lowlands of such food trees as *Mangifera minor*, *Artocarpus utilis*, *Canarium indicum*, *Pangium edule*, *Syzgium malaccense*, *Terminalia kaernbachii* and of the canoe tree *Octomeles sumatrana* (White 1976b). Wildlife is also extensively used. Animals are eaten, the plumes or furs are used as decorations, skins are used for drums and bones are used for tools. Commercial forest exploitation therefore necessitates a way being found to combine the new with these traditional forms of forest utilization.

Table 2.3 Subsistence base of New Guinea societies

Society	District	Location	Gathering	Hunting	Fishing	Animal husbandry	Agri-culture
Motu	Central	C	10	0	40	0	50
Mailu	Central	C	10	0	30	10	50
Wogeo	E. Sepik	C	20	0	20	10	50
Busama	Morobe	C	10	10	10	10	60
Manam	Madang	C	0	0	30	10	60
Lesu	N.Ireland	C	0	10	40	10	40
Lakalai	W.N.B.	C	20	10	20	10	40
Trobriands	Milne Bay	C	10	0	30	10	50
Dahuni	Milne Bay	C	0	10	30	10	60
Dobuans	Milne Bay	C	0	0	30	10	60
Russel Is.	Milne Bay	C	30	10	30	10	30
Kiman	Irian Jaya	C	20	10	0	0	60
Mirindanim	Irian Jaya	C	10	20	20	10	40
Mimika	Irian Jaya	C	40	10	40	0	10
Waropen	Irian Jaya	C	30	10	30	10	20
Koita	Central	C/L	10	20	10	10	50
Orokaiva	Northern	L/C	20	10	20	10	50
Buka	Bougainville	L/C	10	10	20	10	50
Koiari	Central	L	10	20	0	10	60
Mekeo	Gulf	L	10	10	10	10	60
Keraki	West	L	0	10	10	10	70
Wantoat	Morobe	L	0	20	0	10	70
Ngarawapum	Morobe	L	10	20	0	10	60
Kwoma	E. Sepik	L	30	20	0	10	40
Arapesh	E. Sepik	L	20	10	0	10	60
Abelam	E. Sepik	L	20	10	0	10	60
Banaro	E. Sepik	L	20	10	10	10	50
Usiai	Manus	L	20	10	0	20	60
Suiai	Bougainville	L	20	10	0	20	60

C = Coastlands   L = Lowlands
Source: Lea (1976)

Part of the problem lies in determining just what level of site disturbance might be acceptable to village people. Anthropologists studying traditional societies have sometimes concluded that resource usage patterns are well-matched to resource availability. Implicit in this view is the idea that traditional societies maintain a harmonious balance with their environment and that such societies have developed conservational practices that regulated their pattern of resource usage. There are, in fact, many examples of practices in PNG that do tend to conserve natural resources. For example, the harvesting of plants and plant products can be regulated by the restricted access provided by the land ownership system. Further, forest regrowth after shifting cultivation can be hastened by keeping the seedlings or coppice of forest trees weed-free during the gardening period. In some places, bans or tabus can be placed limiting harvesting from particular plants at particular times (Powell 1982, Paglau 1982). Similar controls may be placed on hunting certain animals, or restricting access for hunting to particular areas, as well as banning the eating of certain species (Dwyer 1982, Gaigo 1977).

What is questionable about many of these practices, however, is the extent to which their *intent* was conservational. Bulmer (1982) argues that in the case of hunting rights, for example, the purpose of restricting access was to benefit a small and specific section of society, perhaps just a man and his heirs; there was no intention that the restriction should lead to the sustained harvesting by the wider human population of the region[1]. Bulmer concludes that many conservational practices were not necessarily intentional but arose through circumstance. They were the effects of environmental and cultural restraints on rapid population growth as well as the limits imposed by pre-metal technology. There are, in fact, various examples of degradation that have occurred as a consequence of 'traditional' practices. The best known of these in PNG are the large areas of anthropogenic grasslands created by fire. It is also likely that various animals and birds may have become extinct because of humans. Further, there is ample evidence that Papua New Guineans, like people everywhere, have been eager to take advantage of new labour saving technologies. Thus, the steel axe has been adopted for clearing garden sites and the shotgun for hunting. The overall effect has been to increase the rate of resource harvesting.

This appears to raise a paradox. Why should people, for whom plants, animals and the natural environment are such important components of their economy and mythology act in a way that leads to the demise or degradation of these resources? One answer may be that this damage is not being recognized as such. Carrier (1982) has pointed out that village people in PNG perceive their environment in a way quite distinct to that of westerners. For example, a western scientific model of the environment might hold, first, that all species are unique, second, that these species are part of an integrated whole – the ecosystem, third, that any change in this is undesirable until proven otherwise and, fourth, that human action is the most significant source of disruption. All of these concepts might be foreign to a PNG villager. They might not be interested in the ways species are unique but rather in their value as food, medicine or building materials. They might not see these species as part of any functionally integrated whole but as individuals pursuing their existence more or less independently. Changes in these species populations are not necessarily a bad thing and are not necessarily caused by humans. The species were created by God and will continue to exist as long as He wishes.

These perceptions are probably a consequence of the limited environmental damage caused by most villagers and a belief that the damage is minor in relation to the overall resource. Bulmer (1982) has used the example of a man clearing forest and living on the forest edge. His own access to the plants and animals of the forest has not changed because he has shifted with each shift of the ecological boundary. Similarly, Chapman (1985) has suggested that the environmental perception and conservational attitudes of Pacific Islanders may be more acute on the smaller islands with fewer natural resources and more variable environments than on larger, more resource-rich islands.

This is not to say, of course, that significant environmental damage passes unnoticed in PNG. As in all societies, there are many concerned about environmental degradation just as there are those willing to sacrifice the common good for the sake of their own self interest. Nor does it mean that village land owners are unconcerned about damage to their lands or forests. On the contrary, such damage quickly leads to claims for compensation. The question of just how much compensation a government should pay its citizens for the rights to harvest timber from the nation's forest will be discussed further in a later section.

COMMERCIAL USE OF THE FOREST

Unlike the traditional users of the forests, PNG's Forestry Department knew little about the forest when it commenced operations in 1938. Prior to 1938, exploratory surveys had concluded that the forests had a significant potential value but that the diversity and number of relatively unknown

Plate 3　The early stages of a shifting cultivation garden in young regrowth forest

timber trees present made them difficult to utilize (Lane-Poole 1925). The initial operations of the Department were halted by the advent of World War II. Some timber harvesting for military purposes occurred during the war and a few resource surveys were also carried out, but it was not until several years after the war that forestry activities resumed. When they did, most efforts were simply concentrated on producing timber for post-war reconstruction and building.

The earliest official statement on forest policy was issued in June 1951 by the then Minister for Territories in the Australian Parliament, P.C. Spender. He stated that action was to be taken to:-

(i) locate, assess, and regulate the availabilities of the natural forest resources of the territory so as to bring them within reach of development;

(ii) afford all reasonable encouragement for the investment of private capital in the development of these resources;

(iii) ensure that the indigenes of PNG were able to participate to an ever increasing extent in the fruits of this development.

Following this statement, an active programme of ecological research and resource surveys was commenced and an attempt was made to establish a national forest estate. This proved difficult to achieve because of the decision by the colonial Administration to maintain the traditional system of land ownership. Some small areas were purchased but most exploitation was carried out in areas temporarily acquired using a Timber Rights Purchase (TRP). By this device, the Forestry Department purchased from land owners the rights to harvest timber on their land for a certain period, often up to 40 years. The Department was then able to allocate the timber resource to a logging company or sawmill. Ownership of the land remained, however, with the traditional owners. This was hardly a satisfactory method for long term forest management, but it did allow exploitation of the forest to take place before the complex problem of land tenure was solved.

Spender was followed as Minister by Mr. P. Hasluck in 1951. As already mentioned, Hasluck had firm views on the way in which development and change should occur in PNG and was convinced of the necessity for political and economic gradualism. He also held this view in relation to the commercial utilization of the forests and was concerned that 'exploitation of national resources should take place in conditions that safeguarded the future of the people and should not have priority over but go hand in hand with their social advancement'. Further '...I did not believe in giving measures for economic advancement over measures for other forms of advancement leaving the field of economic opportunity wide open to all comers', and '...my objective was to get the development without impairing the chance of future indigenous development.'[2]

Progress by 1957 was slow despite several years of surveys and research.

Answers to the questions of where PNG's timber resources were and how these could be utilized were still cloaked in a degree of uncertainty. In Hasluck's view –

'The Administration had made detailed studies of forest resources but there was still some uncertainty in the advice given to me about the potential for development. There were still many problems of accessibility of stands of timber, the mixed growth and varying quality of timber in the virgin forests and methods of regeneration to give perpetuity to the forests and continuity to the industry. In general, except where the ultimate intention was to clear land for agriculture, there was much caution (in the Forestry Department) about commercial exploitation of the forest. On the whole, I thought cautiousness at a time of limited knowledge was commendable.'[3]

On the other hand, the Minister also believed that progress towards establishing a permanent national forest estate had been too slow, and, in 1957, he directed that acquisition and reservation of forested land should take place with the objective of acquiring 1.6 million hectares within 10 years and 8.1 million hectares within 20 years. He also outlined a programme of reforestation throughout PNG together with experimental afforestation on limited scale in the extensive grassland areas of the highlands. A forestry training school was to be established as well as research into timber utilization. The PNG Administration subsequently issued a Five Year Forestry Plan for 1962–1967 providing details of how these objectives were to be accomplished. As it happened, however, this plan was overtaken by subsequent events.

Hasluck moved to another Ministry in 1963. At the end of his term of office, the area of land available to the Administration was about 548 000 ha. This area seemed substantial but was still far short of his 1957 objective of 1.6 million hectares. Furthermore, the bulk of the area was in the form of temporary TRP forest (Table 2.4). There were 82 sawmills. Only five of these had capacities of more than $35\,m^3/day$ and 59 had capacities of $12\,m^3/day$ or less. The total daily capacity of all mills was only $930\,m^3$.

Table 2.4   Classification of PNG forest areas (1963)

Forest	*Area* (000) ha
Reservations	
Territory Forests	29.1
Timber Reserves	8.9
Other Administration Land	
Purchased for Forestry Purposes	36.0
Timber Rights Purchase	398.6
Land and Permits and Licences	75.3
	547.9

Source: International Bank for Reconstruction and Development (1965)

Most of the timber areas for which permits to log had been issued were also small. Of the total of 88 permits, only two were on areas greater than 20 000 ha and 64 were for areas of less than 4000 ha. This impression of a fairly small timber industry is reflected in the export statistics. For most of the period prior to 1962, annual log exports totalled less than $5000 \, m^3$ and sawn timber exports less than $8000 \, m^3$ (Office of Forests 1979). The only major timber development was the large ply mill based on the *Araucaria* forests at Bulolo.

The policy of gradual and cautious development of forestry and the timber industry under Hasluck changed sharply with the acceptance by Barnes, his successor, of the 1964 World Bank report. In the World Bank's view, the forests of PNG were one of the country's major assets and had the potential to assist more in the development of the country than had hitherto been the case. The report argued that, with over 400 000 ha of forest already available and with at least another 600 000 ha easily accessible, the forest resource was large. The timber on this area was estimated to be around 16.5 million m^3, with even more on steeper ground. The Forestry Department had advised the World Bank consultants that the forest had a mean annual increment of $2–3 \, m^3/ha/yr$ but the consultants believed this estimate was far too conservative. Even if half of the logged forest was converted to agriculture, they estimated the remaining forest could sustain an annual cut of 1.2 million m^3, a figure many times greater than the then present log harvest. The report concluded –'On the assumption that these figures are reasonably based it is obvious that timber production potential is sufficiently great to warrant an aggressive policy of commercial development'. Such a policy would allow PNG to take advantage of a major timber deficit which they forecast would occur in South Asia, East Asia and Oceania by 1975. Overall, the report argued that the Five Year Plan initiated by Hasluck was far too modest[4].

Several difficulties stood in the way of an expansion in the timber industry. First, there was the fact that the diversity of timber trees in PNG was high and the quantities of each species were often small. This had meant in the past that sellers often had to offer 'mixed parcels' to the market. These were not attractive to buyers having only a limited knowledge of the species involved. Second, the terrain of PNG was such that heavy machinery was necessary for logging and consequently logging costs were high. This made timber sales difficult in a competitive world market. Each of these problems, the report argued, pointed to the need to attract large companies with the necessary marketing skills, managerial abilities and financial resources to make the enterprise successful. There was little prospect that the smaller companies then operating in PNG would be able to cope with these problems and increase output to the extent envisaged in the report. If the PNG Administration wanted to attract such large companies, it would have to offer them large timber concessions to warrant the capital investment necessary.

The new Minister and the Administration accepted the overall economic strategy recommended in the World Bank report and with it the more expansionist forestry policy. Large forest areas at Bougainville (44 500 ha) and Madang (50 000 ha) were offered for sale in 1963 and 1964 by public tender and there was a steady increase in the area of forest acquired by TRP. The rate at which resource surveys were carried out was also increased and, using helicopters, over 3.6 million hectares were assessed between 1964 and 1969.

By 1967/68, it was clear the timber resources were much greater than originally believed. Further, the Forestry Department now had some 1.1 million ha under TRP compared with about 317 000 ha in 1962/63 (the other categories of forest available to the Department remained much the same as in 1963). The volume of logs harvested increased from 183 000 m^3 in 1962/63 to 421 000 m^3 in 1967/68, an increase of 230 per cent in 6 years. However, this was still well below the target suggested by the World Bank and was made up, in part, from logs harvested in a salvage logging operation associated with agriculture clearing. Most of this timber was exported as logs, but sawn timber exports also increased and a greater volume of timber was used in the local market within PNG.

Other areas of the PNG economy were also expanding, and, in 1968, the Administration prepared a Five Year Plan to set further targets for development. The Forestry component of the Plan provided for further production increases and for an increase in the degree of local processing of timber. These objectives were to be achieved primarily by establishing large integrated (e.g. sawmills combined with plymills or veneer mills) industrial complexes located on permanent forest estates. The Five Year Plan also sought to improve the supply and quality of forest products for use in PNG, to increase the opportunities for employment and training of Papua New Guineans and to allow for some PNG equity in the new industrial complexes. Production targets were set allowing for a rapid increase from the expected harvested volume of 557 000 m^3 in 1968/69 to 979 000 m^3 in 1972/73. As these targets suggest, the plan was an optimistic document.

At the same time that PNG was attempting to increase timber production from its forests, changes were also occurring in the timber industry in some of the neighbouring countries of south east Asia. The most important of these were in Indonesia. For much of the decade, Indonesia had suffered considerable political instability. Following the replacement of President Sukarno in 1968, the new Government was keen to increase export income through timber sales. Within a short space of time, massive areas of forest were allocated to loggers. By December 1969 there were 21 major timber concessions in Indonesia, mainly in the province of East Kalimantan[5]. One of the largest of these was a concession of 324 000 ha held by the US timber company, Georgia Pacific[6]. The next year, a Phillippino Company was awarded rights to a timber area of 1.2 million hectares[7]. Over the next few years, log production from Indonesia soared (Fig. 2.1).

All countries in the region were to feel the effect of the emergence of Indonesia as a major timber exporter. The Indonesia timber concessions were many times larger than those in PNG, and the controls placed on the companies were minor compared with those being asked in PNG. It was hardly surprising that investors flocked to Indonesia instead of PNG.

By the end of the decade, it was clear that the World Bank target would not be met, and that although the 1968 Five Year Plan still had some time to go, it too was unlikely to succeed (Fig. 2.2).

SILVICULTURAL PROBLEMS

The attempts to increase the rate of exploitation of PNG's forests were made on the assumption that they could be relogged on successive occasions

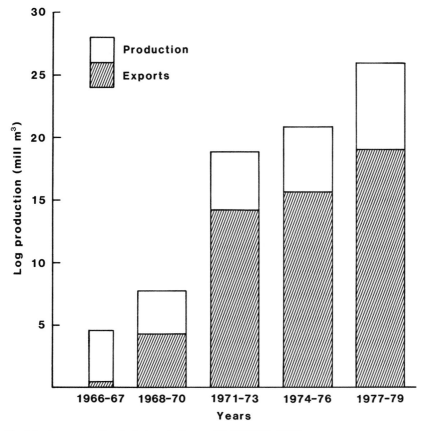

Fig. 2.1   Log production in Indonesia Source: FAO/UNEP (1981)

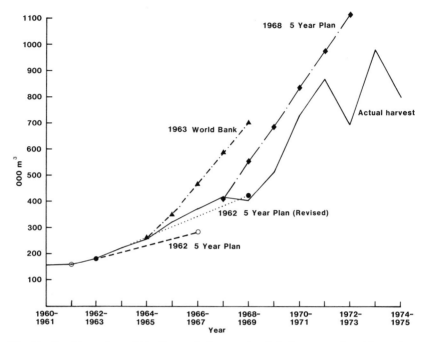

Fig. 2.2 Total log volume (000 m³) actually harvested and the harvest projected by various reports and plans (Source: International Bank for Development and Reconstruction 1965, Territory of Papua New Guinea 1968, Office of Forests 1979)

to provide a sustained yield. In fact, the World Bank report stated they should be seen as an improving asset rather than a wasting asset. The problem was what sort of silvicultural system should be applied to achieve this aim?

Tropical silvicultural systems fall into two broad groups – monocyclic systems and polycyclic systems. The monocyclic systems (often referred to as uniform systems) are those which remove all saleable trees in a single (i.e. uniform) felling. The systems depend on there being a pool of seedlings of the appropriate species on the forest floor which can respond to this canopy opening and grow up to form a new forest. The canopy openings resulting from logging are large and, in some versions of the system (e.g. the Malaysian Uniform System), unsaleable trees not felled are poisoned to assist seedling growth. The length of time between successive harvests is the time it takes for the regenerating trees to reach a merchantable size. In the Malaysian Uniform System, this was 70 years.

Polycyclic systems are those in which only the largest trees above a certain size class are removed. This results in much smaller canopy openings. Since the number of large saleable trees is usually small, the system results in a series of small scattered canopy gaps. Successive harvests depend on smaller residual trees growing into the harvestable size class; that is, it depends on these residual trees rather than on seedling regeneration. Seedling regeneration does occur but it contributes to the harvest at a much later date. The cutting cycle is, therefore, much shorter than under a monocyclic system and is commonly 30–40 years. The yield at each harvest is, of course, less than with a monocyclic system.

Research to develop an appropriate form of silviculture of PNG's forests began at Keravat on the Gazelle Peninsula of New Britain in 1953. Observations on hill and ridge forests showed these were dominated by commercially useful species such as *Pometia tomentosa, Dracontomelum mangiferum, Terminalia* sp., *Calophyllum* sp. and *Canarium* sp. *Pometia* was especially common and regenerated prolifically following disturbance whether by gardening or logging. Seed was apparently produced every couple of years and the seedlings were capable of persisting in shade on the forest floor for several years. A monocyclic system of silviculture was developed, similar to the Malayan Uniform System of the time which encouraged the subsequent growth of the seedlings after logging by removing the remaining non-commercial species in the overstorey. By 1965, about 1000 ha had been treated in this way and a further 400 ha were being treated each year.

Successful natural regeneration was also achieved with forests dominated by *Anisoptera polyandra*, one of the few species of Dipterocarpaceae present in PNG. This species occurs on the coastal ranges east of Lae on the north coast of the mainland. The species apparently produced seed in most years and there was massive seedling regeneration following logging disturbance. Prospects for some kind of uniform system in these forests were also good.

However, research in other areas of PNG began to suggest that forests that could be silviculturally treated in this way were the exception rather than the rule. Surveys in forests at Vanimo on the north west coast of the mainland, Open Bay on the north coast of New Britain and at Brown River west of Port Moresby on the south coast of the mainland all pointed to an apparently low potential for regeneration by commercially desirable species. Some results obtained by White (1976c) at Vanimo illustrate the situation. Counts of 'seedlings' were made in 2 m x 2 m plots in striplines through the undisturbed forest. The 'seedlings' present were counted in various height classes. Young saplings taller than 6 m but with diameter less than 18 cm were also enumerated in 4 m x 4 m plots in the same striplines. The data are given in Table 2.5 and show that, although all plots contained tree regeneration, the numbers of plots with 'seedlings' or saplings of commercially desirable species were less than 10 per cent.

These results suggested that a monocyclic system of silviculture such as that practised in Malaysia, for example, would not be appropriate in these forests. Unfortunately, the prospects for a polycyclic system were often not promising either. In many forests, there was apparently insufficient advanced

Table 2.5 Percentage of plots containing regeneration in various size classes. Plot size for regeneration < 6 m = 2 m x 2 m; for taller regeneration the plot size was 4 m x 4 m. Nineteen species were regarded as commercial

| Forest type | Number plots | Species | Proportion of plots with trees in size class (%) | | | Height – Diam. | |
| | | | Height | | | | |
			0–2 m	2–4 m	4–6 m	> 6 m	< 18 cm
Hill	450	Commercial	7	3	1		0.4
		All spp.	—	—	—		
Hill	524	Commercial	9	2	0.5		2
		All spp.	100	74	54		96
Lowland	402	Commercial	4	1	1		0.5
		All spp.	100	96	58		100

Source: White (1967c)

growth of commercially desirable species to enable replacement of logged trees by younger trees just below the cutting limit. Surveys in several widely separated forest areas in different parts of PNG showed advanced growth of these species in the 30–50 cm stem diameter class was usually less than 20 trees per hectare (Table 2.6). In comparison, the Indonesian selective logging system (a polycyclic system) specifies a stocking of at least 25 trees per hectare in the 35 to 50 cm size class. By such a standard, these PNG stands were understocked.

A further difficulty limiting the use of natural regeneration as a silvicultural technique was the ever-present problem of land ownership. Most of the forest available to the Forestry Department was acquired using a TRP. That is, the Department had no long term control over the land and no legal authority to do any post-logging treatments such as the release treatments necessary in the *Pometia tomentosa* forests on the Gazelle Peninsula. If the land owners decided to clear the regenerating forest for a

Table 2.6 Stocking of commercially desirable species in lowland rain forest in Papua New Guinea. Data based on preliminary analyses of large scale resource surveys in each area

| Area | Number commercial species | Trees per hectare in diameter class | |
		30–50 cm	50 + cm
Cape Rodney	9	8.0	7.2
Vanimo	12	20.0	5.8
Open Bay	10	15.2	10.5
Gogol	12	11.8	6.0

Source: Department of Forests records

cash crop such as coffee or copra they were fully entitled to do so. The Department's tenure over its alienated land was not much more secure. Some of this land had been acquired following the Administration declaring it 'waste and vacant' when there were no apparent owners and some had been purchased. Much of the silviculture research and natural regeneration at Kerevat on the Gazelle Peninsula of New Britain had been carried out on purchased land[8]. The disturbances and rioting over land by the Tolai people described previously eventually resulted in much of this regenerating forest being turned over to Tolai settlers. The remainder was occupied by squatters a few years later in the belief it was unused waste land (Department of Forests 1970/71). Similar sorts of problems occurred with other land purchases elsewhere in the country.

The overall effect of all these factors was to lead the thinking of silviculturalists away from systems of natural regeneration towards plantations of fast growing tree species. Plantations were capable of rapid growth and were far more productive than natural forests[9]. Smaller areas of land could be used and this would reduce (but obviously not solve) the problem of land ownership. Rather than having a variety of timber species, the species planted could be chosen according to the desired end use. Management would be simpler and there would be no chance of misunderstandings over whether the land was being used or not as this would be obvious to all.

Plantations were established in various parts of the country using the native species *Eucalyptus deglupta*, *Araucaria cunninghamii* and *A. hunsteinii* as well as exotics such as Teak, *Eucalyptus* and *Pinus* species. In some cases, lands such as swamps and grasslands were used (e.g. at Bulolo, Goroka and Mt Hagen). In other cases, natural forest areas nearer to ports or major industrial centres were cleared (e.g. at Keravat near Rabaul, Brown River and Bulolo). Land acquisition for these plantations was invariably difficult and the areas purchased at any one time were usually small. By 1970, the total plantation area had reached 11300 ha and the annual planting rate was 770 ha (Department of Forests 1970/71).

UTILIZATION PROBLEMS

Besides these silvicultural problems, it was also proving difficult to develop a timber industry of the sort outlined in the World Bank strategy. Most loggers simply wanted to fell the best trees and export these as unprocessed logs. The problems in attracting larger, more permanent industrial development were:

Low timber yields

The standing volume of timber in PNG forests is around 100–130 m³/ha and, of this volume, around 30 m³/ha was thought to be utilizable according to the commercial standards then prevailing. This volume was less than half that available in the dipterocarp forests of Malaysia and the Philippines (Table 2.7). The low yield had the effect of increasing harvesting costs by increasing the road network and the haulage distances necessary to harvest a given volume.

Species diversity

There are probably about 200 timber species in PNG forests and few areas of forest are dominated by a single species or genus. Commonly 30 to 50 species may contribute around 80 per cent of the standing volume. This diversity has several consequences. First, it is difficult to accumulate large volumes of any desired species. Second, it is difficult to market the wide range of species present. Before World War II, three or four species were logged. By 1970, there were still only about 30 species potentially saleable on overseas markets.

Wood quality

The timber of the various species ranges from light balsa-like wood to extremely dense and heavy timber. There are relatively few species with timber with highly desired characteristics like *Dracontomelum* (Walnut), *Pterocarpus* (Rosewood) and *Toona* (Cedar) that have gained cabinet timber status. The volume of these in most forests areas is low and usually less than 10 per cent. In this respect, PNG again suffers in comparison with neighbouring countries in SE Asia where many timbers are more uniform in colour, texture and quality. Rot is prevalent in some logs causing further difficulties.

Tree form

Tree boles have a variety of shapes. Many have buttressing, fluting and bends. These reduce the value of logs, especially for veneer. When sawn

Table 2.7 Gross volume and presently commercial volume in undisturbed productive closed broadleaved forests

Country	Gross volume m³/ha	Commercial volume m³/ha	% gross
PNG	130	30	23
Indonesia	265	27	10
Malaysia	291	69	24
Peninsular	(323)	(45)	(14)
Sabah	(313)	(90)	(29)
Sarawak	(266)	(75)	(28)
Philippines	305	90	30

Source: FAO/UNEP (1981)

timber could be sold for export, it was necessarily only high quality material. This left the industry with the problem of disposing of larger volumes of second grade timber on a small local market.

Infrastructure

Most of the large timber areas are in relatively isolated areas and have little in the way of a local infrastructure. Commonly there are no towns, roads, electricity or ports. Few areas are near any shipping route. A new timber industry being developed at one of these sites would therefore have to provide all these facilities itself.

Markets

The internal PNG market was small and so most of the increased harvest had to be exported. As mentioned above, however, most PNG timbers were not well known in the world's market places, although a considerable research effort had defined properties and potential uses for many species. Even where particular species were known, many importers preferred to buy timber as logs so that the processing was done by themselves.

As a result of this combination of factors, no large integrated industrial enterprises were commenced in the years following the adoption of the World Bank strategy. The large concession at Bougainville awarded in 1963 failed and no satisfactory agreements were ever concluded in the Madang concession offered in 1964. By 1970, there were 91 sawmills, only nine more than the 82 present in 1963 and most of these were still processing less than 8 m^3 each day. The plymill established during the 1950's to process *Araucaria* logs from the natural stands near Bulolo was still the largest integrated timber mill in PNG. Despite the increasing economic necessity for PNG to develop an export income (amplified by a political need for rapid growth), it seemed circumstances had combined to prevent the country from exploiting one of its most valuable natural resources.

SOLUTIONS

Two solutions suggested themselves. The first was to advertise the resource areas more widely. The rationale was that markets for tropical timbers would be increasing in the near future and that the limitations described above would be more than compensated for by the large volumes of timber available in PNG. A series of bulletins and a more detailed small book entitled 'New Horizons' which described the forests and timber resources of PNG were widely distributed. The book was followed up with trade missions to Australia, Japan and, later, China. Even with hindsight, it is difficult to assess the exact impact of this marketing activity although it was probably successful in making PNG timbers more widely known. In any event, a second solution to the dilemma presented itself.

The second solution involved a radical new form of timber utilization. If sawlog timber volumes were low and marketing the diversity of species was difficult, why not use a form of utilization that overcame both problems – namely harvesting all species for pulpwood?

The first time woodchipping appears to have been considered as a possibility in PNG was in 1966 when the Sangyo Pulp Co. Ltd. carried out an investigation of the Open Bay timber area in New Britain and included woodchips as one possible form of production. Then CSIRO in Australia and the Japanese Honshu Paper Manufacturing Co. successfully tested the suitability of a variety of timber species from PNG for pulpwood. Pulpwood logging, or woodchipping as it became known, seemed, in the words of one observer, a 'golden opportunity' for the industry to break through the silvicultural and utilization limitations experienced up until that time (Endacott 1971). It would allow the achievement of economies of scale and profitability, two attributes mostly absent from PNG's timber industry. As well, markets in Japan seemed assured with the prospect of other markets in Korea and China. At last it seemed the forests of PNG might be used to help fund the rapidly increasing process of development then underway. Negotiations commenced with a Japanese consortium in 1968. These culminated in 1971 when a woodchipping industry was established based on the forest resources of the Gogol Valley near Madang.

Note 1: Dwyer (1982) records the story of a Papua New Guinea friend who heard on the radio a programme suggesting people should not kill wildlife. He agreed with what he had heard and told Dwyer he would abide by the recommendations. A few months later he went hunting and the catch was good. Dwyer reminded him of the radio programme and of his former intentions. 'Ah yes', he said,'but I was hunting on my own land'.

Note 2: Hasluck (1976) p. 291.

Note 3: Hasluck (1976) p. 292.

Note 4: K.J. White (former Assistant Director, Department of Forestry) believed the majority of senior officers in the Department of Forestry at the time were opposed to the World Bank's targets and believed them to be too optimistic especially since little recognition had been given to the quality of the resource (personal communication).

Note 5: Australian Timber Journal, December 1969.

Note 6: Australian Timber Journal, November 1969.

Note 7: Australian Timber Journal, July 1970.

Note 8: According to K.J. White, (personal communication), the Forestry Department was able to purchase this land from its owners, the Baining people, because they wished to establish an Administration-controlled buffer between themselves and the more aggressive Tolai. In the event their strategy failed.

Note 9: Many lowland forests in PNG had a standing volume of 100–130 m^3/ha of which perhaps 30 m^3 might be commercially useful. The mean annual increment was probably less than 2 m^3/ha/yr. By comparison, an average quality *Eucalyptus deglupta* plantation in the lowlands might easily produce a mean annual increment of at least 25 m^3/ha/yr. The oldest *E. deglupta* plantation at Keravat had a standing volume of 485 m^3/ha at 19.5 years.

CHAPTER 3

THE GOGOL VALLEY – A BACKGROUND

INTRODUCTION

The town of Madang, around which the Gogol Timber Project (GTP) is based, is an attractive district centre on the north coast of the PNG mainland. It is built on an old uplifted coral terrace and looks out across a seascape of small coral islands topped by coconut palms. Behind the town, across a narrow coastal strip, are the foothills of the Adelbert Ranges. To the south, lies the Gogol River. Further south are the rugged Finisterre Ranges. Apart from coconut plantations along the coastal strip, most land in the district is covered by tall forest or forest regrowth resulting from shifting cultivation.

Madang is the administrative centre of the district. Although it has an airport and harbour, it was not linked by road to any other major town until 1974 (when a road to Lae was built) because of the difficult terrain surrounding it. A coastal road extends north for 50 km but no roads penetrated far inland. At one time, Madang was an important transit point for goods being air freighted into the highlands. This role ceased in the early 1960's when a road link to the highlands from Lae was completed. Since then, Madang's economy has been based primarily on agriculture. Extensive coconut plantations have been developed on the flat coastal land. Other crops grown by subsistence farmers include cocoa and coffee. Some commercial fishing is also carried out. Towards the end of the 1960's, there was increasing interest in cattle although cattle numbers were then still low. Because of the terrain, most of these agricultural developments were close to the coastal roads.

The GTP is composed of four separate TRP's or blocks. Two of these are located in the Gogol Valley (one centred on the Gogol River itself and the other on the Naru River, a tributary of the Gogol River). A third, the small Gum TRP, lies between Madang and the Gogol River while the fourth, the North Coast TRP, is 20 km north of Madang (Fig. 3.1). A map of the Gogol and Naru TRP areas is given in Fig. 3.2.

CLIMATE

The climate of the area is warm and moist and typical of much of the lowland forest area of PNG. It falls within Köppen's tropical wet climate

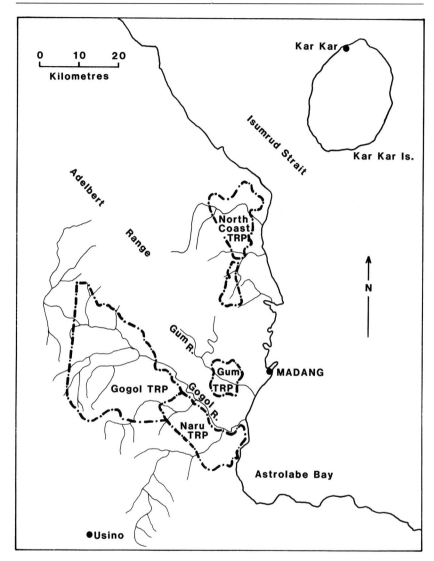

Fig. 3.1 Madang region showing the location of the main Timber Rights Purchase areas

(Af) classification and Thornthwaite's Perhumid tropical rain forest type (AA'r). The temperatures at Madang normally range between monthly mean maximum and minimum of 30°C and 23°C, with little seasonal variation. The rainfall averages 3518 mm at Madang on the coast, but is 2985 mm at Baku inland in the centre of the Gogol TRP (Table 3.1). There is a distinct seasonal pattern, with most rain being received between November and April. Average rainfall in the driest month (August) is 111 mm at Baku. Long term (21 years) records at Madang show the

Fig. 3.2 The Gogol and Naru Timber Rights purchase areas showing the main road network established by 1978 and some of the villages. The Jant base camp is near the Department of Forests headquarters at Baku. The Balek wildlife sanctuary was outside the project area but close to the benchmark reserve near Malaga Village

coefficient of variation of the annual rainfall is 14 per cent. Most rain falls in frequent showers, and heavy storms are less common.

A water balance model has been developed to estimate the soil moisture regime using the Madang rainfall statistics. Table 3.2 shows a frequency distribution giving the mean number of weeks per quarter in which moisture is depleted below certain levels. The driest period is in the third quarter of the year. At this time, the soil moisture store may be depleted by more than 50 per cent for nearly 3 weeks.

Rainfall in the Adelbert Ranges and Finesterre Ranges maintains flow in the Gogol River throughout the year. Heavy rains, especially between December and May can cause flash flooding and the Gogol River has been known to rise 6 m in a few hours. Similar flash flooding can occur in

Table 3.1 Rainfall statistics for Baku (1970–79) in the central Gogol Valley and Madang (21 years)

Month	Baku mm	Baku Raindays	Madang mm
January	409	23	359
February	367	22	292
March	362	22	344
April	298	20	443
May	269	17	337
June	133	13	209
July	118	11	166
August	111	10	128
September	177	10	144
October	225	14	301
November	264	16	387
December	252	18	397
Total	2985	196	3507

Source: McAlpine *et al.* (1975) (Madang), Department of Forests records (Baku).

Plate 4 Streambank erosion on the Gogol River causing a break in the main road into Madang

the various tributaries including the Naru River. No regular discharge measurements are made, but volumes in excess of $192 \, m^3/sec$ have been observed (Bureau of Water Resource records). Some extended dry periods have occurred in the past although these are not well documented. In the 1900's, the Gogol River reportedly dried up for 3 years and another dry period occurred in 1942 (Davidson 1983).

44

Plate 5   Floodplain of the lower Gogol Valley

Table 3.2   Mean number of weeks per quarter at Madang with soil moisture storage at specified levels

Quarter	Storage level			
	Full	*1–49% depleted*	*50–99% depleted*	*Empty*
Jan–March	11.2	1.8	0	0
April–June	10.8	2.2	0	0
July–Sept.	6.0	4.3	2.7	0
Oct.–Dec.	10.7	1.7	0.3	0.3

Source: Short (1976)

GEOMORPHOLOGY AND GEOLOGY

The Gogol River drains the southern part of the Adelbert Range and the northern flanks of the Finesterre Range. The Adelbert Range is a low coastal mountain range mainly below 1300 m consisting of steep sided ridges and an upland area of rounded hills. The Finesterre Range is a much more elevated (over 3000 m in places) mountain system with steep sided ridges. The tributaries of the Gogol River run from these into a broad wide flood plain about 12 km south of Madang.

During the upper Miocene and lower Pliocene, the present Adelbert Range was probably a string of islands lying off shore from the mainland. Uplifting during the Pliocene and Miocene lead to the coastline being demarcated by a series of low hills. Surfaces of low relief were formed during this period during a pause in the uplifting and then dissected during further periods of uplifting. Seismic activity and upraised coral platforms and alluvial plains along the coast show uplifting is continuing at present. Continued earth movements have intensified the tendency for rapid erosion in higher areas and extensive deposition in the lowlands (Reiner and Mabbutt 1976).

In most of the Gogol Valley, the resulting topography is a mixture of steep low hills, broad flood plains, river terraces and swamps. Most of these floodplain and swamp areas are less than 50 m above sea level. Hills are a more dominant feature of the landscape in the southern and northwestern areas. In most places, the hills are usually below 300 m although some more elevated areas do occur. Most of the hills are low and rounded but some are more strongly dissected.

Areas of land in various topographic classes in the Gogol and Naru blocks of the GTP are shown in Table 3.3. Flat and gentle terrain covers 35 000 ha or 52 per cent of the total area. Rugged or broken terrain covers about 17 000 ha or 25 per cent of the area.

The Gum and North Coast Blocks are located on strongly dissected foothills of the Adelbert Ranges. The area is made up of close-spaced, rounded hills with steeper short ridges and some smaller alluvial basins. No detailed terrain analysis has been carried out on the area.

The most common rock types in the area are mudstones, siltstones and sandstones although there are also localized areas with limestone. The mudstones are readily weathered and the thick, impermeable weathering mantle results in a dense drainage pattern with closely spaced, short tributary valleys. Saturation of the weathered mudstone can lead to mudflows and minor land slips. Where sandstone is combined with mudstone in a thin layer, this gives some protection to the mudstone and gives stronger relief than is the case with mudstone alone (Reiner and Mabbutt 1976).

Table 3.3 Areas of various topographic classes in the Gogol and Naru Timber Rights Purchases. Relief refers to the difference in elevation between valley floors and ridge tops. Grain refers to the horizontal distance between adjoining ridge tops

Topographic class	Terrain description	Area ha	Per cent
Flat	Slope 0°–2°	23 300	34
Gentle	Slope 0°–30°, relief < 50 m	12 000	18
Moderate	Slope 20°–35°, relief 35–120 m, grain 400–800 m	15 600	23
Rugged	Slope 25°–40°, relief 70–220 m, grain 600–800 m	12 300	18
Broken	Slope 30°–45°, relief 35–80 m, grain 100–150 m, narrow ridges and V shaped gullies	4 500	7
		67 700	100

Source: Whyte (1975)

FORESTS

Like the lowland rain forests of Papua New Guinea in general, the forests of the GTP are rich in species. A number of these species lack formal scientific names, although most of the genera present are reasonably well known. Vegetation surveys in the region have been carried out by Robbins *et al.* (1976), Saunders (1976) and Whyte (1975) has classified the forests of the GTP into a number of categories. These studies have shown it is difficult to assign genera or species to even broad categories such as 'hill forest' or 'terrace forest' and floristic associations may be of only local importance. However, while a species may not be definitive of a forest type, differences in abundance do occur. The main vegetative types, according to Whyte (1975), are as follows:

(a) Hill forest

The canopy of this forest type is commonly 35 m tall with emergents sometimes reaching 50 m. On ridges, the canopy height is usually less and may be as low as 10–15 m. Some of the main species in the canopy include *Intsia bijuga, Celtis philippinensis, C. nymanii, C. latifolia, Canarium acutifolium, C. indicum, Pometia pinnata, P. tomentosa, Cryptocarya depressa, Garuga floribunda, Hernandia papuana, Spondias cytherea* and *Terminalia, Pimeleodendron, Dysoxylum* and *Ficus* spp. There is a well developed subcanopy layer and shrubs, epiphytes and climbers are common.

(b) Well-drained terrace forest

The forest structure of this forest type is similar to that of the hill forests. However, the range of girth sizes of canopy trees is more variable and there are more widely spaced, large-girthed individuals and fewer emergents. Flange buttresses are common and palms may be locally dominant. Common tree species include *Pometia pinnata, Vitex cofassus, Celtis luzonensis, Terminalia* spp., *Ficus* spp., *Intsia bijuga* and *Teysmanniodendron bogoriense.* Climbers are common and the ground flora include *Donax, Elatostemma,* and *Selaginella.*

(c) Poorly-drained terrace forest

The canopy level in this type is usually lower than the other forests and may average around 30 m. The canopy tends to be made up of smaller crowned trees and is more broken and uneven. Characteristic trees are *Octomeles, Terminalia, Nauclea, Campnosperma, Planchonia, Celtis, Ficus* and *Pometia pinnata. Calamus* and *Donax* are common elements of the ground flora. Large stilt rooted *Pandanus* are common.

(d) Swamp forests

Small areas of swamp forest occur in old river ox bows and at the rear of some flood plain terrace systems adjacent to hill areas. These are commonly occupied by *Pandanus* or *Metroxylon sagu* with various scattered trees sometimes up to 20 m tall.

(e) Secondary regrowth and grassland

Large areas of secondary regrowth and grassland occur in both the Gogol TRP and the Naru TRP. The grasslands are invariably dominated by *Imperata cylindrica*. The secondary forest regrowth has originated from shifting cultivation and landslips but the origin of the grasslands is less certain. In some cases, these too may have resulted from shifting cultivation. It is interesting in this respect, however, that there are reports that the population in the Gogol Valley may once have been much higher than at present (Cavanaugh 1976). If true, these grasslands may be a legacy of these higher population densities. A third possible explanation is that the grasslands originate from wildfires that burnt through parts of the Gogol Valley during earlier drought periods (Johns 1986).

(f) Other plant communities

Smaller areas of palm swamps (*Nipa frutican*) and *Saccharum* grasslands occur along waterways, especially near the coast.

The areas covered by these various vegetation types within the Gogol and Naru Blocks of the GTP are shown in Table 3.4. Hill forests cover the largest area and make up 53 per cent of the total. Most of the hill forest are, of course, in the more mountainous terrain, but nearly 40 per cent of the hill forest is on terrain classed as rugged or broken. Floodplains and terrace forests account for 25 per cent of the total while secondary regrowth and *Imperata* grasslands cover 16 per cent and 3 per cent respectively. The regrowth and grassland occurs mainly in the flat and gentle terrain classes but are also found in the more mountainous terrain classes as well. The other vegetation types only cover three per cent of the area.

Table 3.4 The distribution of various vegetation types across different topographic classes in the Gogol and Naru Blocks of the GTP

Vegetation type	Topographic class					Total ha	Per cent
	Flat	Gentle	Moderate	Rugged	Broken		
Hill forest	780	7530	12830	10400	4440	35980	53
Well-drained terrace forest	4570	740	140	30	10	5490	8
Poorly-drained terrace forest	6270	960	10	70	20	7330	11
Flood plain forest	4300	120	10	—	—	4430	6
Swamp forest	580	20	—	—	—	600	1
Secondary regrowth	5260	1830	2060	1310	60	10520	16
Imperata grassland	460	600	510	470	10	2050	3
Saccharum grassland	860	80	—	—	—	940	1
Sago palm forest	220	70	—	—	—	290	<1
Nipa Swamp	10	—	—	—	—	10	<1

Source: Whyte (1975)

Vegetation in the Gum and North Coast blocks of the GTP is mostly hill forest, with some secondary regrowth following shifting cultivation or landslips.

DISTURBANCES

Forests in the area are subject to a number of recurrent disturbances.

(a) Earthquakes

Earthquakes are common and occur in most years. Particularly severe earthquakes occurred in 1910, 1933 and 1970. The latter caused considerable structural damage to buildings in the town of Madang and extensive earthslipping occurred in the Adelbert Ranges in the upper reaches of the Gogol River. Surveys showed an area of 240 km^2 was affected. Within this area, avalanches completely denuded 60 km^2 of forest leaving bare soil. Altogether about 27.6 million m^3 of soil was estimated to have moved into the river system (Pain and Bowler 1973). The greatest amount of earthslipping occurred on slopes greater than 46° with poorly developed shallow soils. Avalanches were apparently less common where the vegetation was mainly secondary regrowth perhaps because the root mass was denser and better able to bind the soil.

(b) Volcanoes

There are also a number of active volcanoes in the region (Fig. 3.3). The closest of these is on Kar Kar Island which is only 30 km from the North coast TRP but is some 80 km from the Gogol TRP. All these volcanoes have erupted in the recent past. The frequency of eruptions since 1870 is estimated to be as follows (Cook *et al.* 1976):

Kar Kar Island	3 (but possibly 4)
Long Island	6 (but possibly 8)
Manam Island	36 (but possibly 42)

Volcanic ash layers have been found in soils in the Naru Valley (D. Skelton 1986) and folk tales from the Gogol Valley recall great falls of blue ash which killed many people (De'Ath 1978b). One source of this ash seems to have been a major eruption that occurred on Long Island in the mid seventeenth century. Blong (1982) presents evidence showing the tephra or pyroclastic material from this covered a large area of the Madang district and extended inland as far as the central highlands (Fig. 3.3). In the Gogol Valley, the tephra would probably have been about 10 cm thick. The effect of such a fall is difficult to assess, especially since it may have been accompanied by acid rains. Blong's review of the literature on the subject suggested that, at the very least, a shower of this magnitude would have caused many trees

49

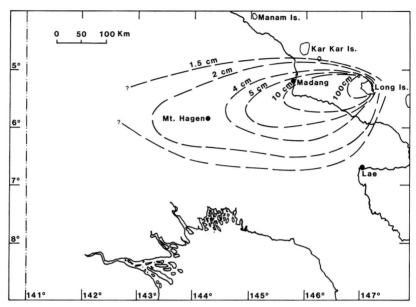

Fig. 3.3 The closest volcanoes to the Gogol Valley are those on Long Island and Kar Kar Island. There is also a large active volcano on the more distant Manam Island. The isopleths on this map show the depth of tephra originating from a mid seventeenth century eruption on Long Island. Source: Blong (1982)

in the Gogol Valley to lose leaves and branches and that a number of plants would have been killed.

(c)   Drought and fire
Severe dry periods have been recorded in the area on various occasions in the past. Thus, Lane-Poole (1925) quotes an observer from the German colonial period that in '1895 a great drought set in in the Astrolabe Bay, which continued during 1896'. Similarly, wildfire has been reported in the Gogol Valley in the early 1900's, 1915 and 1941 (Cavanaugh 1975). How extensive these fires were and exactly what ecological effects they had is unclear. Johns (1986) notes major discontinuities in the size class distribution of trees in the south Naru Valley which he attributes to the 1941 fires. Cavanaugh (1975) also notes that the Gogol Valley has an unusually high proportion of the supposedly fire tolerant species *Intsia palembanica* and *I. bijuga* but only low populations of more fire sensitive species such as *Pometia*.

(d)   Erosion
In the lower reaches of the Gogol Valley, the Gogol River and most of its tributaries have braided water courses and meanders are common. Swamps in old ox bows show the rivers have moved course back and forth across the floodplain to a considerable extent in the recent past.

50

Active erosion and undercutting of river banks is underway at present. Much of the forest in this topographic unit is necessarily relatively young.

Since little is known about the frequency of most of these phenomena, or the area of forest affected at any one time, it is difficult to be too specific about the overall effect they have had. However, it is likely that much of the Gogol Valley is a mosaic of disturbance classes each of differing ages and origins. The large areas of recent secondary regrowth are only the most obvious sign of this. Recurrent disturbances have a selective effect on forest vegetation. Only those species able to tolerate the particular types of disturbances occurring will persist. If these disturbances are frequent and extensive, then the forests will come to be dominated by species with easily dispersed seed or seed stored in soil banks; these species will be fast growing and reproduce early. It is, in fact, the longer lived secondary species which appear to dominate the forests of the Gogol Valley.

TIMBER RESOURCES

The first survey of the timber resources of the Gogol Valley was carried out in 1959. This was a reconnaissance survey to ascertain whether the acquisition of timber rights in the area would be justified and to establish contact with the owners and determine their attitude to such a proposal. The survey covered 15 000 ha and results were encouraging enough for the report to recommend that a more detailed survey should be carried out. The second survey party spent 5 months in the field in 1962 and established 188 sample plots, each 0.8 ha in size in an area of nearly 50 000 ha. A statistical analysis of the data suggested there was a sampling bias which favoured the higher quality *Intsia bijuga* stands. For this reason, a further investigation was carried out in 1963. This used 600 plots each 0.1 ha in area. The information was collected and superimposed on a forest type map prepared from aerial photographic coverage.

These surveys indicated the area contained a commercially useful timber resource and a timber rights purchase was carried out. The resource was then offered for tender by the Administration in 1964. No successful tenders were received and, despite being readvertised, the resource remained uncommitted.

In 1970, a further survey was carried out to determine the volume of timber in smaller-sized trees, following expressions of interest in using the resource for pulpwood. The results of this are summarized in Table 3.5 using a simplified set of vegetation types. The largest volume of sawlogs (girth greater than 1.5 m) as well as the largest total timber volume was located on the flat land of the flood plain ($107 \, \text{m}^3/\text{ha}$) and slightly lower volumes were present in the hill forest areas ($98 \, \text{m}^3/\text{ha}$). Some pulpwood was present in the advanced secondary regrowth but, not surprisingly, this

Table 3.5 Estimated standing volumes (m³/ha) of timber in the Gogol and Naru Blocks of the GTP based on Department of Forests assessments carried out in 1963 and 1970

Vegetation type	Pulpwood (0.25 m–1.5 m girth)	Saw logs (> 1.5 m girth)	Total
Grassland	1	—	1
Secondary regrowth	3	4	7
Advanced secondary regrowth	54	9	63
Flat land	71	36	107
Hill forest	66	32	98

forest contained no sawlogs.

In the forest on the flat land, 30 genera accounted for 72 per cent of the total timber volume (Table 3.7). The most common of these was *Intsia bijuga* which accounted for 12 per cent. *Terminalia* species and *Pometia* species which are also highly regarded timber species accounted for 6 per cent and 2.5 per cent respectively. All of these species were well represented in the forests on the hill areas as well.

Similar surveys were carried out in the Gum and North Coast Blocks and TRPs carried out to cover both pulpwood and sawlog sized trees. The total area eventually included within the Gogol Timber Project was 88 000 ha and this was estimated to contain 7 million m³ of timber (Table 3.6). Though large, the area and its resource were not as big or rich in high quality sawlog species as other timber areas elsewhere in PNG.

SOILS

Most soils of the Gogol and Naru areas are loams, silty clays or clays derived from mudstones or the alluvial sediments of the floodplain. There is usually little profile development.

In the valleys close to the river, the soils are often structureless loams or silts although changes in texture are common within the profile and lenses

Table 3.6 Timber rights purchase areas and timber resources in the Gogol Timber Project

Name of area	Date purchased	Term (years)	Area (ha)	Volume million m³	
				< 1.5 m GAB	> 1.5 m GAB
Gogol	1963	40	52270	—	1.26
Gogol	1971	32	52270	3.00	—
Naru	1971	32	15800	1.00	0.61
Gum	1971	32	4960	0.15	0.10
North Coast	1971	32	14990	0.70	0.47
			88020	4.85	2.44

*GAB = girth above buttresses
Source: Areas and TRP details – Department of Madang Province (1980a);
       timber volumes – Yauieb (1978).

Table 3.7 Composition of main tree genera in valley and hill forest areas in the Gogol Valley based on Department of Forest assessments carried out in 1970

Flat land		Hill forest	
Genera	Percentage of timber volume	Genera	Percentage of timber volume
Intsia	12.01	Intsia	9.13
Terminalia	5.78	Celtis	9.22
Teysmanniodendron	4.78	Ficus	5.51
Celtis	4.60	Pometia	5.14
Myristica	2.53	Terminalia	3.61
Ficus	2.51	Pimeleodendron	3.42
Pometia	2.49	Dysoxylum	3.07
Maniltoa	2.46	Artocarpus	2.86
Eleaeocarpus	2.22	Sterculia	2.69
Sterculia	2.22	Pterocymbium	2.64
Diospyros	2.22	Spondias	2.13
Spondias	2.20	Myristica	1.83
Artocarpus	1.96	Garuga	1.83
Eugenia	1.96	Hernandia	1.53
Anthocephalus	1.91	Litsea	1.44
Dysoxylum	1.80	Euodia	1.41
Macaranga	1.77	Canarium	1.31
Canarium	1.68	Mastixiodendron	1.22
Pimeleodendron	1.61	Maniltoa	1.19
Cananga	1.60	Endospermum	1.18
Neonauclea	1.43	Polyalthia	1.16
Pterocarpus	1.38	Diospyros	1.14
Parinari	1.37	Cryptocarya	1.12
Alstonia	1.19	Eugenia	1.09
Endospermum	1.13	Chisocheton	1.07
Euodia	1.09	Dracontomelum	1.04
Garuga	1.09	Teysmanniodendron	1.01
Litsea	1.07		
Polyalthia	1.05		
Cumulative percentage			
Vol. =	71.11		= 69.99
Volume per hectare of trees of 25 cm girth (m^3/ha) =	107		= 98

of coarser material can occur. Further away from the river, textures become heavier and silty clays predominate. Surface drainage is slow because of the flat topography and internal drainage is poor because of the heavy textures. The depth to the water table varies. In the wet season, flooding is common in some areas and the water table is frequently within 50 cm of the surface. In the dry season, it may drop to more than 100 cm. Because of these seasonal changes, mottling is common in many soil profiles and gley layers are often found in soils of the low lying terraces and swamps.

Soils of the hill areas of the Gogol Valley are mostly silty clays or clays derived from mudstone or siltstone. Most have massive structures and plastic consistencies. Except for shallow ridgetop soils most are usually at least a metre deep. Although internal drainage is limited by texture, surface drainage is generally good and mottling and gley layers are not common. Some impeded drainage can occur however in small valley bottoms within the hills and in some, mottling may develop.

Some reports have suggested the fertility of soils in the Gogol Valley might be low. These views were based on the large amount of secondary regrowth and grassland in an area with a relatively low density of shifting cultivators. Soil chemical analyses suggest this is not the case and that the level of most plant nutrients is moderate to high by agricultural standards. A summary of the analyses is given in Table 3.8. This summary shows that calcium, magnesium and potassium concentrations are high in all soils, while nitrogen concentrations are moderate to high in most topsoils but lower in subsoils as might be expected. The phosphorus concentrations are

Table 3.8 Average soil nutrient concentrations in various land classes in the Gogol Valley

	Flood plain levee	Poorly drained terrace	Well-drained terrace	Hill	Swamp
No. samples	10	10	10	10	3
(a) Topsoil (0–5 cm)					
pH	6.58	6.37	6.36	6.68	6.30
Avail. P ppm	22.0	17.0	17.0	5.0	25.0
Ca meq%	27.8	30.7	32.5	41.2	30.7
Mg meq%	9.2	15.7	13.3	9.5	20.8
K meq%	1.68	1.21	1.66	1.71	1.42
Na meq%	0.26	0.21	0.13	0.23	0.30
Total meq%	38.7	47.7	47.4	57.7	53.2
CEC meq%	50.1	53.3	52.1	49.2	67.2
C %	3.2	5.4	5.2	3.7	9.3
N %	0.33	0.48	0.50	0.39	0.72
C/N	9.7	11.2	10.2	9.45	12.7
(b) Subsoil (50 cm)					
pH	6.77	6.73	6.71	6.62	6.70
Avail P ppm	12.20	8.00	7.0	2.0	17.0
Ca meq %	37.7	28.9	27.5	38.0	28.7
Mg meq %	10.6	14.9	16.4	11.3	20.5
K meq %	0.83	0.66	0.54	0.87	0.84
Na meq %	0.53	0.52	0.47	0.32	0.51
Total meq %	45.7	45.0	45.0	54.1	50.4
CEC meq %	47.3	45.3	45.6	45.2	52.2
C %	0.60	0.82	0.57	0.14	0.76
N %	0.10	0.12	0.10	0.12	0.11
C/N	5.7	7.5	5.6	6.4	6.6

moderate in most soils although lower in the hill areas. The cation exchange capacity of all soils is high and is generally saturated, the dominant ion being calcium. Soil pH levels are mostly about 6.5.

Most of the undifferentiated alluvial soils in the valleys can probably be classed as Tropofluvents (Bleeker 1983). These are widespread in the tropics and commonly regarded as highly fertile. Productivity is usually only limited by drainage. Most of the hill forest soils of the GTP can probably be classified as Eutropepts or Brown Forest Soils. These are amongst the most common soils in PNG and are usually found to be moderately fertile (Bleeker 1983).

The Gum and North Coast Blocks have soils similar to the hill forest areas of the Gogol Valley. The soils are immature and, in places, shallow. The textures are usually heavy clays. Some are imperfectly drained leading to mottling in parts of the profile. No detailed chemical analyses have been carried out in these areas but the fertility of the soils is likely to be similar to those in the hill areas of the Gogol Valley.

WILDLIFE

Scientifically speaking, little was known, let alone published, about the wildlife of the Gogol Valley before 1970. A series of surveys since then has produced successively larger species lists. The latest data summary shows a total of 251 species of fauna (Table 3.9). These are dominated by 167 species of birds. Endemism is high, ranging from 36 per cent for mammals to 70 per cent for frogs. Sixty per cent of the wildlife are dependent on forests to varying degrees, especially the mammals (Liem 1978a).

Among the birds, the most common groups appear to be the pigeons and doves, parrots, kingfishers and flycatchers. A number of species appear to be rare. These include some that are naturally rare (*Cophixalus rostellifer, Gallicolumba beccarii, Hemiprocne mystacea, Peltops blainvillii* and *Euaegotheles insignis*) as well as some species made rare because of excessive hunting such as *Harpyopsis novaeguineae* (kapul eagle), *Aceros plicatus*

Table 3.9 Estimates of wildlife species present in the Gogol Valley

Animal group	Total no. species	Endemic sp.		Species dependent on forest	
		No.	%	No.	%
Mammals	27	10	37	20	74
Birds	167	77	46	102	61
Reptiles	34	19	56	15	44
Frogs	23	16	70	15	65
	251	122	49	152	60

Source: Liem (1978a)

55

(hornbill), *Casuarius unappendiculatus* (single wattled cassowary), *Probosciger aterrimus* (palm cockatoo) and *Goura victoria* (victoria crown pigeon) (Liem 1978a). There is some uncertainty associated with these assessments because only 4 years earlier Pippett (1974) noted hornbills and cassowaries were common throughout the Gogol Valley.

The mammals present include several species of fruit bats, bandicoots, wallabies, bats and cuscus. Little is known of the distribution, numbers or ecology of most of these species in the GTP area.

THE HUMAN INHABITANTS

Living within the valleys and hills of the GTP area are a number of shifting cultivators. These are the owners of the forests and lands and were to be the chief beneficiaries of the development logging would bring.

Populations and clans

In 1969, the human population in the four areas of the GTP totalled 4398 persons, giving a population density for the area of five persons per 100 ha (Table 3.10). This density varied from a low in the Gogol area of two point three persons per 100 ha to a high in the Gum area of 13.8 persons per 100 ha.

Roughly half of this population, some 2324 persons, lived in the Gogol and Naru areas. Early missionaries reported these areas were much more densely populated in the 1880's. Not long after this date, the population apparently declined sharply, supposedly because of malaria. The population decrease was so drastic that the mission stations were closed and it wasn't until the 1940's that population numbers began to increase once more (Cavanaugh 1976).

The people of the Gogol and Naru areas of the GTP speak at least eight separate languages and Z'graggen (1975) reports there are some 21 languages

Table 3.10 Population and number of land owning clans in the four timber rights purchase areas of the Gogol Timber Project in 1969

	Total	Gogol	Naru	Gum	North Coast
Population	4398	1183	1141	687	1387
Number of villages	34	11	7	5	11
Number of clans	508	168	93	73	174
Area (ha)	88 020	52 270	15 800	4960	14 990
Population density (No./100 ha)	5.0	2.3	7.2	13.8	9.2
Area (ha)/clan	173	311	170	68	86

Source: Department of Forests records, Colton (1976)

in the vicinity of these two areas. Most people can speak at least one other language besides their own. In addition, many can speak Pidgin English and the Lutheran Mission language called Bel or Graged and a few can communicate in English.

Plate 6 Braided course of the Naru River. Such meandering is typical of the Gogol River and its tributaries and causes much erosion and forest disturbance

Plate 7 An old grassland community in the Gogol TRP. There are 4000 ha of such grasslands scattered through the area

Land in the Gogol and Naru areas is owned by 261 clans (Table 3.10). The Gum and North Coast areas have 73 and 174 clans respectively making a total of 508 clans in the whole GTP area. The amount of land owned by each clan varies. Simple averages suggest that clans in the Gogol area own more land (311 ha per clan) than those in the Gum area (68 ha per clan). In fact, the differences between clans are probably much greater than these. The overall effect is that some clans are relatively well-off while others are comparatively short of land. Most of this land is held in small areas interspersed with the land of other clans.

In the past and now, a dispute over land was sometimes a source of great bitterness. Claims and counterclaims could lead to strained social relationships even after an official decision had been reached.

Social structures

Despite the social diversity implied by the numbers of languages and clans, the work of anthropologists in the Madang District (e.g. Lawrence 1964, 1970; Morauta 1973, 1974; McSwain 1977) suggests there are many similarities between the various groups. In each group, membership of a clan and the associated rights of land usage are normally acquired at birth. In some areas, however, non-cognates can also be incorporated into a clan. For example, a man might adopt a son or a host might give land to a war refugee. Such persons are treated thereafter as full clan members (Morauta 1974). More commonly, however, non-clan members are only allowed the temporary use of land without acquiring any long-term rights. Such persons may be simply friends or affines who wish to temporarily move from their own land for some reason. An example of this occurred in the northern Gogol TRP area following the 1970 earthquake which destroyed gardens and forest in parts of the Adelbert Range. Many people were able to shift temporarily into land belonging to other clans.

All economic, political and religious activities are carried out within the clans. Hence, they provide a person from birth to death with a fixed social milieu governing most of their behaviour and contacts. A person's allegiance is, therefore, primarily to the clan to which they belong and only secondarily to the village in which they live.

All clan decisions are made by consensus since there is no centralized authority or sytem of rank. There are, however, a number of potential leadership roles. The most important of these is that of the 'Big Man'. This is not a hereditary position but one achieved by the nature and force of personality. A man might achieve 'Big Man' status among his fellow clansmen through prowess in hunting, warfare or perhaps because he is articulate in discussion; alternatively, he might be wise in solving disputes or he might be a generous man. Such Big Men hold no formal office but achieve their position through their ability to pull strings, persuade or achieve popular endorsement of the activities they organize. The position of Big Man is widespread in village society throughout PNG.

A second leadership position is that of land leader. Morauta (1973) describes this as being simply the position occupied by the most senior active member of a clan. The land leader does not have to be especially talented, but, because of his seniority, the office holder is usually a respected figure and focal point for the clan. Finally, some clans have specialist magicians able to influence warfare, fighting, hunting, gardening etc. The magician acquires his powers through selective inheritance. The influence of magicians is such that activities for which they are responsible cannot go ahead without their consent. This does not give them right of veto but rather power to influence the timing of activities (Morauta 1973).

Not all clans have all leadership roles filled at any one time and group decisions can still be taken without prominent Big Men, but where Big Men exist they have political significance as politicians. Importantly, however, this significance is confined for the most part to the vicinity of a Big Man's village and rarely extends far beyond.

Spiritual beliefs strongly influence people's lives. Traditionally, people believed in a number of superhuman beings who were credited with creating the natural environment, the economy, society and culture. They were thought to be the source of all true knowledge and power. Spirits of the dead were not seen as creators but as guardians of their living descendant's interests. To ensure economic or political success, a person had to harness the power of the deities by means of ritual. Provided this was done, the deities were believed to guarantee in perpetuity the material requirements for existence.

All people placed a high value on materialism and the possession of material goods was a prerequisite for social relationships. As Lawrence (1964) points out,'Where there was no exchange of goods and services, there could be no sense of relationship, mutual obligation and value, but only suspicion, hostility and the risk of warfare'. Material culture, apart from its immediate and most obvious uses, is the symbol of all important relationships and social status. Ambitious men might envisage profit but for the most part, this would be in terms of the prestige achieved by display or distributing material wealth to clansmen and others.

Traditional religion supported this system by defining the deities' role in creating material goods and the manner by which these might be acquired. Some things such as the natural environment and the form of the social structure could be taken for granted but resources, artefacts or the relationships necessary for producing and distributing wealth could not and had to be explained by elaborate myth buttressed by ritual.

These beliefs profoundly affected the way in which the people of the area reacted to the arrival of Europeans and to changes in economic circumstances.

Plate 8   A typical small village in the lower Gogol Valley

Cargo Cults

The arrival of Europeans presented a dilemma for people of the Madang District. The Europeans had great material wealth that arrived as cargo in an apparently endless series of ships. They explained this wealth as being the end result of work and accumulation, but no such cargo had ever arrived for the villagers themselves despite work and the strict adherence to traditional rituals. In time, people came to believe there must be other deities and rituals responsible for the Europeans' material success. Since all knowledge had a divine source and a man's success depended on his ability to address that source, the problem was one of identifying the deity or deities responsible for this new cargo. Observations and reasoning like this has led to the so-called Cargo Cults that are widespread throughout Melanesia. These have taken many forms, although all have the goal of achieving by mystical means an increase in the material welfare of their adherents. In some cases, cult members have destroyed their possessions and neglected their gardens in order to demonstrate to their deities their confidence that the deities would recognise their needs. In other cases, cult members have rejected the economic methods offered by governments and Christian Missions believing these to be useless without the enabling ritual.

Cults in the Madang district have a long history and have been described in some considerable detail by Lawrence (1964). The earliest began in 1871 during the German colonial era and Lawrence has recognised five distinct stages since then involving at various times pagan deities, the Christian God and a pagan-Christian syncretism.

Some of the cults making up each of these stages were short-lived and localized, but others were highly influential and attracted adherents from far beyond the bounds of the cult leader's village. The most recent of Lawrence's five stages began in 1948 with a cult lead by Yali Singini, a man from a coastal village to the east of the Gogol River. Detailed descriptions of Yali's activities are given in Lawrence (1964) and Morauta (1974). Yali's cult achieved widespread support through the Madang district and probably achieved its political zenith at the time of the 1968 elections for the National House of Assembly. According to Harding and Lawrence (1971), the main issue of the campaign for electors in the Gogol Valley was the choice between the pathway to development offered by the cultists and the western model offered by the Administration. The cultists were defeated in the poll and, with Yali's death in 1975, have since lost influence. However, many people still support Yali's cult and many others who may have discarded Yali as a leader still find other forms of cargo cultism intellectually satisfying. Needless to say, such beliefs have influenced people's reaction to development opportunities following logging[1].

Health

Little was known about the health of people living in the Gogol Valley until several years after the GTP commenced, apart from casual observations by visiting health workers and Patrol Officers. In 1976, a detailed survey was carried out in a number of villages by the Institute of Medical Research (Serjeantson 1978). Although post-dating the commencement of logging, the report probably gives a reasonable picture of the health situation of the human population before the GTP commenced since most of the villagers surveyed had only just been reached by the new roads or were still some distance away.

The major health problems were malaria and anaemia. Up to 40 per cent in some childhood groups had malaria parasites and the average for all ages was 29 per cent (Table 3.11). Less than 10 per cent of the population

Table 3.11 Malarial parasites in human population of Gogol Valley by age group

Age group (years)	No. examined	Parasite rate %
0–1	43	27.9
2–4	61	39.3
5–9	103	40.3
10–14	125	36.0
15 +	276	19.7
All ages	608	29.1

Source: Serjeantson (1978)

Table 3.12 Medical conditions other than malaria showing a high incidence in the Gogol Valley

Condition	Children no. examined	% affected	Adults no. examined	% affected
Tinea imbricata (grille)	314	10.8	250	10.8
Other skin disease	314	15.6	250	14.8
Trachoma	285	24.9	247	11.3
Perforated ear drums	280	8.9	212	5.2
Respiratory disease	312	1.0	249	10.0

Source: Serjeantson (1978)

had haemoglobin levels within the range defined as normal by WHO. Other conditions having a high incidence were respiratory diseases, perforated ear drums and trachoma (Table 3.12). Skin diseases including *Tinea imbricata*, *Tinea versicolor*, scabies and *Molluscum contagiosum* affected more than 25 per cent of the population. The incidence of decayed, missing or filled teeth was low although peridontal disease was common. Only two cases of severe malnutrition were observed in the survey although the situation may be the same as elsewhere in PNG where Riley (1983) observed that,'one's clinical impression is that many children are in a state of precarious balance, rather than that malnutrition *per se* is a major national problem'. Interviews with mothers suggested infant mortality levels were rather higher than in urban Madang.

TRADITIONAL RESOURCE USE

Like the people of the lowlands elsewhere in PNG, villagers in the GTP make extensive use of the various resources of the forests. Most people are subsistence farmers and practise shifting cultivation. Within the Gogol Valley, three main gardening sites are recognised. These are the hill areas, the well-drained terrace areas (in pidgin *nambis*, or near water) and the levee strips (*waitsan* or sandy soils). No gardening is carried out in the swamp areas (*tais*). Within each of these sites, different soils are distinguished and judged to be either favourable or unfavourable for gardening. Clearing for gardening usually starts around June–August. The debris is burnt in September, heaped and reburnt in some places and planting is carried out following the early wet season rains in October or November. Before the GTP commenced, secondary regrowth forest was favoured over primary forest for gardening sites, a practice common to much of PNG. Although the advantages of having long fallow periods are recognized, regrowth as young as 6 years old could be used. This may reflect the location, amount and type of land available to particular clans.

No ethnobotanical studies have been carried out within the GTP area,

62

but it is clear that, like all PNG forest dwellers, the people of the Gogol Valley make extensive use of plants in the forest on their clan's land. Likewise, considerable use is made of the forest wildlife. Of the 251 species of animal known to occur in the area, 68 species are used by villagers. These include 16 species of mammals, 42 species of birds, eight species of reptiles and two species of frogs. Of the total of 68 species, 58 species (86%) are used for food, 32 species (46%) for adornment or ornaments, seven species (10%) sometimes kept as pets, four species (5%) used for making implements, two species (3%) for bride price or compensatory payments and six species (9%) for various other purposes. About 31 species (45%) had entered the cash economy by 1978 and were regularly available for sale in local markets. These included pigs, cuscus, wallabies, bandicoots, wildfowl and their eggs, monitor lizard skins and various bird feathers and mammal pelts (Liem 1978b).

There seems to have been few customary hunting restrictions in the area except that traditionally, a person would only hunt for sufficient wildlife for their needs. However, this attitude was changing with the advent of the cash economy and the increasing market for wildlife. One survey in 1977 found shotguns were then owned by 10 per cent of the hunters (Liem 1978b). These have obviously increased the capacity of hunters to take advantage of the cash market for wildlife. They have also meant that some animals previously regarded as difficult to catch could now be more easily hunted.

EVENTS IN THE GOGOL VALLEY SINCE THE ADVENT OF THE COLONIAL ERA

The early years

The first European to visit the area was the Russian scientist Nicholas Mikloucho-Maclay who visited and lived on the coast just east of the Gogol River several times between 1871 and 1883[2]. Mikloucho-Maclay admired the people of the area and made strenuous efforts within Russia and Europe after his departure to limit the adverse effects of the colonialism then about to overtake the country. In the event, he failed and German economic and colonial ambitions led to settlements in and around Madang from 1895 onwards.

Large areas of coconut plantations were established along the coast especially to the north of Madang, but there was little direct disturbance to the people of the Gogol Valley. Some worked as indentured labourers in the coastal plantations, but the comparative lack of access into the hinterland meant that life styles probably remained more or less the way they had always been.

Lutheran and Roman Catholic missionaries were active in the region generally and missions were established in the Gogol Valley at Utu (Roman

Catholic) and Amele (Lutheran). Just what the effect of the missions' activity was is unclear. Health and education of people in the immediate vicinity benefited but the extent to which Christianity surplanted the old ways and beliefs is less obvious. Certainly the missions were the fiercest opponents of the Cargo Cults suggesting they viewed the cults as significant ideological competition. Administrative controls were established by a network of appointed village officials (known as Luluais) who acted as representatives of the colonial authorities and were supposed to report serious misdemeanours.

Events remained in this disturbed but basically unaltered state until the Second World War. There was military action in the area during the war but afterwards the situation soon returned to pre-war conditions.

Economic changes

Few economic changes occurred in the Gogol Valley for much of the post-war period. Elsewhere in the country, agricultural extension officers actively promoted cash crops like coconuts, coffee and cocoa. However, the Gogol Valley was given a low priority by the Agriculture Department because of the supposedly poor soils in the area.

In 1963, the first TRP was carried out and a payment of $50,000 was made to landowners for the larger trees on their land. Forestry officers spent some months on foot patrols in the area explaining the changes likely to occur and the possibilities open to the people once logging commenced. One of the most eagerly awaited consequences was a road system. As already mentioned, the 1963 tender was unsuccessful and no logging occurred. However, the expectation of roads in the future led to considerable interest among landowners in cash cropping. When it became evident that new roads might not be built after all, some people in more isolated parts of the Valley attempted to build their own (De'Ath 1980).

In 1967 and 1968, a road was finally built by the Administration along the northern side of the Gogol Valley bridging the river at Mawan near the middle of the Gogol TRP. Records of coconut plantings show these immediately increased in the years following the road (De'Ath 1980). Overall, however, governmental agricultural officers were rather disappointed with the response to the improved access because 6 years after the completion of the road the numbers of coconuts and cocoa in the area were still far below those in areas adjoining the Gogol TRP or on the North Coast. This is an unfair comparison since many Gogol villages were still some distance away from the road and the North Coast area in particular had had a much longer time to take advantage of road access. However, as will be discussed later, this perception of an unenthusiastic response to the agricultural opportunities offered by the new road was important because it influenced the judgement of land use planners later trying to estimate the availability of land for tree plantation establishment after logging.

Political changes

Although the network of Luluais appointed by the Administration had been in place for many years, there was no real sense of political affinity between different villages in the valley. Trade links did exist between many but the clan was the all-important grouping.

In 1957, the Ambenob Local Government Council was formed covering much of the hinterland of Madang. Initially it included people from the Gum area but not those from the Gogol Valley. These later joined in 1967. Each councillor represented a ward, and each ward was composed of about four villages. The purpose of the Councils was to organize mutual help projects such as road building and maintenance and taxes were levied to complement funds received from the Administration for these tasks.

The Council was dominated by councillors from areas close to Madang. These men tended to be more experienced, better educated and knew each other well through common church membership or affinal links. This dominance was at the expense of councillors from some of the more inland areas. One year after the Gogol people joined the Council, one member of the Executive and Finance Committee could not name a single fellow councillor from south of the Gogol River. As a consequence, members from more remote inland areas such as the Gogol Valley had little influence on Council affairs (Morauta 1974).

The Council was not very popular and in 1969 only 38 per cent of eligible voters bothered to vote[3]. In Morauta's view, this was due to dissatisfaction with the Council rather than just apathy since there was also a rising number of tax defaulters. The Council was seen by many voters as inept and unresponsive to public opinion. This may have been due to unrealistic expectations of what the Council could do but it was probably also not too far from the truth[4]. From the outset, the main request that the Gogol councillors asked of the Council was support for more road construction within the Valley. The Council decided it was unable to afford this. Not surprisingly, therefore, the Council did nothing to create a sense of common purpose or political unity among people in the GTP.

National elections for the second House of Assembly were held in 1968. One of the main issues was economic development. All candidates for the Mabuso Open electorate, which included the Gogol Valley, were firmly in support of more roads which they believed would assist economic growth. As already mentioned, however, the campaign also concerned the two rival approaches to development – one was the utopian view of the cargo cultists and the other was the more conventional view espoused by the Administration. Although the supporters of the cargo cult movement were defeated in the election, their support was widespread. This is probably best illustrated by the fact that about 11 per cent of the vote in Mabuso Open electorate was for the cult leader Yali although he was not a candidate in the electorate. This figure probably underestimates his support since many other voters would have realised that a vote cast for him would have been informal. At Mawan in the centre of the Gogol Valley, Yali received 318 votes while the legitimate candidates received only 81 votes (Harding & Lawrence 1971).

Absenteeism

Of all the changes occurring in the Gogol Valley in the late 1960's, perhaps the most dramatic was the gradual increase in absenteeism; i.e. the temporary emigration of people from the area. By 1969, it had reached quite serious proportions. The census carried out in that year showed some 25 per cent of the total population in the Gogol and Naru areas was absent (Table 3.13). Since most of these persons were probably young men, and men in the 16–45 year old age group accounted for 42 per cent of the population, the census suggested a very high proportion of the able-bodied men in the area had left.

There may be a number of reasons which explain this phenomenon but the most probable cause was the perceived lack of economic opportunity in the Gogol Valley area compared with that in Madang. Elsewhere in PNG, absenteeism has been found to be greater in villages further from roads than in villages near roads (Conroy 1976). Roads allow cash crops to be marketed and increase economic opportunities in villages.

Commenting on the data, a District officer of the Administration observed,'The people themselves told me they held little hope for their future as more and more men were wanting to leave the area and some had been away for years and had never come back'. In his view,'the various social systems in the Gogol Valley were disintegrating and the rate of disintegration was becoming more and more rapid and I could see no way at the time of giving people meaningful development plans within the then financial restrictions' (Colton 1976).

In view of the Administration, the people of the Gogol Valley lived in a comparatively well developed district. There were many others living in more isolated parts of PNG who were much more deserving of support. The prospects of increased financial aid for roads and other development in the area was slight.

Table 3.13 Absenteeism in the Gogol Valley in 1969

Area	Population	16–45 *year age group*		*Absentees*	
		No.	%	*No.*	%
Gogol	1183	574	48	343	29
Naru	1141	411	36	228	20
Total	2324	985	42	571	25

Source: Colton (1976)

IN SUMMARY

The forests of the Gogol Valley and the associated TRP areas nearby were probably typical of much of the lowlands of PNG. They were rich in species, and, being subject to a number of natural disturbances, they contained a variety of habitats and vegetation types. In comparison with other lowland forest areas, they probably had rather more regrowth forest and grassland areas than is usual. As a timber resource the forests had not proved to be particularly attractive to loggers.

The forests were occupied by a small human population whose density was similar to that in many other lowland forest areas of the country. These people lived as shifting cultivators and relied on the forest to provide virtually all their needs. As in other parts of PNG, food production was not especially difficult but surveys of the people's health showed that their existence was not entirely idyllic.

People in the Gogol Valley were aware of some of the changes occurring in the wider society of PNG and were keen to participate in the economic opportunities being created. They had various views on how economic gain might be achieved and when their aspirations remained unfulfilled, many found it intellectually satisfying to seek explanations in some of the older beliefs. Despite an interest in economic advancement few people were willing to sell their land. Instead, an increasing proportion of younger men decided it was necessary to leave their village and look for opportunities elsewhere.

In the Administration's view, the hinterland of Madang, including the Gogol Valley, was an area that had already benefited from considerable funding. There were other more isolated communities in PNG needing the limited financial resources it had at its disposal. All this meant that, when the proposal to develop an intensive logging operation based on the Gogol Valley was received, it seemed an attractive proposition.

Note 1: Towards the end of his life, Yali maintained he was never the leader of a Cargo Cult but had simply wanted development for his people (Tua Kaima 1986).

Note 2: Some believe the present name of this area – the Rai Coast – is a corruption of his name.

Note 3: In 1969 the Council also became a multi-racial body. The change occurred without any of the controversy that took place in Rabaul.

Note 4: This situation did not improve with time. De'Ath 1980 quotes a provincial local government officer writing in 1975, "As with all councils, the greater majority (if not all) of tax revenue is eaten up paying salaries, allowances and general running expenses. Capital works programmes (the only thing people can see and understand") are entirely reliant on Rural Improvement Programme grants (a grant from the then National Government), cash contributions by Councils becoming less and less and self-help (free labour etc.) is virtually non existent. A certain amount of blame rests with council members themselves. Almost any task they perform (major or minor) must be paid for. At every meeting, one can hear the members' attitudes – 'the national government must provide money for this or that' not 'what can we (the Council and the people) contribute towards this?' The present day, much bandied phrase of 'self-reliance' does not exist in practice. Considerable funds are wasted in staff and general expenses. Superfluous staff are often employed. Council members either do not wish to or are still unaware that they should be controlled and checked on by them. Almost the only item of work that the majority of Council Executive Officers can be relied on to do fairly efficiently and promptly is to write a voucher and cheque for their salary each fortnight'.

CHAPTER 4

THE GOGOL TIMBER PROJECT

INTRODUCTION

The advent of the Gogol Timber Project appeared to be the answer to a number of problems. For the colonial Administration concerned with large trade deficits and the likelihood of some form of political independence in the near future, it was a much needed new industrial development. It would diversify the export base of the country and buffer it against the vicissitudes of international agricultural markets. For the Forestry Department, it was a way of overcoming the limitations imposed by having small volumes of numerous commercially unknown species. It also came at a time when the possibility seemed to be increasing that Papua New Guinea would be left behind in the market place by the developing timber industry of Indonesia. For the people of the area, it was a chance for 'development', a way to acquire roads and a way in which to participate in the economic changes occurring elsewhere in Papua New Guinea.

THE NEGOTIATIONS

The Gogol Timber Project formally commenced in August 1971 when an agreement was signed by the PNG Administration and a Japanese consortium known as Japan and New Guinea Timber Co. Ltd. (later to become incorporated in PNG as Jant Pty. Ltd.). This agreement gave to the consortium the rights to harvest timber from the area. The agreement marked the end point in a series of unsuccessful attempts by the Administration to utilise these forests. As mentioned earlier, the timber rights were first offered for public tender in 1964, but no satisfactory tender was received. The rights were offered again in 1966 with the same result. In 1968, the rights were offered a third time. On this occasion, a Japanese consortium submitted an application and began feasibility studies on making pulp from the variety of species present in the forest. Members of the consortium included a prominent financial company, Nomura Securities, and one of Japan's largest paper companies, Honshu Paper Co. Ltd. The

Administration was sufficiently impressed with the application to carry out a survey of the pulpwood resources in the area and arrange for a TRP over these and others nearby.

Details of the initial negotiations are not public. According to De'Ath (1980) the application was unsuccessful because the consortium were unable to satisfy the requirement for a majority Australian or PNG equity in the project. The application officially lapsed at the end of 1968, but, in January 1969, the equity requirements were altered and the Japanese were invited to reapply. At the same time, however, a small PNG sawmilling company known as Wewak Timbers also expressed an interest in the area and was given a permit to extract a small amount of sawlog timber. This operation was to function as a pilot project to verify timber volumes per hectare and determine logging costs (Anon. 1969a). Perhaps the Japanese could eventually use the smaller logs for pulp and Wewak Timbers the larger logs for sawn timber? The next 3 years involved negotiations between the Japanese group, Wewak Timbers and the Administration. Attempts were made by the Administration to force a partnership between the Japanese and Wewak Timbers. This was apparently unacceptable to the former. Finally, an agreement was reached in which Wewak Timbers became, in effect, a sub-contractor to Japan and New Guinea Timbers. The latter was given rights to harvest all pulpwood material from the whole GTP area. On the other hand, Wewak Timber was given rights to all sawlogs. Japan and New Guinea Timber was to operate in the Gogol, Naru and Gum TRP areas while Wewak Timbers was to operate in the North Coast area. Clear-felling would be carried out at both areas and logs would be exchanged in Madang (at appropriate prices).

The negotiations leading to the final agreement in 1971 were lengthy, but all parties appeared determined to achieve a successful outcome. From the Administration's point of view, the project was of considerable importance in several respects. First, it would be a demonstration of the viability and worth of woodchipping. If successful in the Gogol Valley, it could be applicable elsewhere in PNG. Second, the timber resources of the Gogol Valley were regarded as a relatively low grade resource because of the large areas of secondary forest. They had been unattractive to industry despite having been advertised on several occasions. The Japanese proposal seemed to be an ideal way of using these resources and providing an economic boost to the Madang district which had undergone a slump since the new highway to the highlands from Lae had been completed and Madang's role as a major air transit port had ceased. Finally, the project offered the chance of significant rural development to the Madang district because of the roads it would generate and the opportunities for cash cropping on the logged-over lands. This was seen as particularly important in those areas where emigration away from the villages was occurring and where cargo cults were well established.

One may question the extent to which the people of the area shared the Administration's enthusiasm for the project. There is not much doubt that the Administration genuinely believed the project would be beneficial and took this message to landowners. It is also clear that Patrol Officers and Foresters reported people seemed willing to sell their timber if it meant roads could be constructed. Apart from roads, however, their only concerns seemed to be that they would get the first choice of any new jobs in the project and that people from the populous highlands would not be able to move into the area along the roads and squat on their land.

Despite this, it is doubtful whether people really appreciated the implications of the choice they were being asked to make. Who can envisage the impact of chain saws and bulldozers if they have never seen them? Recognizing the difficulty, the Administration made an attempt to overcome it by taking some leaders to the large forestry operation and plymill at Bulolo. What help or influence this was is unclear. After all, it was a significantly different operation and did not involve clear-felling. In the event, the clans agreed to sell the timber rights over most land in the valley and participate in the project[1]. Some did so enthusiastically in the hope of immediate material gains. Others probably did so with less enthusiasm, or at least with less certainty about their future prospects.

The Japanese were probably interested in the Gogol Valley for several reasons. Until that time, Japanese companies in PNG had been only concerned with exporting unprocessed timber as logs. The originator of

Plate 9 An aerial view of clear-felling. Not all trees are removed. Those remaining are mainly *Ficus* species or smaller individuals. Note the considerable numbers of logs left on the site as waste

71

the Gogol woodchipping project seems to have had a more idealistic vision. According to De'Ath (1980) the originator was Mr. T. Okumura, the then chairman of Nomura Securities. Okumura had visited PNG in 1968 and believed he could establish a joint venture that would be a model for other Japanese companies. It would be an example of shared development which would combine the financial resources of Japan with the timber resources of PNG. Okumura's vision seems to have provided the driving force for the Japanese negotiations and sustained them during the lengthy discussions. At the same time, it is perfectly clear that the Japanese were motivated by more worldly considerations as well. An increasing proportion of Japan's pulpwood needs was then being met from overseas imports and most of this was in the form of chips. Thus, in 1955, only 0.2 per cent of Japan's pulpwood came from chips, but, by 1975, the proportion had soared to 74 per cent. In 1965, imports of chips were 2.8 per cent of the market, but, by 1975, imports totalled 39 per cent (Shimokawa 1977).

The technological knowledge allowing pulp to be made from a mixture of tropical species had attracted considerable interest from around the world. FAO was cautiously enthusiastic about the possibilities (King 1975) and PNG was an obvious potential source of this new material. In 1977, the then Director of the Planning Division of the Forestry Agency of Japan, said of the mixed species chips from PNG, 'Further utilization of this kind of woodchip is strongly desired from the viewpoint of securing a stable supply of raw material' (Shimokawa 1977). It seems fairly clear therefore that, besides satisfying Okumura's vision, the Gogol Project was another step in establishing a number of sources of pulpwood for Japanese mills from around the world[2].

The consortium realised that the Gogol Valley resources were not as valuable as those in other parts of the country. However, the Gogol Valley was preferred over those such as at Open Bay and Vanimo because, unlike these, there was a town, electricity supply, water and a good port at Madang. Since the project was to be, in many respects, a pioneering venture for the companies involved, they wished to minimise the additional infrastructural costs that would have been involved in the more isolated areas. The resource itself was virtually a secondary consideration (Lembke 1974).

THE AGREEMENT

The Administration wanted an industry and associated infrastructure established and it wanted a timetable for progress. Ideally, the industry would be 'integrated' in the sense that an optimum use would be made of each log. The best timbers would be either sawn or used for veneer production. The remainder would be chipped and exported for pulp production. At some time in the future, the Administration hoped that the pulping could be carried out at Madang. The companies would be responsible for building the plant and port facilities at Madang and establishing the road network and bridges in the forest. Some of these roads would be incorporated into the national road system. The Administration anticipated that plantations of fast growing species would be established to replace the original forest and that these would reach maturity at about the time that the original forest was finally harvested. This was expected to take 20 years. The Administration also expected the project would become profitable and that the people of PNG could share in these profits by obtaining equity in the companies[3].

For its part, the consortium wanted an assured supply of raw material and was prepared to take a few risks to ensure a favourable future position in PNG. There seems to be no reason to believe that it was not also interested in using woodchips from plantation species in the future after the natural forest had been logged. However, it also wanted some security over its investment and was not entirely happy with the form of land tenure in PNG and the uncertainties this could involve, especially in terms of reforestation. It was unwilling to form a partnership with the small local company, Wewak Timbers. It was, however, willing to have the Administration take up equity in its operations.

The agreement, finally signed on 11 August, 1971, remains confidential. However, the main provisions were apparently that:

(a) A permit would be issued for clear-felling within the TRP areas for 20 years.

(b) The Company would have rights to the Gogol, Naru, Gum and North Coast TRP's (at the time of the agreement the final purchase arrangements for these had not been completed. These arrangements were completed later in 1971).

(c) The Company would use its best endeavours to reach a suitable arrangement with a local sawmill for conversion of the sawlog component of the forest. Failing that, the Company was to establish a sawmill of its own with an annual capacity of $24\,000\,m^3/yr$. (No time scale was placed on this requirement, but an agreement was quickly reached with Wewak Timbers).

(d) The Company would build a veneer mill and would study the feasibility of establishing a pulpmill in the area.

(e) The Administration had the option to take up 20% of the total share capital of the Company within 5 years.

(f) There would be consultations to determine the prices for wood chips that Jant would receive from its parent company Honshu.

(g) The Company would be responsible for building port facilities and roads and pay a share of the maintenance costs of existing public roads.

(h)   The Administration would supply electricity to the company.

(i)   The Administration would endeavour to obtain land for reforestation such that the industry could be maintained at a viable level. (However, there was no date set by which this should be done nor was it made clear who would be responsible for actually carrying out reforestation).

(j)   The Company would train local staff and progressively replace expatriate staff with local people.

(k)   The two parties agreed on a capital structure that could only be changed with Administration approval.

(l)   The Company would submit plans for pollution control and working plans for the field operations (the latter, however, did not have to be submitted until 12 months after the agreement was signed and there were no penalties for damage to the environment or a performance bond).

Japan and New Guinea Timbers was renamed as Jant in December 1971 and a permit issued to Jant on 1 November, 1973. Interestingly, the Memorandum of Association for Jant filed in the Registrar of Companies Office in Port Moresby provided for Jant to engage in a wide range of businesses other than the timber industry. These included aquaculture, fishing, ship building, and the importing and distributing of machinery and chemicals. The principals of the Company were evidently keeping their future options as open as possible.

Woodchip prices

One of the most difficult problems in negotiating the agreement concerned the price that Jant would charge its parent company, Honshu, for woodchips. It could, for example, charge an artificially low price which was less than its cost of production. In this case, Jant would not make a profit and would not be liable to PNG tax. In effect, the profits would be transferred to Honshu. On the other hand, it was difficult to say before the operation actually started just what the real production costs would be and thus what a 'fair' price would be. The solution chosen was to compare the PNG chips with those from other sources, in particular those being produced from eucalypt forests in Australia since in both cases the chips were used for kraft pulp.

There are a number of technical considerations in making such a comparison (Higgins and Philips 1973c). The factors influencing the price of chips include wood quality, freight, pulp yield, pulp quality and processing costs. An outline of the significance of each is given in Appendix 2.

The main differences in the PNG mixture – Australian eucalypt comparison, concerned basic density, pulp yield and transport costs. The negotiations were carried out accordingly although various other factors were considered at different times.

Initially there was considerable experimental data but little commercial experience in making pulp from the mixed species. Accordingly, a price was established for the first few years of K38 per Bone Dry Unit (BDU). This was lower than the K41 which the Administration estimated was equitable in comparison with Australian *Eucalyptus* chips. However, Jant argued that the PNG chips were 'new' and needed to be discounted accordingly.

The first price review took place in 1977, three years after the first shipments of chips from Madang. The Administration brought in specialist consultants from Australia's CSIRO to help in the negotiations. Jant argued that the price should be dropped. The chips were inferior to those from elsewhere and they were taking a risk with the lower grade resource. Moreover, they said, no one else wanted these chips[4].

The Administration argued the price should be higher and asked for K40 fob per BDU for the next year. Jant responded with an offer of K35.50 per BDU. The final ageed price was K40 for 2 years with further negotiations to take place in 1979. By comparison, the weighed average price for eucalypt chips from Australia in the first quarter of 1977 was K43.34 fob per BDU.

In subsequent negotiations, prices have been affected by changes in the international markets. For example, in 1979, international prices increased because of a slump in the U.S. timber industry and a fall in the amount of sawmill waste going into woodchips.

Problems with the agreement

In retrospect, the final agreement suffered from two major weaknesses. One of these was the uncertainty over reforestation and the other concerned environmental protection.

Both the Administration and Jant were interested in reforestation to sustain the industry once the natural forest resource had been logged. The Administration wished to play a key role in establishing these plantations. This was partly because it wished to ensure they were established correctly (Honshu, after all, had little or no tropical experience). The Administration was also concerned because it realised acquiring land from the landowners would be a complex and lengthy task.

Landowners in the GTP area had different views over reforestation. Those in the Gum and North Coast Blocks were not interested. Following the logging operation, they proposed using the cleared land for cash crops. The old logging roads would enable these crops to be taken to market. The people of the Gogol and Naru Blocks were less certain. Some were interested in cash crops and others were interested in reforestation. The inherent problem with reforestation, however, was that it required a commitment to that land use for perhaps 20 years or more, a period beyond the life times of many senior clan members. Understandably, this aspect of the proposal was not appealing to such people. There was no prospect of landowners selling land to the Administration and the idea of land leasing was treated with suspicion by some people. If the Administration or Company planted trees on their land, would they then not be entitled to claim the land as their own?

There were, however, other people less concerned by such worries and more interested in the idea of plantation reforestation, perhaps because they had seen the Forestry Department's research plantation at Baku. However, they wanted someone else to take the first step and prove that tree growing really was as profitable as coffee or coconuts. They had already committed their land to clear-felling and that was enough for a first step.

At the time the negotiations were under way (1968–1971), the Administration was seriously worried about the political turmoil on Bougainville and the Gazelle Peninsula. In both cases, land ownership was a root cause of the problems. The Administration's attempts to resolve the complexities of multiple ownership with the Land Bills of 1970 and 1971 were strongly opposed in the House of Assembly. It was obviously not a time for radical new solutions to the problems of long term land management in the Gogol Valley. Feedback from villagers to Patrol Officers and Foresters suggested that some form of land leasing could probably be arranged but that it would take time. That seemed the only choice.

For its part, the new company was unwilling to commit funds over a long time period in land over which it had no control. It was aware of the likelihood of Independence in the near future and uncertain what attitudes a new Government might have towards such an investment. The result was that the problem was deferred.

The second problem with the agreement concerned environmental protection. The agreement provided for environmental safeguards for the town and harbour of Madang near where the chipmill and sawmill were to be built but there was nothing explicit in the agreement, governing the way in which logging should be carried out, wildlife protected or soil and water resources safeguarded. The only safeguards were the general guidelines and penalties available under the various existing Forestry and Water Resources Ordinances. These were quite inadequate for a logging operation of the size of the GTP.

INITIAL ACTIVITIES OF JANT AND WEWAK TIMBERS FOLLOWING THE COMPLETION OF THE NEGOTIATIONS

Prior to the completion of negotiations, field parties from Honshu Paper Co. carried out surveys in Madang and the GTP area. With the signing of the agreement Jant immediately embarked on a vigorous construction

Plate 10 The chip dump and conveyor belt system associated with the loading facility

Plate 11 The woodchip mill and loading facility at Madang

programme. In terms of the engineering aspects of the project, it seems clear that the company carried out fairly detailed planning. Construction of the chipmill and loading facilities began at a site on the waterfront in Madang. Consultants were called in to ensure mill noise levels would not be obtrusive and pollution would not drain from the site into the Madang Harbour. The mill had log loaders to transfer logs onto chain conveyors, a debarker, saws to break down the larger logs and two chippers with 3 m discs. It had a capacity to handle up to $400\,000\,\text{m}^3/\text{yr}$ (two shifts). Some of the technical details are described by Lembke (1974).

In the field, a base camp with dormitories and an engineering workshop was established near Baku in the centre of the Gogol Valley. With the completion of this base camp, efforts were directed at establishing a logging road network.

Two classes of roads were constructed. The main roads provided the primary access into various parts of the GTP and branch roads were constructed off these. The standards initially set were very high. Main roads had pavement widths of 10 m and up to 30 m clearway on either side to ensure they dried out quickly after rain. Slopes were kept to 10 per cent or less. The branch roads had 6 m pavements set in 18 m clearings. The cost of some of these roads was probably up to K50 000 per km, compared with the K12–20 000 per km being spent elsewhere in PNG for main logging roads (Gardner, 1980). The cost of this programme was obviously too high, and eventually the main road standard was relaxed to that of the branch road standard and the latter became 4 m wide. The roading plan called for 200 km of main roads and 500 km of branch roads. This represents a road density of around 3.2 m per ha of main road and 7.9 m per ha of branch road – an overall density of 11.1 m per ha (calculated on an assumed accessible forest area of 63 000 ha). This road density is much higher than that at the Baja Calima pulpwood logging operation in rain forest in Colombia, which had a total road density of 2.9 m per ha (Frisk 1978)[5].

Several hundred men were hired as plant operators, truck drivers and labourers. Since employment preferences were to be given to people from the Madang District in general and the GTP area in particular, the company was obliged to mount an intensive training programme to teach the new skills necessary. Some instructors were brought from Japan by some of the companies supplying the equipment (virtually all equipment being used in the field was of Japanese origin) and other instructors were hired from other large PNG companies like Bougainville Copper that had formal programmes of employee education[6].

The road clearings generated the first woodchips. These were added to and stockpiled as logging commenced until the arrival of the specially designed bulk chip carrier, the 23 000 dwt MV Madang in June 1974. The shipping of the first consignment of chips marked the formal opening of the chipmill at Madang. By this time, Jant had completed the chipmill and loading facilities, established the field base camp, built 50 km of roads and had over 400 employees. The investment in chipmill and loading facilities was A\$4.4 million and in loading and logging equipment A\$3.6 million (Table 4.1).

The Wewak Timbers operation differed from Jant in many aspects. It was a much smaller operation and the original owners of the Company had had a good deal more experience in logging in PNG conditions. A controlling interest in the company was subsequently bought by a New Zealand timber company, Fletcher Holdings and the new owners built a sawmill on a site at Madang next to the Jant chipmill. The logging roads the Company built on the North Coast Block were much less sophisticated than the Jant roads in the Gogol Valley, and its early logging costs were probably appreciably lower. The company had less success, however, with its sawmilling operations. These problems will be described later.

While the engineering aspects of Jant's early operations in particular were evidently carefully planned, there is less evidence that this was true of the early logging operations of either company. No detailed working plans were submitted by either company during negotiations or, as the agreement provided, within 12 months of it being signed. As will be explained later, early fluidity may have suited the Administration in some respects, but it also hampered its ability to monitor and control the early stages of the project. There was no knowledge, except in the most general terms, of what areas were to be logged, when these would be logged, and how big each area would be. This information was critical, of course, for the Administration's attempts at post-logging land-use planning.

Table 4.1 Status of Jant's operation 1974

	June 1974	*Expected*
Facilities		
Chipmill	complete	
Port facilities	complete	
Base camp – Gogol Valley	complete	
Veneer mill	—	by 1975
Pulp mill	—	feasibility study by 1977
Roads		
Main roads (kms)	26	200 by 1984
Branch roads (kms)	24	500 by 1984
Workforce		
Papua New Guinean	400	1200
Japanese	20	?
Australian	4	?
Production		
Timber harvested	—	300–380 000 m^3 by 1976/77
Veneer output	—	24 000 m^2 by 1976/77
Annual sales	—	A\$6 million

Source: Lembke (1974)

EARLY ADMINISTRATION ACTIVITIES

It is probably not unfair to say that, like Jant, the Administration had not developed detailed plans for the GTP at the time the agreement was signed. Trial plots of various plantation species had been planted in the Gogol Valley since 1968 and studies of the financial viability of a major plantation programme had been carried out in 1970 and 1971 (A.E. White 1975). However, detailed planning was still incomplete. In part, this may have been caused by the fact that the Administration was essentially responding to the Honshu proposal. It did not have a detailed prescription for the project of its own. It was also due to the limited staff available for the planning needed. In retrospect, it was fortunate that few of the timber projects advertised in 'New Horizons' in 1973 were taken up in the early 1970's. The Department of Forests would have been unable to maintain any semblance of control. Two important early decisions were made after the operation started, however. One of these was to create a co-ordinating body in Madang to handle the day-to-day developments of the project. The second was to commence detailed planning for the post-logging land use.

Madang timber working group

The Madang Timber Working Group (MTWG) was formed in 1972 as a sub-committee of the Administration's existing Madang District Coordinating Committee. The MTWG was made up of representatives of the Departments of Forestry, Agriculture, Lands and the Chief Minister's Department and, at a later stage, seven elected village representatives. Its role was to coordinate the roles of these various departments and to act as a focal point for and liaison between the Administration, the Companies and landowners.

The first major task carried out by the Group was to patrol the GTP area to inform people of the current state of the project and the likely future developments, to make known the MTWG as a point of contact, and to seek people's views on the project and future operations. It quickly became the main Administration management agency for the GTP and, in light of the considerable uncertainty amongst all parties as to the way the project would develop, the best single decision the Administration made in the early years of the project. In time, its role included compiling geneologies, distributing royalty payments, acting as a mediator between landowners and the company, and surveying clan boundaries.

Land-use planning

The Department of Forests began planning the post-logging land-use in 1971. It was clearly too late to be able to consider all land-use options because the agreement allowing unrestricted logging was completed. However, the planning was carried out in an attempt to reconcile economic and social requirements against ecological desiderata. The Administration was in an awkward position. It had no ultimate control over land-use – that still remained with the clans. However, it wanted to promote several particular land uses, especially reforestation. There was also a general feeling that parts of the area should remain unlogged in some form of a reserve.

Planning was only carried out in the Gogol and Naru Valleys because, as already noted, landowners in the Gum and North Coast areas already had definite ideas on post-logging land use and did not want the Administration to become involved. Reforestation was not high on their list of priorities.

The planning process has been described by Whyte (1975). The basic steps involved were to:

(a)   classify and map the vegetation.

(b)   classify and map the terrain.

(c)   combine the vegetation and terrain maps into a single 'land type' map (a land type was defined as land which had uniform vegetation and terrain attributes and which, it was assumed, would therefore have a uniform suitability for any particular use).

This process yielded a total of 20 land types, ranging from well drained terrace forest on flat land to hill forest on broken terrain. Each of these land types were then ranked on a scale of 1 to 5 for their suitability for various purposes such as plantation establishment or different forms of agriculture (Table 4.2). In planning for reforestation, the five rankings were rearranged as follows:

1 and 2:	comparatively well suited for intensive reforestation.
3a:	less suited for intensive reforestation because of seasonal inundation; special techniques (e.g. dry season planting) or species needed.
3b:	less suited for intensive reforestation because of rough terrain; enrichment planting possible.
4a:	low suitability for reforestation because swampy.
4b:	low suitability for reforestation because very rough terrain (i.e. desirable as protection forest).
5:	unsuitable for reforestation because swampy or extreme liability to flooding and river erosion.

At the same time, the MTWG drew up a list of possible land-uses for the area. These included:

Table 4.2 Land suitability matrix for Gogol and Naru Valleys. A rating of 1 = most suitable or liable to erosion while 5 = least suitable or liable to erosion

Terrain class	Vegetation type	Land type	Area (ha)	Roading	Logging	Erosion	Reforestation	Agric.	Cattle	Subsist. gardens
Flat	Secondary Forest	1	5250	1	3	4	1	1	1	2
	Kunai	2	460	1	5	4	2	2	1	3
	Pit-pit	3	860	4	5	1	5	4	4	4
	Floodplain forest	4	4300	1	1	4	1	1	1	2
	WDT forest	5	4570	1	1	4	1	1	1	1
	PDT forest	6	6270	2	1	4	3d	2	1	4
	Swamp forest	7	580	3	1	4	4d	4	4	5
	Hill forest	8	780	2	2	3	2	2	1	1
Gentle	Secondary forest	9	1840	2	3	3	2	2	1	2
	Kunai	10	600	2	5	3	2	2	1	3
	WDT forest	11	740	1	1	4	1	1	1	1
	PDT forest	12	960	2	1	4	3d	2	1	4
	Hill forest	13	7530	2	2	3	2	2	1	1
Moderate	Secondary forest	14	2060	2	3	2	3t	3	2	2
	Kunai	15	510	2	5	2	3t	3	2	3
	Hill forest	16	12830	2	2	2	3t	3	2	1
Rugged	Secondary forest	17	1310	2	4	1	4t	4	3	2
	Kunai	18	470	3	5	1	4t	4	3	3
	Hill forest	19	10400	3	3	1	4t	4	3	2
Broken	Hill forest	20	4440	4	4	1	4t	4	4	3

Notes: d = poor soil drainage is major constraint; t = terrain is major constraint; Kunai = Imperata grassland; Pit-pit = Saccharum; WDT = well drained terrace; PDT = poorly drained terrace.
Source: Whyte (1975)

Plantation reforestation
Experience with plantations elsewhere in PNG suggested an area of 20 000 ha with trees grown on 10–12 year rotations would be sufficient to maintain the Jant operation once the natural forest had been logged. Trials had been commenced in the Gogol Valley in 1968. These trials, and experience elsewhere in PNG, showed that the endemic species *Eucalyptus deglupta* Blume was a very promising plantation species, with mean annual increments (MAIs) of $25\,m^3/ha/yr$ or more. A number of other species also showed considerable promise.

Enrichment planting on selectively logged forest
Although the agreement negotiated with Jant did not specify how logging should be carried out, it was generally expected that large areas of forest might be only logged selectively, especially forests on steeper topography and perhaps some of the advanced secondary regrowth forests. Although a certain amount of natural regeneration would occur after logging, enrichment planting was considered another possibility[7].

Small scale agriculture
Most landowners would continue to practise subsistence agriculture and this would obviously be a major future land-use. With the advent of roads, however, opportunities would also exist for small scale cropping of cash crops such as coffee, cocoa and copra.

Large scale agriculture
The Agricultural Department believed there could be some prospects for cropping of rice in parts of the Naru valley. A United Nations consultant was brought to PNG to advise on the matter. He eventually recommended against the venture, but the possibility was included in the early planning stage.

Large scale cattle project
Many landowners were impressed with beef cattle because of the high value these could command and because they conferred considerable status on the owner. Besides having small individually owned herds, there seemed to be some potential for a larger cattle herd, perhaps run by a co-operative.

Reserves
Two so-called 'benchmark reserves' were allowed for. One of these was a well-drained floodplain forest in the upper Gogol Valley, and the other was an area of more poorly drained forest near the mouth of the Gogol River. No reserves were located in steeper terrain since it was expected that these would be achieved by default[8]. In addition, a series of smaller 'village reserves' were planned. In theory, these were to occupy small watersheds

and safeguard village water supplies or protect natural forest near villages as sources of traditional natural products such as medicinal plants etc. Detailed planning and mapping of these reserves was not carried out since they were small (about 40 ha) and were to be finalised after discussions with each village.

Using the various land types recognised earlier, a series of eight possible 'scenarios' or land-use plans were drawn up giving different weights to these various uses and showing the distribution of each in the area. All included the plantation option, although the area allocated varied. In general, the plantation lands were located on the more gentle slopes (which coincidentally have the chemically more fertile soils). The different combinations of plantation reforestation and agriculture are shown in Table 4.3.

The plantation land-use was planned making certain assumptions. It was known that many landowners were interested in plantations being established. The problem was in persuading enough of the 261 land-owning clans holding adjoining land to participate. To be viable, the plantation had to be more or less contiguous and not split into numerous small patches. At the time that planning was being carried out, Patrol Officers and Foresters working in the area believed that somewhere between 67 per cent and 75 per cent of landowners in some of the flatter topography would eventually be willing to join a plantation scheme. Plans were therefore drawn up to include each possibility. One particular area north of the Gogol River was excluded from the reforestation proposal. The people in the area (which included the Catholic Mission station at Utu) were unwilling to be involved in any Administration-promoted reforestation or agriculture, and, like the people of the North Coast and Gum areas, believed they would need all their land for their own purposes.

Eight land-use plans were considered by the MTWG and one, Scenario 3, was modified to widen the options still further. Scenario 3B was finally forwarded to the Cabinet in Port Moresby for its approval and was adopted as the basic planning document for the area in 1974. Scenario 3B included plantation reforestation, large scale agriculture, large scale cattle reserves and a residual area that could be reforested either by enrichment planting or by allowing natural regeneration. The plan is shown in Fig. 4.1.

Although this plan constituted the most desirable final land-use plan for the area, at least from the viewpoint of the MTWG, it did have two areas of uncertainty associated with it. One of these was the extent to which clear-felling or selective logging would be carried out in the more rugged terrain. The formal agreement signed by Jant provided for no restrictions in this respect, but, in practice, it was expected that substantial areas in the hill forest zone (those rated 4B in terms of their suitability for reforestation in Table 4.2) would remain untouched. The second uncertainty was the

Table 4.3 Various land-use plans (scenarios) considered for the Gogol and Naru TRPs after logging (areas in hectares)

Land-Use	Scenario									
	1	2	3	3A	3B	4	5	6	7	8
Small holder agriculture no reforestation	3900	3900	3900	3900	3900	3900	3900	3900	3900	3900
Benchmark reserve	1300	1300	1300	1300	1300	1300	1300	1300	1300	1300
Reforestation	25 100 **	26 900 *	25 600 **	25 600 **	26 900 **	27 800 *	25 900 **	28 400 *	26 300 **	28 500 *
plus small holder agriculture (land for reforestation)	(18 800)	(17 700)	(19 200)	(19 200)	(20 200)	(18 300)	(19 400)	(19 000)	(19 700)	(19 100)
Large scale agriculture	—	—	—	1200	1200	—	4900	4900	4900	4900
Cattle	—	—	4800	—	3100	4700	—	—	4600	4700
Selective logging and enrichment planting	34 400	32 600	29 200	33 000	28 600	27 100	29 000	26 300	23 800	21 500
Swamps and river edges	3000	3000	3000	3000	3000	3000	3000	3000	3000	3000
TOTAL	67 700	67 700	67 800	68 000	68 000	67 800	68 000	67 800	67 800	67 800

* Assume 66 per cent available for reforestation
** Assume 75 per cent available for reforestation

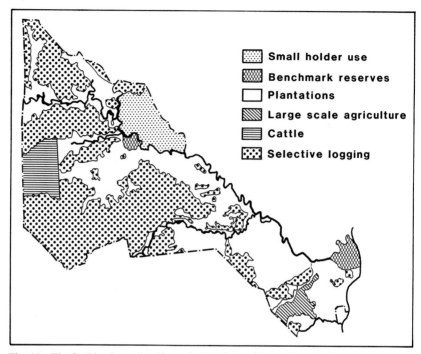

Fig. 4.1 The final land-use plan (Scenario 3B) chosen for the Gogol Valley

exact location of a number of village reserves. The location of these was not something for the MTWG alone to decide but could only be discussed after villagers themselves had held lengthy consultations. However, the expected land-use after logging is shown in Table 4.4. In essence, 51 per cent of the area was expected to be clear-felled, 18 per cent partially logged, and the remaining 31 per cent was expected to remain unlogged. In the clear-felled areas, the bulk would be used for plantation forestry or intensive agriculture, while the remainder would be used by landowners for small scale agriculture or would be abandoned to revegetate naturally.

It is necessary to reiterate again at this point that the formal agreement between Jant and the Administration preceded the development of this plan. However, Jant agreed to the excision of the benchmark reserves and village reserves from its logging areas – it would have been insensitive to do otherwise.

LOGGING OPERATIONS

Jant eventually established a number of logging teams to work in different parts of the forest simultaneously. By 1980, three teams were working in the Gogol Valley, and two others were based in the Naru Valley. At times, up to eight teams were at work in various parts of these two areas. The

Table 4.4 Post logging land-use in the Gogol and Naru Valleys anticipated in 1974 based on Scenario 3B (approximate only)

Land-use		Area (ha)	Percentage Partial	Total
(a)	Clear-felled			
	Plantation forestry	20 000	29	
	Cattle Project	3140	5	
	Large scale agriculture	1160	2	
	Smallholder agriculture	9980	15	51
(b)	Selectively logged			
	Enrichment plantings	12 000	18	18
(c)	Not logged			
	Benchmark reserves	1280	2	
	Village reserves	900	1	
	Swamps, rivers etc.	3000	4	
	Hill forest on rugged terrain (land type 4B)	16 600	24	31
	TOTAL	68 060		

advantage of this number was that it dispersed road traffic and reduced the hazard of congestion, especially during wet weather. It was also easier for Jant to maintain work rates among its new workers. From an ecological point of view, it had the important effect of diffusing the impact of logging. This aspect will be described further in the next Chapter.

The operation was a learning experience for all parties. Few of the newly hired Madang people had significant logging experience. On the other hand, few of the Japanese supervisors had tropical experience, and no one in the Administration had had to deal with intensive clear-felling operations. The result for the first year or so was a constantly changing routine until methods and harvesting rules were established[9].

In the view of some outside specialists, Jant's original logging operation showed signs of a lack of planning and too great a road density (Groves 1975 quoted by Webb 1977). All of Jant's logging was carried out using Komatsu D65 crawler tractors. In many respects, this dependency was a disadvantage. Crawler tractors can be used for breaking out logs from where they have been felled and bunching these on a snig track. However, where there are favourable grades to a log landing (i.e. loading point) of less than 20° and/or adverse grades of no more than 12°, rubber tyred skidders can be used to snig logs along cleared tracks more quickly than crawler tractors. Slopes up to 20° can be negotiated by skidders provided they are short i.e. less than the length of the winch rope (Groves 1975). A major advantage of the skidders is that they can reduce the density of logging roads needed to service a particular area. By 1980, Jant had three rubber tyred skidders and were considering buying a yarder, but were still experimenting with logging systems. Wewak Timbers on North Coast used crawlers, tractors and skidders from the beginning of their operations.

Monitoring of the roading and logging operation by the Forestry Department led to a number of controls being established on environmental grounds. These controls will be discussed in the following Chapter.

The original expectations were that the annual logging rate would reach about 4200 ha within a few years of operations commencing. At the end of 5 years, some 19 000 ha were to be logged. At this rate, the natural forest would sustain the industry for 20 years. After this time, the plantations would take over as the main resource. In fact, the rate of logging never reached this expected level. By December 1978, that is 5 years after logging commenced, the area logged in *all* areas (Gogol, Naru, Gum and North Coast) was only 14 000 ha.

A lower annual logging rate should have led to a longer life for the natural forest resource. Instead, it soon became evident that the natural resource would be logged well before the 20 year period. By the end of December 1979, 6 years after logging started, only 36 100 ha of commercially available forest were estimated to remain out of the total forest area of 88 000 ha in the GTP. There were several reasons for this. One was that the effect of topography had been underestimated when the original estimates of the resource life were made. In practice, Jant did not log the steeper slopes (roughly corresponding to the land type 4b mentioned earlier). Another was that the importance of grassland and secondary regrowth also appeared to have been under-estimated. Finally, areas of commercially utilizable forest were excised from the concession for village reserves, benchmark reserves and later, buffer strips along rivers and streams. All of these reduced the size of the natural resource at a time when the prospects for establishing a plantation forest within the original timetable seemed uncertain.

A temporary solution to the problem was to increase the size of the natural forest resource available to Wewak Timbers. An area of 10 900 ha, 85 km north-west of Madang and accessible from the coastal road, was surveyed in 1975. This became known as the Far North Coast Block. The timber rights for sawlogs only were purchased and allocated to Wewak Timbers. Some consideration was also given to extending the resource available to Jant by making a second extension on the western boundary of the existing Gogol TRP. This extension had been assessed for sawlogs (but not pulpwood) in 1966 and roads into the area could have ultimately been part of a road to the highlands. The problem with such an extension was that the haulage distances were considerable and possibly uneconomic, and, unlike the Far North Coast Block, the population was low. There were, therefore, considerable difficulties in developing economic future land uses after a clear-felling operation. By 1981, no decision had been made on this extension.

MILLING OPERATIONS

Jant's main difficulties in the field lay in organizing its logging operations to deal with the particular combination of forest and terrain of the Gogol Valley and to do this under the developing series of environmental controls imposed by the Department of Forests. In the mill operation, it faced another series of difficulties. In the first place, it was restricted by limited electricity supplies for the first 2 year's operations. The Administration had agreed to supply Jant with power from the Ramu hydroelectricity scheme in the highlands. A delay in installing the Ramu generator and connecting this power to Madang meant Jant's production was substantially limited because it was not able to operate after 6 p.m. when domestic electricity consumption peaked. There were also difficulties in processing the variety of species and log sizes arriving at the chipper. Eventually, however, these problems were overcome.

Although Jant had agreed to install a veneer mill after the chipping operation was established, it did not do so. When the time came, it argued that the market for veneer was declining and it pointed to the number of plywood mills in Japan then in serious financial difficulties. Furthermore, Jant claimed it was still too far in debt to be able to afford any further outlays on a veneer plant. Prospects for a pulpmill at Madang had never been good because of the very high costs and the large timber requirements. It seems unlikely that even the ritual of preparing a feasibility study, as required under the Agreement, was ever carried out.

Wewak Timbers also had difficulties with its new mill. Like Jant, the new owners of the company insisted on using technology and management methods imported from their home country. A New Zealand bandsaw and oil operated shotgun carriage was installed. The equipment was more suited to softwood timbers than hardwoods and proved to be insufficiently robust for the logs being sawn. It was also difficult to service and needed a specialist technician to be flown from New Zealand to handle major problems. Eventually, it had to be replaced (Gardner 1980). Initially, the mill only received kwila (*Intsia bijuga*). By 1977, however, other species were being taken as well although kwila remained the dominant species. In the absence of a veneer mill, efforts were made to optimize the use of the resource by converting as many species as possible into sawn timber rather than woodchips. On average, it seemed about 25 per cent of the logs cut were of sawlog size and about half of these were commercially acceptable species. Much of Wewak Timbers early production of sawn timber was exported, but, by 1980, most was used for prefabricated housing construction and was sold in PNG.

REFORESTATION AND OTHER LAND-USES

By 1980, 6 years after Scenario 3B had been adopted as the preferred land-use plan for the area, it was apparent that the actual pattern of land-use was likely to be somewhat different to that originally envisaged. The benchmark reserves and most of the village reserves were still intact, but neither the cattle project nor the large scale agricultural project had eventuated. Similarly, enrichment planting had been tried, but little of the area was treated in this way. On the other hand, plantation forestry had commenced and was beginning to achieve acceptance amongst landowners as an appropriate land use. The circumstances surrounding each of these land-uses were as follows:

Reserves

The benchmark reserves remained undisturbed, although some minor boundary adjustments were carried out. For example, the large reserve near the mouth of the Gogol River was found to inadvertently contain all the land of one clan from Maraga Village and the boundary was adjusted to alter this situation. Part of this success with the two benchmark reserves may have been due to the fact that the owners had received payment for the land through the original TRP payment. There was, however, still no formal agreement that guaranteed the reserve's integrity after the completion of logging. The only realistic safeguard was a continued acknowledgement by the owners of the worth of such reserves.

The village reserves had a more chequered history. Some remained intact and were used as intended. Others were partially cleared and used for gardening, and others again were broken up and located on intersecting boundaries of several clan lands so that each group had its own small reserve. In the latter case, the difficulty was that the reserves were sometimes located on the land of only one or two clans. This meant that either these clans restricted access to the reserves to members of their clans, or that they had the burden of providing reserve forest to all members of a village, including those from other clans. One solution could be to have a reserve for each clan. This would necessitate abandoning the idea of a reserve occupying a small undisturbed watershed and would probably mean each reserve would have to be smaller than the nominal 40–50 ha currently used, but this might make the whole idea impractical. Overall, it was clear that the size and location of each village reserve would have to be settled on a village by village basis according to clan land holdings.

In the late 1970's, an additional wildlife reserve was declared in an area less than a kilometre outside the GTP north of the junction of the Gogol and Naru Rivers (Fig. 3.2). It covered part of the steep escarpment opposite Asuar village and although small, was a significant addition to reserves in the area.

Cattle and large-scale agriculture

The cattle project was to be established in grasslands near Tebensarik Village in the west of the Gogol TRP. However, this area was not due to be logged until late in the life of the project, and, by 1980, no road had been built to the site. In the meantime, some cattle were brought into the Gogol Valley and were grazed along road sides, but it seemed that enthusiasm for cattle amongst landowners had waned. In the early 1960's, many aspired to own cattle. Twenty years later, in the 1980's, only a few were interested in building herds. The Department of Forests also tried running cattle in fenced off areas within its experimental plantations but eventually abandoned the idea. There was not enough feed and trampling damage was high.

The large-scale agricultural project foundered because of a lack of land. People in the chosen area were unwilling to allocate land to the project and it seemed more appropriate to the MTWG that smallholder agriculture take precedence over some still undefined large scale cropping system. Details of small scale agricultural development will be discussed later in Chapter 6.

Enrichment planting on selectively logged land

In early land-use planning, it was expected that clear-felling would give way to selective logging in forest on steeper hillsides and that the most appropriate technique to deal with this land would be enrichment planting (White 1976b). In fact, the lower timber yields on the steeper terrain and the higher extraction costs limited the areas of such land over which any logging occurred.

Enrichment planting was also considered in some of the regrowth forests developing after clear-felling on more gentle topography. Trees were planted in striplines cut every 10 m–20 m through the regrowth. The technique appeared promising but was eventually abandoned. In the first place, ownership of the land was still unresolved. Secondly, further trials showed that the cost of clearing the young regrowth was not as high as expected (commonly it cost less than 12 man days per hectare) and it made more sense to establish a fully stocked pulpwood plantation than an enriched sawlog forest.

Plantations

Plantations of species suitable for pulpwood were the largest single land-use proposed to follow logging. Trial plantings had been carried out annually since 1968 on a small 160 ha block of land the Administration had been able to purchase at Baku in the centre of the Gogol Valley. By 1973, 23 species had been planted at Baku and in the region generally. A list of the species planted is shown in Table 4.5.

Experience elsewhere in the PNG lowlands suggested *Eucalyptus deglupta* would be an especially useful species and the trials confirmed this suggestion. It occurs naturally in PNG (as well as in Indonesia and the Philippines)

Table 4.5 Potential plantation species included in trials in the Gogol Valley up to 1981. Those endemic to PNG are shown with an asterisk

(a)	Good growth; some potential as plantation species
	*Anthocephalus chinensis**
	Gmelina arborea
	*Eucalyptus deglupta**
	*Terminalia brassii**
	*Acacia mangium**
	Elaeocarpus multisectus (= *sphaericus* ?)*
(b)	Moderate-poor growth; less potential as plantation species
	*Acacia auriculiformis**
	Albizia falcataria
	Albizia stipulata
	*Araucaria cunninghamii**
	*Araucaria hunsteinii**
	*Casuarina oligodon**
	Callitris sp.
	Fraxinus uhdei
	*Eucalyptus brassiana**
	Eucalyptus camaldulensis
	Eucalyptus grandis
	*Eucalyptus papuana**
	Eucalyptus robusta
	*Eucalyptus tereticornis**
	Eucalyptus torrelliana
	Eucalyptus urophylla
	*Intsia palembanica**
	Leuceana leucocephala
	*Melaleuca leucodendron**
	Podocarpus blumei
	*Octomeles sumantrana**
	Pinus caribaea var. *hondurensis*
	Pinus caribaea var. *bahamensis*
	Swietenia mahogoni
	Tectona grandis
	*Terminalia catappa**
	*Terminalia complanata**
	Toona surenii

as an early colonizer of river banks and on recent volcanic deposits. On these sites, it forms virtually pure stands. The trees can grow to over 60 m tall, with girths of about 6 m. In time, an understorey of other rain forest species develops preventing the light demanding *Eucalyptus* seedlings from regenerating and the species disappears with further successional development. The first plantations of *E. deglupta* in PNG were established in the late 1940's and others in different parts of the country have followed. Growth is usually rapid and yields in the order of 250–300 m³/ha in 10 years are common. In many respects, the plantations are a mimic of the natural situation, since a diverse understorey of forest tree and understorey species commonly developed beneath the plantation canopy. The species has some insect pest problems, the most common of these being a buprestid beetle, *Agrilus opulentus*, which tends to girdle young trees. The trees most affected, however, are usually less vigorous or suppressed and the losses are commonly regarded as tolerable.

A variety of research involving *E. deglupta* and other promising species was carried out at Baku. This included nutritional research and fertilizer trials, spacing trials, tending and weed control trials and provenance testing (i.e. comparing the performance of trees of a particular species grown from seed collected from different geographical locations) (Lamb 1976a, Skelton 1981). In general, the research suggested *E. deglupta* would have few nutritional problems and would be relatively productive on the alluvial terrace soils, although perhaps not as productive as on the volcanic soils of New Britain. The best provenances (i.e. seed sources) to use were from East New Britain and from the Philippines. Weed control was critical in the first 2 years but could be reduced after that time.

Other early research concerned methods of plantation establishment. Trials suggested good growth could be achieved without the need to burn logging debris after clear felling (Lamb 1976b).

Tests were also carried out with a number of nitrogen fixing cover crops such as *Macroptilium atropurpureum* (siratro), *Pueraria phaseoloides* (puero), *Bracharia mutica* (para) and *Stylosanthes guyanensis* (stylo) to explore their use in plantations and in covering road verges.

All this research was done on a restricted area on flat river flood plain soils and more extensive trials were needed in a wider variety of conditions. But these trials could only be commenced after the whole problem of reforestation on clan-owned land had been resolved. The initial agreement between the Administration and Jant had left this matter unresolved. However, in 1974, a meeting was held at which a number of Gogol people voiced their strong interest in plantation establishment in partnership with Jant. The Department of Forests suggested the land lease and reforestation option. There was some support for this suggestion among landowners and Jant were also interested. However, a key concern of Jant was the security of any reforestation investment. Colonial rule had virtually ended in 1973 when PNG became self-governing and local politicians had control of the Administration, except in a few key areas such as foreign relations and defence in which Australia retained control. Jant (and indeed most other investors in PNG) were waiting to see how this new government would act. Although pressed by the Administration, Jant was apprehensive about committing itself to reforestation. It could see, for example, that most of the Department of Forests own main plantations were subject to disputes over land ownership or purchase payments (Table 4.6). In the absence of any clear set of national land laws, Jant saw leasing as a risky procedure.

In 1974, the Administration set about finding overseas aid to fund

Table 4.6 Disputes involving major Department of Forests Plantations during the mid 1970s

Area	Size (ha)	Nature of dispute
Keravat	2500	Squatters occupy alienated land reserved for plantation expansion.
Wau	3600	Long standing dispute over the price of land sold for the plantation
Brown River	1500	Rival claimants over original land ownership; one group claims payments wrongly made to a clan not owning the land.
Mount Hagen	1400	Swampland the Administration had believed to be unclaimed by any clan was drained and planted. Subsequent claimants demanded compensation.

Not all of each area was necessarily involved in each dispute. Only two other plantation areas in PNG exceeded 1000 ha.

reforestation. The next year, a mission from Japan's International Co-operation Agency (JICA) arrived and carried out a preliminary study. This study was followed by a further mission in 1976. These missions reported favourably on the viability of the reforestation programme, and Jant was finally persuaded to undertake a pilot planting programme in order to establish costs and procedures suitable for an enlarged operation. The Administration undertook to acquire land for this operation and low interest finance was provided by JICA.

In November, 1977, following 2 more years of negotiations, the Gogol Reforestation Company (GRC) was formed and an agreement was reached between the government of the newly independent state of PNG, Jant and the GRC on reforestation in the Gogol and Naru areas. The GRC was jointly owned by Jant and the Government with Jant holding 51 per cent of the shares. The new company had a paid-up capital of K100 002 and received loans from Jant of Y 205 472 000 (K650 000). Directors of the company included representatives of Jant, the Government and the Gogol people (initially nominated by MTWG but later selected by the Trans Gogol Council). Reforestation was to be carried out on land leased from the various landowners by the Government who would then sub-lease the land to the GRC. The Lands Department wanted land leasing terms to be common throughout PNG and recommended a rate based on 5 per cent of the unimproved capital value of the land. Negotiations led to an annual rent of K0.50/ha paid 5 years in advance plus 2.5 per cent of the final crop with the rate to be renegotiated after 5 years. The lease period was for 30 years, which would allow two pulpwood rotations. The GRC planting target was 400 ha/yr for 6 years. Because this programme was inadequate to provide for future needs of the industry, and because the Department of

Forests wished to maintain its own reforestation expertise, a government financed plantation programme to last 5 years was also commenced. Together, the two operations were expected to result in 700–800 ha/yr of plantation. Assuming a conservative MAI of $20\,m^3/ha/yr$, this programme would yield $150\,000\,m^3/yr$ of timber in 10–12 years, which would be roughly 50 per cent of Jant's requirements.

The initial response of landowners was one of cautious interest. In 1977, six groups offered land for leasehold joining seven others who had already done so. By December 1980, a total of 2900 ha of plantation had been established (Skelton 1981). The annual planting rate at this time (400–500 ha/yr) was still less than that hoped for, but at least a beginning had been made.

Because of the nature of clan land ownership, much of the land being offered for leasing was in dispersed small blocks. The plantations established on these were costly to service and administer, roading was more expensive, and fire protection was more difficult. It was hard to reconcile the need for larger contiguous areas of plantation with the fragmented nature of clan land holdings and the extent to which various clans were willing to lease a portion of their land for reforestation. Another early difficulty was the fact that leasing arrangements were sometimes completed months after logging such that secondary regrowth then occupied the site. This meant the site had to be cleared once more before planting could be carried out. With time, however, a better co-ordination between logging and reforestation was achieved.

Although reforestation was slow to develop, it gradually became accepted as a valid land use by more people and seemed likely to become more widespread in the area in the future. One sign of this acceptance was a decision by the clans owning a large 4000 ha block of land in the north of the Gogol TRP near the Catholic Mission station at Utu to ask that some of their land be leased for reforestation. The area had originally been classed in the Scenario 3B land-use plan as being for small holder use only since it was expected that the higher population density in the area would lead to extensive agricultural development. This development did not occur, and, in time, the reforestation option evidently began to seem more attractive to these people.

SUMMARY AND CONCLUSION

The GTP commenced in an atmosphere of optimism but also of considerable uncertainty. The Forestry Department was not sure of Jant's immediate logging plans or timetable, and had not resolved how reforestation should be accomplished. Jant was also uncertain about reforestation and about the guidelines under which it was to operate. The landowners were not certain just what effects clear-felling would have on their lands. They had, in effect, sold their forests in exchange for roads. This feeling of uncertainty enveloped the project from the beginning and the planning that did occur was essentially an iterative process – a constant readjustment in the face of experience.

Such feedback is necessary in even the most planned situations, but is no substitute for good initial planning. One consequence of many uncertainties surrounding the project was that it soon became evident that Jant was harvesting the accessible resource at a faster rate than expected. This was due to unexpected topographic limitations and requests by the MTWG that various areas remain unlogged as benchmark reserves, village reserves or buffer strips along streams. Jant also lost timber to Wewak Timbers when, in the absence of a veneer mill, potential sawlogs were sent to Wewak Timbers for sawing instead of to the chipper.

One obvious way of overcoming this difficulty would have been to increase the rate of plantation establishment so that a conversion from natural forest to plantation timber could have been made earlier, but neither the landowners nor Jant were willing to facilitate this option. Both professed an interest in reforestation, but, for different reasons, wanted it to be done more slowly. None-the-less, by the end of the decade, two important milestones had been passed. One was the establishment of the GRC as a vehicle by which plantation establishment could be carried out. The other was the increasing acceptance by landowners of plantations as a viable and profitable land use.

In the light of these events, one can question the value of a land-use plan drawn up after an agreement on pulpwood logging had been signed. While it did not, in retrospect, define the actual patterns of land-use that developed, it did act as a focal point for the MTWG and Jant in discussions on plantation development and did help define the choices open for future land use. The background documents (e.g. the land type maps) were also invaluable in planning for plantation land acquisition.

Note 1: It is important to note, however, that agreement was not universal. Some land in the Naru Valley was excluded because the owners refused to sell.

Note 2: Besides importing woodchips from America, Australia, New Zealand and Malaysia, Japanese companies were also establishing joint afforestation schemes with companies in Brazil for producing pulp and paper at about the same time as the GTP was starting in PNG.

Note 3: The Administration's own economic analyses showed this to be the case, e.g. Davidson 1983, A.E. White 1975.

Note 4: As already noted, in the same year the Director of the Planning Division of the Forestry Agency of Japan was arguing that PNG woodchips were highly desirable (Shimokawa 1977), and a few years later Jant was selling trial shipments to Taiwan.

Note 5: At this time this was the only other pulpwood logging operation being carried out in tropical rain forest.

Note 6: Like all Japanese companies, Jant was keen to instil in its employees a sense of belonging to and identifying with the company. Safety helmets and tee-shirts with the company logo flourished. In the early days all the field labour force were obliged to participate in an exercise programme before beginning work. The music from a small tape recorder was blared out via a loudspeaker over the hillside on which the early base camp was constructed and several hundred bemused Papua New Guineans went through a routine of keep fit exercises probably designed for office clerks in Tokyo.

Note 7: Enrichment planting is a silvicultural technique used to enhance the commercial productivity of an otherwise less valuable forest (usually one that has been recently logged). Fast growing and commercially desirable species are usually planted at low densities along widely spaced lines. The intention is that these should take advantage of temporary gaps in the canopy left by logging and soon form part of the canopy themselves.

Note 8: Several other reserves or 'natural parks' were being considered in the locality outside the TRP at this time. These included the Balek wildlife reserve just outside the eastern GTP boundary.

Note 9: A significant setback occurred in this early stage when a Papua New Guinean truck driving instructor accidentally killed a young girl from a roadside village who ran into the path of his truck. The villagers immediately set up a roadblock to stop traffic and demanded compensation. The instructor resigned in fear of a 'pay-back' killing and Jant lost one of its few skilled indigenous technicians.

CHAPTER 5

ENVIRONMENTAL CONSEQUENCES

INTRODUCTION

It is difficult not to be shocked when seeing the effect of pulpwood logging for the first time. The damage seems complete. Instead of forest, there is a wasteland of bare soil, stumps and broken branches. Instead of cool shade, the soil is exposed to sun and rain.

Surprisingly, however, revegetation usually commences within a few weeks. Within months, many logged areas can be covered in greenery once more. It is obvious that some sort of recovery process is underway. What sort of forest will this be? Will it contain the same species that were present once before?

Our knowledge of rain forest ecology is such that it is difficult to confidently predict too much about this recovery process. It appears that most rain forests are made up of a mosaic of patches, each being the result of a gap formed by some previous disturbance and each being at a different stage of successional development. The size of these patches may vary widely. There are some naturally occurring disturbances that leave small gaps in forests. For example, a large branch might fall off a tree, or a single tree itself may die of old age or be hit by lightning. In such cases, the gaps are usually short-lived and are mostly filled by the growth of young, shade tolerant plants already established under the forest canopy. Much larger gaps in the forest canopy can be created by landslips or storms. In these cases, the more easily dispersed pioneer plants can quickly occupy much of the gap. It is usually only later, when these short-lived and shade intolerant pioneers begin to die, that the less easily dispersed species representative of mature forests can become more dominant at the site.

Since all forests are subject to a number of naturally occurring disturbances which produce a range of different sized gaps in the canopy, the composition of a natural forest is a dynamic mix of species of different ages, longevities and physiological responses.

In all situations, the recovery process after a disturbance will be greatly affected by the nature of the disturbance itself; apart from the size of the area affected, the intensity of disturbance, the time of year, and the duration of the disturbance may all be influential.

Pulpwood logging represents a rather different kind of disturbance to those normally occurring in rain forests. The key elements of this difference are the areas involved and the intensity of the impact. Forest dwellers have long felled forest as part of the shifting cultivation cycle, and, to a large degree, these forests have recovered because the areas involved were small and usually only 1 or 2 hectares in size. Clear-felling for pulpwood, however, may involve several thousand hectares being cleared in any one year. Obviously, any recovery process will be quite different. Further, clear-felling represents an intensity of disturbance quite different to that occurring in large gaps created by storms or landslips. Nutrients are removed from the site, the topsoil may be highly disturbed by machinery, and the hydrological cycle may be altered because of the road and track network. There are, of course, many naturally occurring disturbances such as wildfires or volcanic blasts that also have an intense impact, but clear-felling does represent a potentially highly damaging combination of area and intensity. The question is, therefore, whether clear-felling as practised in the GTP area will allow forest regeneration to occur? Or is the scale and intensity such that the forests can never recover their original structure and species richness within time scales relevant to their human populations?

This chapter describes the scale and nature of the logging disturbance and attempts to assess some of the longer term consequences. The task is difficult given the complexity of the rain forest ecosystem and the fact that, ecologically speaking, the recovery process is still in an early phase. It is

Plate 12 An aerial view of clear-felling. Not all trees are removed. Those remaining are mainly *Ficus* species or smaller individuals. Note the considerable numbers of logs left on the site as waste

also made difficult because of the paucity of descriptive data. Unlike the economic and political facts described in earlier chapters, many of the ecological facts are still incompletely known. The reason for this is that very few specialist staff were available to work on the GTP. Shortly after the project commenced, other large logging operations started, or seemed likely to start, at Open Bay, Vanimo and Kapaluk. Staff involved in the GTP also had to begin planning the development of these operations. At the same time, several other large mining and engineering projects were underway or being planned elsewhere in the country. These included the large copper mines on Bougainville and at Ok Tedi, west of Mt Hagen, and the huge hydro-electric scheme on the Purari River on the south coast of the mainland. Each of these projects dwarfed the GTP. The Purari hydro-electric scheme, for example, was expected to have 12 major dams and a total generating capacity of over 7000 MW of electricity. These were being built in one of the most densely populated watersheds in the country. Not surprisingly, PNG's environmental specialists worked mostly on these larger projects. In effect, the GTP was overtaken by events and was never able to rate highly enough in the Administration's list of priorities to have the specialist staff necessary to monitor the operation[1]. The account that follows therefore uses observations made in the Gogol Valley, plus reports from comparable situations elsewhere in the humid tropics to draw conclusions about the likely long-term consequences of the operation.

Plate 13 An aerial view of clear-felling. Not all trees are removed. Those remaining are mainly *Ficus* species or smaller individuals. Note the considerable numbers of logs left on the site as waste

ENVIRONMENTAL CONTROLS ON FIELD OPERATIONS

Before describing the way in which logging was carried out and the effects this had on the forest ecosystem, it is necessary to outline the environmental controls placed on Jant's operations. When logging started, environmental safeguards were not given a particularly high priority. The actual agreement between Jant and the Administration seems to have referred to environmental controls in only the broadest terms. Presumably existing legislation such as the Forestry Acts and the Water Resources Ordinances were thought to be sufficient. In any event, it became obvious in early 1974, shortly after logging commenced, that there was a difference of opinion between the two parties as to what were acceptable standards for controlling erosion arising from road construction. The result was the development later that year of a set of standards for minimising erosion, not only from roads but from logging operations generally. These standards involved, amongst other things, specifications for road locations, provision of road drainage and the leaving of unlogged buffer strips 20 m wide on each side of all permanent waterways (this later became 30 m). There was also a requirement that cross drains be established on all old snig tracks on steep slopes, and that old log loading areas be deep ripped to aid revegetation. Logs were not to be dragged through stream beds, if at all possible, and crowns falling into streams were to be removed.

In 1974, the Forestry Department also sought advice from several consultants on appropriate environmental standards for the project and other logging operations in PNG. Their recommendations covered a variety of land-use planning techniques and methods of safeguarding the forest environment (Nagle 1976, Webb 1977). Many of these were subsequently absorbed into standard operating procedures and guidelines used in other projects in PNG. Both consultants also made specific recommendations on ways of reducing the adverse effects of clear-felling operations in the Gogol Valley. Nagle suggested a 'mixed cover strategy' involving alternating patches of clear cut and lightly logged forest. Each of the clear-cut areas would be up to 100 ha in area (Fig. 5.1). Webb suggested restricting each logging coupe to 20–40 ha. These could be up to 300 m in width and 1–2 km long, and would involve no more than one-half to two-thirds of any particular area. He argued these would allow the dispersal of seed from most species to quickly recolonize the new 'gaps' (Fig. 5.2).

Neither of these suggestions were immediately acted upon. Relationships between the Forestry Department and Jant were amicable but the Department was reluctant to impose yet another requirement on the Company's operation, especially when the company could argue it had no legal obligation to agree. The MTWG was then negotiating with Jant almost weekly and asking it to modify its operations. For example, the location of proposed logging roads was frequently changed in response to requests

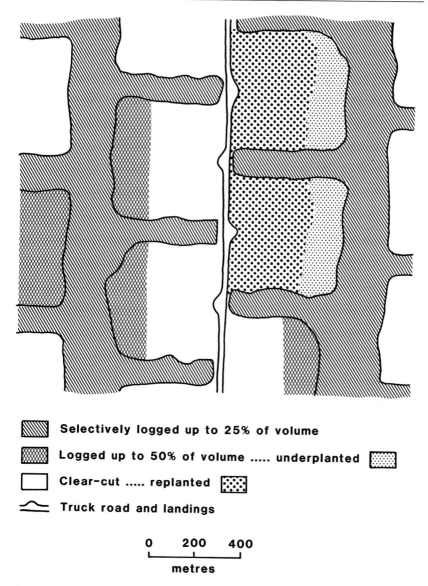

Fig. 5.1 Logging pattern suggested by Nagle (1976) showing how part of the area might be selectively logged and part might be clear-felled. The selectively logged area could be followed by underplantings (= enrichment planting) while the clear-felled areas could be converted to plantations if desired

from villagers for roads to their village, and Jant was also asked to agree to the excision of reserves and greenbreaks from the logging area. The consultants' proposals would have required a major change in the whole

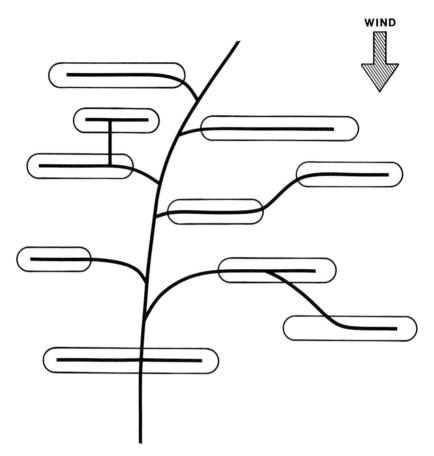

Fig. 5.2 Logging pattern suggested by Webb (1977). Each coupe might be up to 1–2 km long but would be broader than 300 m. The area of each coupe would be 20–40 ha and the total logged area would cover no more than 50–60 per cent of the total area

operation and the Department decided to defer the approach until a later time.

What all this meant, therefore, was that environmental controls were never as strict as they should have been. Standards did improve for a while after the 1974 guidelines were developed, but, in later years, there was a tendency for these to be by-passed.

PATTERN OF DISTURBANCE

When Jant commenced logging, its objectives were to generate a rapid cash flow and to train its unskilled machine operators. Both objectives could be best met on the more productive forests on gentle terrain. The earliest

Plates 14 (above) **and 15** (below) Forest strips running through these logging coupes are streamside buffer strips

logging started on the flat areas around Jant's base camp at Baku and then moved south into the hills towards the Kokun River (Fig. 5.3). The areas logged in late 1973 and 1974 were done in an almost continuous swathe. The terrace forests were completely cleared, but, as logging extended into the hillier areas, the intensity varied. This was partly due to the fact that

105

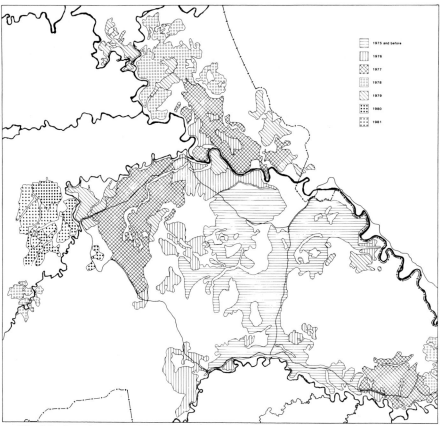

Fig. 5.3 Actual pattern of logging in part of the central Gogol Valley between 1973 and 1981. The location of coupe boundaries is approximate only. Streamside buffer strips and residual secondary forest patches are not shown

the logging teams were still gaining experience and partly because the area had a high proportion of secondary growth.

In 1975, the pattern changed and three widely separated areas were logged. In 1976, the number increased to 17, and, in subsequent years, was around seven or eight. The conversion to a patchwork pattern of logging was not done for environmental reasons but because it allowed greater management flexibility during wet weather. If rain prevented work at one site, production could be maintained at the other sites. Again, by having several logging crews operating at different sites truck traffic jams could be avoided because the heavy logging trucks were dispersed. Jant also believed it was easier to maintain worker productivity in a number of smaller sites than in a few large crowded sites.

The size of each of these logging areas, or coupes, varied. One way of expressing this variation is to measure the maximum distance from the middle of any coupe to the nearest boundary of unlogged intact forest. This is the maximum distance over which seed must be dispersed for colonization to occur in the middle of the coupe. Data from each of the coupes logged in the first years of the operation are shown in Fig. 5.4. Most distances were 400 m or less, although several larger coupes were also present. The areas ranged from less than 50 ha to over 600 ha.

The overall pattern that appeared to be developing in the Gogol TRP in the first few years, therefore, was one of a patchwork of coupes of various sizes dispersed throughout the forest. This pattern subsequently changed as further logging occurred adjacent to the initial patches and increased the size of contiguous disturbed areas. However, there was often a period of several years during which an intact forest capable of acting as a seed source remained adjacent to the coupe.

By 1981, the situation in the Gogol TRP could be summarized as follows (see Fig. 5.3):-

(a) Road 1 north towards Ninam River: a patchwork strip of logging coupes felled between 1976 and 1979; maximum width of the strip about 2.5 km.

(b) Road 7 south across hills to the Kokun River: a large area felled between 1973 and 1975. Though forming a continuous strip up to

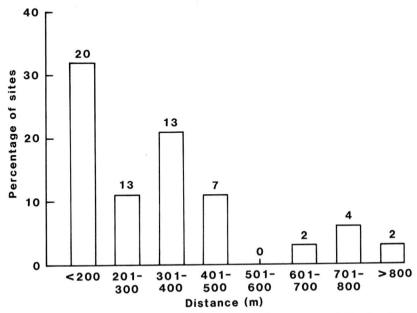

Fig. 5.4 Frequency of non-contiguous logging areas of various size classes in the Gogol TRP between 1973 and 1981 (n = 61). The distance is the maximum distance from within any area to the nearest unlogged forest existing in 1981

3 km wide the area contained many patches of unlogged secondary forest.

(c)   Road 2 west through Sapi River watershed: intensively logged area; felled between 1976 and 1981; about 3 km wide at widest point.

(d)   Road 8 along the Kokun River: a mostly narrow strip logged between 1975 and 1978.

The actual pattern of logging was thus not the highly dispersed mosaic of small coupes suggested by Nagle (1976) and Webb (1977). Though composed of patches, the logging areas were larger than those recommended and tended to form linear aggregates. On the other hand, most of the logged areas were not cleared completely but contained residual forest in the form of streamside buffer strips, small village reserves or secondary forest. The pattern of logging disturbance was broadly similar in the Gum and North Coast TRP's, where the topography and proportion of secondary forest were similar to the Gogol TRP. The Naru TRP, however, was mostly very flat terrain and the logging coupes there tended to be much larger.

There is considerable scope for modifying this logging pattern to ensure coupe sizes are smaller and that intact forest boundaries are retained for longer. This pattern might be more costly since it would necessitate maintaining a large bridge and road network in an environment where both deteriorate rapidly, but these costs might be compensated for by other savings. Interestingly, Australian woodchip loggers were finding at about this time that coupes of 40 ha or less were more cost effective than larger coupes (Humphreys 1977).

In 1980, the Department of Forests adopted an upper size limit of 100 ha on coupes if the logged forest was not to be used for some prescribed land use, and 200 ha if a prescribed land use (e.g. cash cropping, forest plantation etc.) was to follow.

INITIAL EFFECTS ON VEGETATION

By its very nature, clear-felling results in the removal of virtually all canopy trees from a forest. The degree to which this actually occurred in the GTP varied considerably during he first years of the project. Initially, at least, a relatively large number of trees were left in place either because of their small size or because minor variations in topography made them less accessible to the then newly trained machinery operators. Since then, however, the utilization rate increased until the only trees left were either those unsuitable for pulping (e.g. *Ficus*) or were naturally occurring food trees deliberately marked for retention by their owners[2].

Clear-felling was most complete on the level flood plain areas but tended to become more selective in the hill areas as slopes increased. While there was no regulatory upper slope limit, less logging occurred in areas with broken or rugged topography where slopes exceeded 20 per cent. In many areas, ridgetops tended to be left undisturbed because these sites often had only small trees and low timber volumes, perhaps because of past landslips.

Since the minimum acceptable girth for a pulpwood log was 60 cm, many of the sub-canopy trees were left untouched by chainsaws. In practice, however, few survived the logging operation unscathed. No systematic studies have reported on the fate of seedlings on the forest floor prior to logging, but casual observation suggests that most of these were also destroyed.

Despite this damage, forest regrowth was rapid. A dense plant cover was virtually complete within 6 months of logging, except for some of the more badly compacted log loading sites. Within a year, most of these plants were 2–4 m tall, and, by 10 years, tree heights of 20 m were common. Vine and climbers were present in this regeneration but usually not in sufficient densities to inhibit tree seedling growth[3].

Several studies suggest the regrowth had a surprisingly high species diversity. Johns (1976) assessed the patterns of regeneration in some of the earliest logged areas using a series of 0.25 ha plots. Successive annual measurements showed that new species continued to appear in the plots over the first few years, either from the soil seed store or by being dispersed into the site from outside. Plots in 2-year-old regrowth forest contained between 28 and 42 commercially important tree genera. Seedling densities of these genera at the time varied beween 280–650 trees per plot in hill forest sites to 130–140 trees per plot in poorly drained terrace sites. The

Plate 16 Twelve-year-old regeneration

109

Plate 17 New garden site being cleared by a shifting cultivator in 12-year-old post-logging regrowth forest

height growth of some of these species was rapid: in 2 years, *Intsia bijuga* had reached up to 7 m, some *Terminalia* species had reached 6 m and *Anthocephalus chinensis* had reached 8 m. The pattern of regeneration was not uniform throughout the area, and dense stands of *Anthocephalus chinensis* in particular were noticeably more common in some poorly drained sites.

A more extensive survey covering a much larger area was carried out by Whyte (1977). This survey assessed the extent to which 17 commercially desirable (i.e. as sawlogs) tree genera had regenerated in the regrowth forest. Striplines 300 m to 500 m long were established through regrowth forest of various ages in different topographic units. Along these lines, counts were made of the numbers of contiguous plots in which an individual of any of the specified genera occurred. Two plot sizes were used to take account of differences in the size of the regenerating plants. Plots sized 2 m x 2 m were used to assess regeneration smaller than 6 m tall, and plots 4 m x 4 m were used to assess trees that were taller than 6 m but smaller than 15 cm diameter at breast height. The survey found there was usually at least 20 per cent of the 4 m^2 plots, and about 25 per cent of all plots, contained one of the commercially desired species (Table 5.1). Using 4 m^2 plots and this method of assessment, the maximum stocking that could have been measured was 2500 per ha. The data indicate, therefore, a stocking slightly in excess of 500 trees per ha, which is probably lower than desirable, but within the range found by Nicholson (1979) in a number of Malaysian dipterocarp forests after logging.

Table 5.1 Percentage of plots with commercially desirable tree genera* in regrowth forest of different ages and in different topographic units

Terrain	Age since logging (months)	Stripline No.	Regeneration size 0–2 m ht	2–4 m ht	4–6 m ht	6 m– ht	15 cm dbh	Total
Moderate	15	11	7	7	10	–		24
		12	30	4	2	3		39
	27	4	12	3	3	4		22
		5	18	2	1	3		24
	33	2	11	3	2	2		18
		3	8	9	7	0		24
Broken	27	7	20	5	1	9		35
		8	16	4	2	3		25
Rugged	15	14	10	10	5	0		25
		18	6	0	0	38		44

*Genera recorded: *Terminalia, Elaeocarpus, Dracontomelum, Celtis, Buchanania, Homalium, Alstonia, Intsia, Euodia, Spondias, Pterocymbium, Pometia, Plerygota, Anthocephalus, Sterculia, Flindersia, Toona.*

Source: Whyte (1977)

A later study by Saulei (1984, 1985) examined the total complement of species regenerating after logging, including the less commercially important species not included in these earlier investigations. Like Johns, he found plant growth was rapid. Six months after being felled in the previous wet season, a 0.16 ha plot contained 151 plant species. These included 58 secondary tree species, 42 primary tree species and 51 species of shrubs, herbs, climbers and grasses. By 24 months, the number of secondary tree species had increased to 73 and the number of primary tree species had increased to 58 (Table 5.2).

Most of these species originated from seedlings or coppice regrowth rather than residual advanced growth. After 6 months, 53 of the species present had regenerated from seed and 55 species had regenerated by vegetative means (coppice, root suckers). Some species regenerated by both methods. By 24 months, the two regeneration modes were still evenly represented; 78 species present had regenerated from seed and 77 species had regenerated vegetatively (Table 5.3). One of the most striking features about these observations was the relative importance of the two modes for secondary and primary forest tree species; most secondary species regenerated from seed, but most primary species owed their presence in the regenerating forest to their ability to reproduce vegetatively.

The overwhelming majority of individual plants in the regenerating forest were secondary species. At 6 months, for example, 98 per cent of the 6701 individuals present were secondary species, with primary tree species making up the remainder. After 24 months, competition had reduced the total plant density, but the number and proportion of primary species both

Plate 18 In low-lying wetter sites *Anthrocephalus chinensis* is often a dominant component of the regeneration. At this site all other species were removed to leave a nearly pure stand. Note figure in foreground for scale

increased showing these were actively colonizing the site (Table 5.4).

The actual density of trees establishing on logged sites, whether from seed or from vegetative growth, was strongly affected by the extent to which the soil was disturbed during logging. Where little topsoil disturbance occurred, tree density was high, but, where substantial disturbance occurred, the density declined. The relationship is shown in Fig. 5.5.

Saulei (1985) also examined the recovery in species richness over a longer time period, using a sequence of ten 0.12 ha plots located on areas logged during the previous 11 years. In this case, only tree species were recorded. The areas containing these plots had had differing logging histories and varied in terms of intensity of logging, time of year that logging took place and size of the areas logged. Perhaps because of these differences, there was not a significant relationship between time since logging and the number of species present as seedlings. Nor was plot age related to the

Plate 19 Twelve-year-old regrowth forest

Table 5.2 Numbers of plant species recorded in a 0.16 ha plot regenerating after being felled in the wet season

	Time since felling (months)		
	6	12	24
Secondary trees	58	66	73
Primary trees	42	54	58
Shrubs, herbs, climbers, grasses	51	35	21
Total	151	155	152

Source: Saulei (1985)

total number of tree species present (i.e. seedlings plus coppice). However, all plots had at least 23 species present and several had more than 60 species (Table 5.5). Altogether, the 10 plots contained 132 tree species. The majority of these were secondary species, but, as in the previous study,

Table 5.3 Numbers of tree species regenerating from seed or from vegetative regrowth in a 0.16 ha plot felled in the wet season

	Time since felling (months)		
	6	12	24
Seedlings			
secondary trees	50	57	64
primary trees	3	12	14
Total	53	69	78
Vegetative regrowth			
secondary trees	14	18	21
primary trees	41	51	56
Total	55	69	77

Source: Saulei (1985)

Table 5.4 Numbers of secondary and primary trees recorded in a 0.16 ha plot regenerating after being felled in the wet season. Values in parentheses are percentages

	Time since felling (months)		
	6	12	24
Secondary trees	6569 (98)	4236 (94)	3332 (88)
Primary trees	132 (2)	276 (6)	461 (12)
Total	6701	4512	3793

Source: Saulei (1985)

there were also a number of primary species, most of which originated from vegetative regrowth. The regeneration also included a few species left undamaged from the original forest.

It is difficult to compare these regrowth forests with the original forests at these sites since there is no comparable data describing the plant communities present prior to logging. Saulei (1985) described the composition of unlogged forest in a 0.16 ha plot in the vicinity of the 10 regrowth stands. This plot contained 64 tree species, only 19 of which (i.e. 30 per cent) were secondary species. There were 154 trees in the plot. On the basis of this rather simple comparison, it is clear that the young regrowth forests still had a greater representation of secondary trees than the forests they replaced. On the other hand, the rapid height growth of the regrowth and Johns', Whyte's and Saulei's observations also indicate that a succession leading towards a new, diverse forest community which includes primary tree species was taking place once logging had ceased. What further changes might take place in these regrowth forests will be discussed in a later section.

An interesting comparison with these observations is the pulpwood

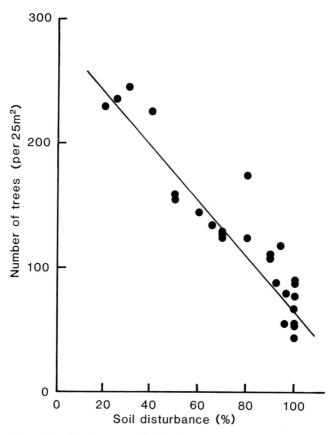

Fig. 5.5 The relationship between soil disturbance caused by logging (expressed as a percentage of area disturbed) and tree seedling density in 25 m² plots. Source: Saulei (1985)

Table 5.5 Number of primary and secondary forest tree species in 0.12 ha plots in regrowth of various ages

	Age of Regrowth (years)									
	1.5	2.5	3.5	4.8	5.8	6.5	7.8	8.8	9.8	10.8
Secondary species										
seedlings	26	31	19	27	34	19	36	25	33	28
vegetative growth plus residual trees	1	4	4	1	3	1	3	11	1	6
Primary species										
seedlings	0	0	1	0	11	2	5	8	5	6
vegetative growth plus residual trees	5	3	18	11	20	1	11	11	7	21
Total	32	38	42	39	68	23	55	55	46	61

Source: Saulei (1985)

logging operation in lowland rain forest at Bajo Calima in Colombia (Carton de Colombia 1985). Apart from the GTP, this is the only other operation that involves clear-felling rain forest to produce wood pulp. The forests grow in a very high rainfall zone (7500 mm annually) and on infertile soils. On average, the trees are smaller than those at the GTP and have diameters of only 27 cm and a canopy height of about 20 m.

Like the Gogol forests, regeneration after logging was rapid and many of the species originally present appeared in the regrowth. Ladrach and Mazuera (1985) carried out an assessment of forest composition before and 2 years after logging in a series of 40 plots having a combined area of 0.8 ha. The primary forest contained 31 families and all but four of these were present in the young natural regeneration. There were 136 tree species in the plots. Seventy-seven of these species were common to both the primary forest and the natural regeneration while 19 species were found only in the natural regeneration. Forty species were present only in the primary forest. Of these, however, half were observed elsewhere in the natural regeneration outside the plots.

In a separate study, Mazuera (1985) assessed the composition of natural regeneration in stands up to 15 years of age. He also recorded a large degree of similarity between the composition of this regeneration and the primary forest. Pioneer species dominated the early years of the succession but primary forest species were becoming more common by 15 years.

Most species in these Colombian forests regenerated from seed with most being dispersed by birds or mammals. In contrast to the Gogol Valley forests, vegetative reproduction was relatively unimportant.

The extent of natural regeneration at the site was attributed to the fact that little soil disturbance occurred since all logging was carried out using an aerial cable system. This had a maximum reach of 1000 m. Unlogged areas were left between the clear-felled zones so that it was rare for the distance for seed dispersal to exceed 500 m.

The Bajo Calima operation differs from the GTP in both the nature of the forest and in the manner of logging. Like the GTP, however, the early natural regeneration developing after logging is surprisingly diverse and includes a significant proportion of species representative of the primary forest.

INITIAL EFFECTS ON WILDLIFE

A changed habitat is a threat to the welfare of many forest dwelling animals. Most studies of the effect of disturbance on wildlife in tropical forests have been carried out following selective logging. The results of such studies have shown that some animal groups are relatively tolerant of disturbance while others are more intolerant (Whitmore 1984). For example, a study by Wilson and Wilson (1975) in East Kalimantan found primates were not affected by moderate habitat disturbance, but that species such as birds and squirrels were more sensitive.

> 'The mammalian order most adaptable to changing habitat conditions in the Malay Archipelago are the rodents and the primates...On the species level...there is great variability of response and success of adaptability amongst primates. Birds and squirrels seem to be the most disrupted by habitat disturbance from selective logging. While some of the other mammals are directly harmed by selective logging, others are only endangered by the hunting and slash and burn farming that can follow the opening up of the forest. Many species, then, can exist in forests that have been selectively logged at the relatively low intensity of 8 trees/ha and perhaps as high as 12 trees/ha when efforts are made to minimise the destruction to other trees during the logging'.

Logging by clear-felling is obviously a different situation. Broadscale surveys carried out in a variety of habitats within the Gogol Valley by the Wildlife Division of the Department of Primary Industry found that about 60 per cent of the 251 species of mammals, birds, reptiles and frogs recorded depended on the forest to varying degrees (Liem 1978a). These species included:

Mammals:	74 per cent (20 spp) dependency
Birds:	61 per cent (102 spp) dependency
Reptiles:	44 per cent (15 spp) dependency
Frogs:	65 per cent (15 spp) dependency

Little is known of the ecology of many of these species but the high degree of dependency implies that the removal of forest could drastically reduce these wildlife populations. Several specific studies have been carried out on particular animal groups.

Small terrestrial mammals

Morris (1978) has described a trapping programme designed to investigate the size of small mammal population in the Gogol Valley and the effect of disturbance on these. Three types of habitat were studied — undisturbed forest, regenerating forest (logged within 12 months) and *Eucalyptus* plantations (up to 5 year old). Traps were baited with a mixture of peanut butter, banana, bread and sometimes papaya, and laid out in the morning and evening. The traps included three different designs of breakback trap and sometimes cage traps as well. Trapping was carried out in June 1977 and July 1977. [June happened to be rather wet while July was dry.]

The overall catch rate was surprisingly low. In June, 630 trap nights yielded only seven animals, a catch rate of 1.1 per cent. In July, when conditions were drier, the catch rate increased to nearly 6 per cent. The mammals trapped included *Echymipera kalabu, Melomys platyops, Melomys lorentzi, Melomys refusceus, Rattus ruber* and *Rattus exulans*. A number of skinks, frogs, toads and a crab were also caught. A summary of the data is shown in Table 5.6.

Although the trapping rates were too low for statistical analyses, Morris drew several tentative conclusions. First, the numbers of small mammals in both the undisturbed and regenerating forest were much lower than expected on the basis of trapping elsewhere. Second, the young *Eucalyptus* plantations had the 'richest' fauna of the three habitats studied.

The reasons for these low numbers were not clear. The heavy rain in June was probably partially responsible because it suppressed mammal activity and also sprang many traps leaving them useless for the rest of the night. Another reason could have been the comparative lack of food at ground level. In comparison with Malaysian dipterocarp forests, there appeared to be fewer seeds and fruit on the forest floor. Ants may also have had a role in reducing the food available to the mammals. Finally, flooding at some sites could have made them inhospitable mammal habitats. Overall, Morris concluded that the mammal densities in the disturbed and undisturbed forest were so low that the displacement of one species by another as a result of logging operations would be difficult to detect.

Studies in other tropical forests have shown that intensive logging can have significant effects on mammals. Harrison (1969) reported that, although the species numbers in undisturbed and highly disturbed sites remained similar, the species composition changed. Commensal rats accounted for a high proportion of species in secondary regrowth forests, while groups such as carnivores and primates were dominant in the undisturbed forest.

Bats

A number of bat colonies occur throughout the Gogol Valley. Morris (1978) observed *Pteropus, Dobsonia, Syconycteris, Rousettus, Hipposideros, Aselliscus, Nyctimene*. Hall (pers. comm.) believes *Macroglossus, Aproteles* and *Paranyctimene* may be present as well. In all, there may be 16 bat species in the area.

Nothing is known of the effect of logging in the GTP on this resident bat population. It is known that many bats show little loyalty to temporary foliage roosts when alternatives are abundant, although they may show greater fidelity to a home area. Bats roosting in hollow trees or caves often have greater roost attachment (Kunz 1982). Most of the species in the Gogol Valley are tree roosting species. Their comparative lack of site attachment and great mobility suggest logging may not greatly affect bat populations in the area, provided there are still areas of undisturbed forests nearby (Hall, 1986). Some newly logged sites may even prove to be more attractive to insectivorous bats.

Birds

Wildlife surveys in the Gogol valley have suggested there are probably around 167 bird species present. Most usually occur within the forests, but

Table 5.6 Numbers of small mammals, skinks, frogs, toads and crabs caught in traps in various sites in the Gogol Valley in June and July 1977. June was a wet month and July was much drier

	Undisturbed forest					Regrowth forest		Eucalypt plantation	
Location	Terrace poorly-drained	Terrace well-drained		Stream side	Terrace well-drained	6 month regrowth	12 month regrowth	Age 15 month	Age 5 years
Sample month	June	June	June	July	July	July (?)	July	July (?)	June
Mammals	0	1	1	3	3	0	1	5	5
Skinks	2	5	0	0	0	2	0	0	2
Frogs and Toads	0	1	0	1	0	0	0	0	3
Crabs	0	1	0	0	0	0	0	0	0
Trap nights	110	150	50	30	87	20	50	48	250

Source: Morris (1978)

13 are common in grassland or along creeks. Even before logging, the populations of some of the larger of these birds such as cassowaries and hornbills had been reduced by hunting. The increased use of shotguns and the spread of logging roads is certain to increase the pressure on such species.

An intensive study of the effect of logging on birds has been carried out by Driscoll (1984). This study was done in two parts. One part dealt with the effect of logging on birds usually present in the upper forest canopy and involved observations from tree platforms at canopy level over a 12 month period. These observations were carried out in sites on intact forest as well as in regrowth vegetation and both sites were on a well-drained river terrace. The second part of the study involved mist netting understorey birds in forest and adjacent regrowth on river terrace, hill and swamp forest sites. The terrace sites were the same as those used in the canopy bird study and were monitored for 18 months. The hill and swamp sites were monitored for 10 months. The age and average height of the regrowth at the various sites was as follows:

Terrace regrowth: 4.5 years old, 12–14 m tall (adjoining intact forest 29 m tall)
Hill regrowth: 4.0 years old, 12 m tall (adjoining intact forest 27 m tall)
Swamp regrowth: 2.5 years old, 7 m all (adjoining intact forest 23 m tall)

The combined observations (canopy plus understorey) at the terrace sites accounted for 123 bird species. Of these, 111 species were present in intact forest, 100 species were in the regrowth and 88 species were present at both habitats. The majority of birds occupied distinct strata, being found either in the canopy or the understorey with only a few interchanging between both levels. There were apparently few birds confined to a middle strata in the forest.

A comparison of understorey netting and canopy observations showed that understorey birds were primarily insectivores while canopy birds were primarily herbivores (Table 5.7). The proportion of carnivores was greater in the understorey but the proportion of omnivores and mixed feeders was similar.

Table 5.7   Percentage of birds at various feeding types in canopy and understorey at intact and regrowth forest sites

	Insectivore	Herbivore	Mixed (insectivore and herbivore)	Carnivore	Omnivore
Canopy	21	41	24	9	3
Understorey	42	11	26	17	3

Source: Driscoll (1985)

120

Effect of logging on canopy birds

Direct counts of canopy birds from the two tree-top platforms found 96 species were present; 86 species were observed in the forest, 77 species in the regrowth and 70 species were present in both habitats. That is, only 16 of the 86 'forest' species were not observed at the regrowth site and only seven of the 77 'regrowth' species were not observed in the forest. The mean number of species seen each day was always significantly higher in the forest site than at the regrowth site.

Many species were comparatively rare. These were excluded from the subsequent data analyses by only considering 'common' species where a common species was defined as one observed perching at the site on at least 10 occasions throughout the sampling. On this basis, 56 'common' species were present at the forest plot, 53 'common' species were present at the regrowth plot and another 52 species were 'common' to both sites (Table 5.8).

A statistical analysis of the observations on these common species found that 15 species were significantly more numerous at the forest site, while nine were more numerous at the regrowth site (Table 5.9). The species more common at the forest site included two pigeons, seven parrots, two flycatchers, a grackle, a butcher bird, a honeyeater and a berrypicker. Ten of these are obligate herbivores and seven eat only fruit. Five of the nine species more numerous in the regrowth were herbivores. These included a lory, a cuckooshrike, two birds of paradise and *Ptilinopus iozonous*, the most common fruit dove in the Gogol Valley, which was found at both sites but was present in much greater numbers at the regrowth site. (The diet of this species is 80% figs, Frith *et al.* 1976.) The other common species at the regrowth site were a treeswift, a dollar bird, a warbler and a shield bill.

Another 33 common species were present at both sites, but the differences in numbers between sites were not statistically significant (Table 5.8). The

Table 5.8 The numbers of canopy birds including those classed as 'common' (see text) in forest and regrowth. The common species are divided into those exhibiting a statistical difference between forest and regrowth and those where there is just an apparent difference

	All species	Common species			
		Total present	Statistically different*	Apparently different**	Total different
Forest	86	56	15	7	22
Regrowth	77	53	9	4	13
Both sites	70	52	—	22	22
Total	93	57	24	33	57

Source: Driscoll (1985)

* details Table 5.9

** details Table 5.10

Table 5.9 Total counts of species *exhibiting a significant difference* in canopy counts between the forest and regrowth. The species are in two lists: those counted more often at the forest plot and those counted more often at the regrowth plot. The last column gives the results of Mann-Whitney U tests based on daily counts (* = $P < 0.05$, ** = $P < 0.02$, *** = $P < 0.002$.) Food types are: i–insectivore, f–frugivore, n–nectivore, g–gramivore, o–omnivore

				Plot		
		Food	Forest	Regrowth	U	
Ptilinopus perlatus	Fruit dove	f	226	26	20.5**	
Ducula pinon	Fruit pigeon	f	374	24	0.0***	
Trichoglossus haematodus	Parrot	n–g	1038	695	36.0*	
Probosciger aterrimus	Parrot	f–g	37	0	6.0***	
Cacatua galerita	Parrot	g–f	555	1	0.0***	
Micropsitta pusio	Parrot	i–g	144	42	34.0*	
Opopsitta diopthalma	Parrot	f	226	38	17.5**	
Psittaculirostris edwardsii	Parrot	f	168	38	17.5**	
Eclectus roratus	Parrot	f	349	54	1.5***	
Microeca flavigaster	Flycatcher	i	263	0	0.0***	
Pachycephala monacha	Flycatcher	i	182	0	0.0***	
Mino anais	Grackle	f	234	14	4.0***	
Cracticus cassicus	Butcherbird	o	81	26	23.0**	
Meliphaga sp.	Honeyeater	f–i–n	86	19	36.5*	
Dicaeum geelvinkianum	Berrypicker	f–i–n	65	19	14.5***	
Ptilinopus iozonus	Fruit dove	f	435	1113	21.5**	
Lorius lory	Lory	n–f	87	183	31.0*	
Hemiprocne mystacea	Treeswift	i	3	667	0.0***	
Eurystomus orientalis	Dollarbird	i	20	608	21.0**	
Coracina tenuirostris	Cuckooshrike	i–f	4	47	22.0**	
Gerygone magnirostris	Warbler	i	0	71	12.0***	
Peltops blainvillii	Shieldbill	i	123	484	4.5***	
Manucodia atra	Bird of Paradise	f	57	100	26.5**	
Paradisaea minor	Bird of Paradise	f–i	105	309	5.0***	

Source: Driscoll (1985)

actual numbers of these species at each site did, in fact, differ appreciably and the lack of statistical significance appears to have arisen from erratic changes in counts, either from one day to another, or from one season to the next. Driscoll grouped these species into three groups; the first as a group of seven species counted at least three times more often at the forest site; the second was a group of four species counted at least three times more often at the regrowth site, and a remaining group of 22 species showing less than a threefold difference between sites. The actual species present are shown in Table 5.10.

The feeding preferences for all of the 'common' species are summarized in Table 5.11. The most striking difference between the two vegetation types was the lower number of frugivorous birds showing a preference for regrowth forest (over half the obligate frugivores were disadvantaged by logging). The numbers of species of nectivores and insectivores was broadly

Table 5.10 'Common' canopy species which did *not* exhibit a significant difference in counts between forest and regrowth. Species are listed according to whether their counts were at least three times as great at the forest (list A), at least three times as great at the regrowth (list B), or if they were counted with less than a threefold difference between forest and regrowth (list C). Food types are: c–carnivore, f–frugivore, n–nectivore, g–gramivore, o–omnivore, i–insectivore

| Species | Food | | Total counts | |
			Forest	Regrowth
List A				
Ptilinopus nanus	Fruitdove	f	55	6
Ducula zoeae	Fruitdove	f	14	1
Chalcopsitta duivenbodei	Lory	n–f	96	14
Chrysococcyx meyerii	Cuckoo	i	34	1
Scythrops novaehollandiae	Cuckoo	f	34	10
Coracina melaena	Cuckooshrike	i–f	64	20
Oedistoma pygmaeum	Honeyeater	n–i	32	0
List B				
Pseudos fuscata	Lory	f–n	51	197
Cacomantis variolosus	Cuckoo	i	2	13
Myiagra cyanoleuca	Satin monarch	i	5	20
Aplonis metallica	Starling	f–n	266	879
List C				
Haliastur indus	Kite	c	17	23
Ptilinopus pulchellus	Fruitdove	f	15	8
Ptilinopus magnificus	Fruitdove	f	26	19
Geoffroyus geoffroyi	Parrot	f–g	289	400
Eudynamys scolopacea	Koel	f	7	16
Dacelo gaudichaudi	Kookaburra	c	37	25
Lalage atrovirens	Triller	f–i	330	386
Coracina boyeri	Cuckooshrike	f	363	289
Coracina papuensis	Cuckooshrike	i–f	198	99
Gerygone chloronota	Warbler	i	5	14
Monarcha chrysomela	Golden monarch	i	71	55
Pitohui kirhocephalus	Pitohui	i–f	12	7
Mino dumonti	Grackle	f	149	164
Oriolus szalayi	Oriole	f–i	68	77
Dicrurus hottentottus	Drongo	i–f	78	57
Nectarinia sericea	Sunbird	n–i	88	146
Chlycichaera fallax	Honeyeater	i	51	21
Meliphaga chrysotis	Honeyeater	f–n–i	41	46
Pycnopygius stictocephalus	Honeyeater	i–n–f	74	112
Pycnopygius ixoides	Honeyeater	f–n	169	75
Philemon meyeri	Friarbird	f–n–i	68	64
Philemon novaeguineae	Friarbird	f–n–i	137	165

Source: Driscoll (1985)

similar in both habitats. Interestingly, many of the obligate herbivore species in the forest canopy were large birds in contrast to the generally smaller species usually found in regrowth areas. The implication of these

Table 5.11 Feeding preference of the more common bird species (see text for definition) found primarily in forest or regrowth canopies. (Based on Table 5.9 and 5.10.)

	Number of species		
Feeding type	*Primarily forest*	*Primarily regrowth*	*Both habitats*
Obligate frugivore	9	2	5
Frugivore	15	7	16
Nectivore	5	3	6
Granivore	4	0	1
Insectivore	8	8	11
Mixed (herbivore and insectivore)	5	2	10
Carnivore	0	0	2
Total species in habitat	22	13	22

Source: Driscoll (1985)

results is that fewer of the birds in the regrowth forest may have a role in seed dispersal. Furthermore, those that may are mostly species only able to disperse small-fruited species.

In summary, logging reduced the species-richness of canopy birds, although the young regrowth still had a large number of species. Logging also reduced the abundance of many of these species. Perhaps, most significantly, the young regrowth areas were especially deficient in frugivorous bird species.

Effect of logging on understorey birds
Mist netting of the understorey birds showed that the numbers of species present was generally greater in intact forest than in regrowth on the well drained terrace and hill sites, but that more species were present in regrowth than intact forect in the poorly drained swamp areas. Driscoll used the patterns of captures with successive netting episodes (160 net-days per plot) to estimate an 'expected' total species-richness at each site. This estimate is shown in Table 5.12. The differences are not striking. Thus, 35 species were captured at the terrace forest and 32 species were captured at the terrace regrowth. The expected maximum number at the two sites was 44 species and 45 species respectively.

The forests on well drained terraces and on the hill areas appeared to have a distinctive complement of up to 20 understorey species. These species were absent or in low numbers in the swamp forest and regrowth areas where a few other species were more abundant. Many transient birds were present at all sites, but, in general, birds remained longer in the forest plots than in the regrowth. Further, there were significantly more residents in the forest than the regrowth. Overall, the bird density was as much as 40% lower in the regrowth and swamp forest compared with the intact terrace

Table 5.12 Number of bird species captured by mist netting in the understorey of various intact forest and regrowth forests in the Gogol Valley with the expected maximum number available for capture at each site (based on 6 rounds of netting, i.e. 160 net-days at each plot)

Plot	Captured	Expected maximum captured
Terrace		
intact forest	35	44
regrowth	32	45
Hill		
intact forest	36	48
regrowth	29	40
Swamp		
intact forest	24	32
regrowth	30	40

Source: Driscoll (1985)

Plate 20 Logging trucks passing 12-year-old *Eucalyptus deglupta* plantation

forest.

Many of the remaining species did not appear to be affected by logging once regrowth became established. These ranged throughout the area, although they may have been slightly less active in some vegetation types than others. The frequency of occurrence of many species could also differ markedly over distances as short as 50 m. If a typical forest species was found in regrowth, it was usually associated with an isolated patch of suitable vegetation. The same was true of some typical regrowth bird species

Plate 21 As logging moves into steeper lands the intensity often decreases and only the larger trees are removed. Enrichment planting trials were carried out in such areas

found in forest areas. The distributions of these birds were presumably related to features of the environment not directly linked to logging, or to conditions created by logging which were also prevalent as a consequence of natural disturbances in unlogged forest.

Driscoll calculated an overlap index for the birds at the forest and regrowth at the well-drained terrace sites based on successive mist nettings of the 10 most abundant species at each habitat. The overlap index of 0.31 was much greater than the values of less than 0.02 found in mature and secondary forests of Panama and Peru reported by Lovejoy (1975). That is, there was a much greater sharing of species between the two types of vegetation in the Gogol Valley. Driscoll interpreted this result as meaning that most of the species found in the regrowth were simply a subset of primary forest birds distributed according to particular structural attributes of the habitat found in both intact and regrowth forest. In contrast to the Neotropics, there is not a distinctive group of secondary forest bird species, which is surprising given the frequency of past disturbances in these forests.

Considering both the canopy and understorey birds, it was apparent that many species found to be abundant in forest were not as abundant in regrowth. The regrowth may have been a satisfactory habitat for some birds, but it was less satisfactory for many others because the environment was harsher and the amount and availability of food was not as great as in intact forests. This limit was substantially lessened where residual trees or patches of forest remained after logging. In the particular case of canopy species, patches of residual forest or even isolated trees in logged areas were especially important in acting as attractants and foci of activity which determined the horizontal distribution of birds.

One of the main effects of logging appeared to be that the various foraging strata in the forest were compressed, making it difficult to separate the direct effects of logging from the indirect effects such as those involving the breakdown of various limitations on competition. For example, there may have been greater competition between herbivores because there were fewer food trees present or because of a change in habitat structure leading to a change in vertical foraging behaviour and more competition between canopy and subcanopy species.

Overall, Driscoll's observations led him to the conclusion that bird activity in the Gogol Valley 'tended to conform to local mosaics of habitat structure that reflected soil and moisture regimes, as well as the effects of disturbance. Bird communities were not delineated on the basis of vegetation types; instead, species were responding to microspatial conditions'. In so far as it seemed that bird communities were associated with particular vegetation types (e.g. forest or regrowth), this was caused by the predominance of their constituent microenvironments over reasonably large areas.

One of the few comparable studies on the effect of severe forest disturbance on tropical birds is that of McClure and Othman (1965). These workers had part of a study area in lowland rain forest in Peninsular Malaysia unexpectedly cleared during airport construction shortly after a netting programme commenced, giving them the opportunity to monitor the immediate changes to the bird populations, something that Driscoll was not able to do. Prior to the felling, there was a constant interchange of birds at any site such that the population was composed of a number of residents plus a large number of non-residents. Of the birds captured, 45% were taken in areas other than where they had been banded.

Felling the forest caused considerable movement among birds in the disturbed and undisturbed area. Only about 5% of the birds from the disturbed areas moved into the undisturbed areas, and the others became wanderers or died. This rather low figure suggests that either the favourable niches in the undisturbed forest were mostly filled, or that there were few niches favourable to the displaced birds. It may be significant that part of the area cleared was disturbed *Pandanus* swamp, forest edge or *Imperata* grassland rather than intact forest. None-the-less, the observations suggested many forest birds were not able to adapt to the disturbance. The same is likely to have been true in the Gogol Valley.

INITIAL EFFECTS ON WATER

Water yield

It is well known that changes to the plant cover in a watershed can lead to changes in the hydrological cycle. The first sign of this in the Gogol

Plate 22   Forest left standing as a buffer strip along a small stream

Plate 23   Trial planting of cocoa beneath *Eucalyptus deglupta* plantation

Valley was an apparent rise in the water table and an increased swampiness in several of the poorly drained terraces at the junction of the floodplain and hills. However, attempts to monitor and quantify the changes occurring failed. The PNG Bureau of Water Resources had a gauging station at the Mawan Bridge near Baku in the centre of the Gogol TRP to measure the flow of the Gogol River at that point. Since the area to be logged represents only a fraction of the total Gogol watershed, this was insufficient to detect any changes occurring as a consequence of logging. Searches were carried out along all the smaller tributaries to locate sites for establishing small gauging weirs. It soon became clear that suitable sites were difficult to find. All the watercourses appeared to run through alluvium or deep soil and there were no points where a good parent rock base could ensure a watertight catchment giving confidence that all the water running off an area was being gauged. The Bureau's ability to cooperate ceased with the advent of the Purari Hydro Electric scheme proposal and thenceforth all its resources were concentrated on the Purari basin.

Of the hydrological research carried out elsewhere in tropical rain forests, that most relevant to the situation in the Gogol Valley is a study reported by Gilmour (1977) in the wet tropics of Australia. The rainfall in his study area was 4037 mm. In this case, the forest was selectively logged and then, 2 years later, totally cleared in preparation for establishing pastures. A control catchment remained unlogged. Pasture establishment did not take place and the forest began to regenerate on the cleared site.

Neither selective logging nor clear-felling produced a dramatic hydrological impact. There was a slight increase in the peak discharge after selective logging but the statistical evidence for this was weak. The clear-felling caused a 10.2% increase in water yield in the subsequent 2 years but this was mostly due to an increase in base flow rather than quick flow (Table 5.13). There was no increase in quick flow volume, quick flow duration or the time to peak. Peak discharges may have increased slightly (Table 5.14). Again, however, the statistical evidence for this was not strong. Gilmour concluded that flood flows at the site were determined more by rainfall characteristics and catchment geomorphology and conditions (e.g. whether wet or dry) than by differences in vegetation cover. There were no details of run off beyond the first 2-year period, but experience elsewhere suggests that the increased water yield that Gilmour observed would diminish with time as forest regrowth developed. For example, Kellman (1969) describes how run off was 0.26% of rainfall in undisturbed primary rain forest in the

Table 5.13 Minimum weekly discharge (cubic feet per second, cfs) following clearing calculated from base flow recession curves for two rain forest watersheds in North Queensland

| *Weekly minimum discharge (cfs)* | | |
Before clear-felling	After clear-felling	Per cent increase
0.05	0.08	60
0.10	0.14	40
0.50	0.58	16
1.00	1.14	14

Source: Gilmour (1977)

Table 5.14 Change in peak discharge as a result of selective logging and clear-felling calculated from a comparison of disturbed and undisturbed watersheds in North Queensland

Peak discharge before logging (cfs)	Peak discharge after selective logging (cfs)	Peak discharge after clear-felling (cfs)
1	1.05	1.21
5	6.10	5.95
10	13.0	12.0
20	27.8	23.6

Source: Gilmour (1977)

Philippines, 1.73% in recently logged-over forest but 0.26% again in a 19-year-old forest fallow. Similar results are reviewed by Williams and Hamilton (1982).

In view of Gilmour's conclusion about the importance of rainfall

Plate 24 Twelve-year-old *Eucalyptus deglupta* plantation. By this age plantations commonly have a considerable understorey. Note figure on roadway for scale

130

characteristics, geomorphology and catchment conditions, it is not possible to directly extrapolate these results to the Gogol Valley. They do suggest, however, that changes to the hydrological cycle caused by pulpwood logging may be short-lived provided forest regrowth develops on the logged areas.

Water quality

The Gogol River, like many rivers in PNG, often carried heavy sediment loads, especially during the wet season. This is due to soil entering the river as a consequence of mass movement (e.g. from landslips), from streambank erosion or from surface slope wash in undisturbed forest[4]. For example, a water sample collected from the Gogol River in November 1970 after severe earth tremors upstream had a suspended sediment load of 1050 ppm, and a turbidity of 5000 Jackson units. The river discharge was then $71\,m^3\,sec$ (2490 cfs) (Bureau of Water Resources 1973). At other times of the year, the sediment loads in the Gogol River are much lower. These high natural levels and the variability that occurs mean it is difficult to detect changes in water quality as a result of changes in land-use.

The approach used to assess changes in water quality was to measure water turbidity. Turbidity is a measure of the optical properties of the water and is caused by suspended sediment. Since different sediments may have different particle sizes or shapes it is usually not possible to relate turbidity, an optical measure, to the mass of the suspended sediment in the water. On the other hand, turbidity is a useful index of changes in water quality and widely used for this purpose (e.g. Patric 1980). For particular watersheds, there may be a linear relationship between turbidity and total suspended sediments when turbidity levels are low (Earhart 1984).

Turbidity levels in logged and unlogged catchments
A network of sampling points was established on streams draining logged and unlogged watersheds throughout the Gogol TRP. These were monitored weekly. Some results from this monitoring programme are shown in Table 5.15 which gives the percentage of weekly sample times that various turbidity levels were reached.

In unlogged watersheds, stream turbidity levels were 10 units or less for 77–84% of the sample period of 59 weeks. High turbidities, greater than 50 units, were found on only 3–6 per cent of the period. In the logged watersheds, turbidity levels of 10 units or less were only recorded on 70–74% of the sample period and turbidity levels greater than 50 units were found on 2–14% of the time. The results show that logging causes erosion but suggest it may not be too severe if considered over a long period.

131

Table 5.15 Effect of logging on stream turbidity showing the percentage of weekly observations in various turbidity classes for streamwater from three logged and three unlogged watersheds in the Gogol Valley (number of weeks sampled = 59)

	Not logged			Logged		
Sample point	Wan	Eun	Gohea	G1	G3	G5
Turbidity class						
0–10	80	77	84	70	70	74
0–20	92	87	89	79	80	86
50 +	3	4	6	14	10	2

Source: Lamb and Beibi (1977)

Change in turbidity levels with time

Comparisons like these of logged and unlogged watersheds using data averaged over a long period can mask significant short-term differences. This effect is shown by examining changes occurring in the weekly results of a monitoring programme on several streams draining logged watersheds which extended over 69 weeks and covered two wet seasons (Table 5.16). Averaged over the whole period, turbidity levels of 10 units or less were found on 61–87% of the sample times and turbidities of 50 units or more were present on 3–15% of the time. Sample point S4 was less turbid than

Table 5.16 Changes in streamwater turbidity in successive years following logging. The data shown are the percentage of weekly observation in various turbidity classes for streamwater from three logged catchments

(a) Over total period of observation May 1974 to May 1976 (number of weeks sampled = 69)

	Sample Point		
Turbidity Class	S1	S2	S3
0–10	65	61	87
0–20	75	74	0
50 +	1	15	3

(b) In successive wet seasons (i.e. November 1974 to May 1975 and November 1975 to May 1976)

	Sample Point S1		Sample Point S2		Sample Point S4	
	1974/75	1975/76	1974/75	1975/76	1974/75	1975/76
0–10	27	75	27	71	71	89
0–20	45	86	45	82	81	89
50 +	23	11	25	15	0	4

Source: Lamb and Beibi (1977)

S3 for most of the period probably because there were no roads in the watershed above S4 and a large proportion of the area was occupied by a village reserve and remained unlogged (Table 5.16a).

There was, however, considerable variation in turbidity levels during the year. Levels in the dry season were invariably low and rarely exceeded 10 units, despite storms with more than 20 mm of rain occurring in all months of the year. Most high turbidity levels were recorded in the wet seasons, but there was a striking difference beween the first and second wet season after logging (Table 5.16b). At sample point S1, only 27% of the samples collected in the first wet season were 10 turbidity units or less showing erosion was high. In the second wet season, however, this increased to 75%. The proportion of high turbidity samples correspondingly declined. Similar results were found at the other points, although point S4 had mostly low turbidity levels from the beginning of the sample period.

The results show that most of the erosion caused by logging occurs during the wet season. The most severe erosion occurs in the first wet season after logging, but revegetation quickly helps reduce this.

These results are similar to those from studies in other tropical forests where the weights of suspended sediment in streamwater or actual soil loss have been measured following logging. For example, Gilmour (1977) recorded a 200–300 per cent increase after selective logging and a tenfold increase after clear-felling. The stream bed load increased as well. However, the erosion responsible for these increases usually declines as the forest recovers. Thus, Kellman (1969) recorded a soil loss of 4.5 g/m² in undisturbed forest in the Philippines, 83.6 g/m² in recently logged forest but only 6.5 g/m² in 19 year old forest regrowth. Similarly, Hatch and Tie (1979) measured a soil loss of 0.14 t/ha from undisturbed forest in Sarawak, 63.6 t/ha from an agricultural clearing but 0.25 t/ha from a secondary forest regenerating after the cessation of agriculture.

NUTRIENT LOSSES

Logging causes nutrients to be lost from a forest site. Some are removed in the harvested logs and others are lost as a consequence of leaching. Nitrogen can be lost by denitrification. The nutrients remaining in logging debris, roots and in soil organic matter may undergo a series of complex transformations after logging as decomposition occurs and microbial populations react to the altered microenvironment. There have been a number of studies that have documented aspects of these changes (e.g. Ewel *et al.* 1981, Uhl *et al.* 1982, Jordan 1980, Harcombe 1977a, b, Cunningham 1963, Nye and Greenland 1960). It was not possible, with the resources available, to carry out such detailed observations in the Gogol Valley. What follows, therefore, is a necessarily simplistic description of the effect of logging on ecosystem nutrients. It includes an estimate of the amount of nutrient removed in harvested logs, the extent to which leaching losses occur and assesses the likely significance of these losses in terms of the residual nutrient reserves of the ecosystem after logging. Note that logging debris was not burnt except where plantations were being established.

Initial effects on direct harvesting losses

Logs are normally taken from the forest to be debarked and chipped at Madang, although debarking is sometimes also carried out in the field. All other material is left to decompose on the forest floor near the stump. The weight of woody material removed can be calculated from the records of timber volumes removed and from the average basic density (oven dry weight per green volume) of the woodchip mixture. These together show that about 44.7 t/ha of logs are harvested from the floodplain forest and 38.8 t/ha are removed from the hill forests (see note 1 of Table 5.17).

There are no estimates of the standing biomass of the Gogol forests but studies in other moist tropical forests have found weights ranging from 300 t/ha to 650 t/ha (Bruenig 1983). Edwards and Grubb (1977) have estimated the biomass of wood and bark alone in lowland rain forest at

Table 5.17 Estimated weight (kg/ha) of nutrients removed from the forest in logs and bark. For comparison the nutrient content of the above-ground biomass of various lowland rain forests summarized in Unesco/UNEP/FAO (1978) are also shown below

Nutrient	N	P	K	Ca	Mg
Woodchip Concentrations %	0.15	0.06	0.26	0.60	0.06
Floodplain areas					
Weight in timber (1)	67	27	116	268	27
Weight in bark (2)	31	12	44	252	7
Weight in logs	98	39	160	520	34
Hill areas					
Weight in timber (1)	58	23	101	233	23
Weight in bark (2)	27	10	39	219	6
Weight in logs	85	33	140	452	29
Nutrient content of above-ground biomass	1000–1800	70–140	350–2980	1200–3580	180–530
Number of studies	5	6	6	5	5

1 The nutrient content of timber = log volume/ha x basic density x nutrient concentration. Harvested log volumes average 100 m³/ha from floodplain forests and 90 m³/ha from hill forests according to Department of Forests records. The basic density of woodchips is 447 kg/m³ for chips from 'valley' forests and 431 kg/m³ for chips from hill forests (E.D. Harries pers. comm.)

2 The nutrient content of bark is estimated from the wood: bark ratios reported by Nye and Greenland (1960) for all elements except N. For N, bark weight was estimated to be 13% of wood weight and the concentration was assumed to be 0.54% (Grubb and Edwards 1982).

about 300–360 t/ha. Against these values, the Gogol Valley woodchip harvest seems very low. There may be two reasons for this. One is that the Gogol forests simply have a low biomass compared with other lowland forests. If so, one factor responsible is almost certainly the basic density of less than 450 kg/m^3. This is a comparatively low value. Chudnoff (1976), for example, found most trees growing in a similar rainfall zone (i.e. 2000 mm–4000 mm) in the Neotropics had values in excess of 690 kg/m^3. The Gogol Valley data probably reflect the high proportion of secondary tree species in these forests. The other possible reason for the low woodchip harvest is that the harvesting operation is inefficient and leaves behind a lot of timber in the form of small, bowed or decayed logs.

The nutrient content of the timber removed has been calculated by multiplying these log weights by the chemical composition of woodchips (Table 5.17). The results show that harvesting floodplain forest removes 98 kg/ha of N, 39 kg/ha of P, 160 kg/ha of K, 520 kg/ha of Ca and 34 kg/ha of Mg. Slightly smaller weights of these same nutrients are removed from the hill forests during harvesting. Again, these weights appear to be a small proportion of the nutrient content measured in the above ground biomass in various other lowland rain forests (Table 5.17). Clearly large amounts of nutrients in the original forest biomass may remain as debris on the forest floor after logging. Just how big this residual, above-ground nutrient pool is remains unknown.

Nutrients exported from ecosystems in streamwater

Immediately after logging, a pulse of nutrients may be released into the soil solution when debris, such as leaves and branches, decomposes, and as some topsoil organic matter mineralizes. In many cases, these nutrients are leached from the top soil but are absorbed in lower horizons (McColl 1978, Harcombe 1977a). In some circumstances, however, a proportion of the nutrient pulse is leached through the soil profile and into streams. Once in the streams, nutrients are lost from the ecosystem[5].

This loss can be detected by monitoring changes in streamwater chemistry during and after logging operations, the loss from the site being the product of the nutrient concentration and the stream discharge rate. The concentration of nutrients may vary as a direct consequence of logging but can sometimes also be influenced by the stream discharge rate irrespective of changes in land use. In fact, different concentration–discharge relationships have been found for the same ion in different watersheds (Jordan and Kline 1972, Likens *et al.* 1970, Lewis and Grant 1979). This means that accurate monitoring of nutrient export following logging should involve measuring changes in both concentration and discharge. In practice, however, such monitoring is often not done, and a number of more qualitative studies have monitored ionic concentrations alone to describe gross changes to the ecosystem nutrient cycle as a consequence of alterations to the forest cover (e.g. Likens *et al.* 1969, Aubertin and Patric 1974, Sopper 1975). This approach was used in the Gogol Valley after Gilmour's (1977) study suggested the streamwater discharge rate might not be too greatly affected by logging. The study implied that the concentrations alone would probably provide a reasonable comparative indicator of the extent to which logging affected nutrient loss.

Water sampling took place several years after logging commenced. By that time, a variety of small subcatchments with differing logging histories were present. Four broad groups were sampled.

(a) unlogged watersheds (three streams sampled).

(b) watersheds logged within the previous 3 months. One of these (T2) was logged 3 months prior to sampling and the other (T3) was partially logged during the sampling period.

(c) watersheds logged 12 months to 18 months previously (two streams sampled).

(d) watersheds logged 2–3 years previously (three streams sampled).

Samples were collected from the streams at weekly intervals at the commencement of the 1976/77 wet season and later, after a short break, towards the end of that same wet season[6]. There were differences in the size of the catchments, the proportions of the catchments disturbed and the timing and duration of logging. The assumption made, however, was that they could be considered as a time sequence and that differences between the four groups were a function of logging and forest regeneration. All catchments retained some undisturbed forest on the steeper slopes.

Overall, there was no striking difference in the nutrient concentrations in water from the different groups of catchments (Table 5.18). For most ions, the concentrations were similar in all the streams sampled. There were, however, several exceptions. Stream T2, which had been logged 3 months before sampling commenced, had higher levels than most other streams of nitrate, phosphate and potassium. In the later wet season, sampling the differences in nitrate and potassium concentrations between T2 and the other streams disappeared, but the phosphate level remained comparatively high. Two to 3 years after logging, the concentrations of phosphate in early wet season samples were apparently still greater than in streams draining undisturbed watersheds.

There was a difference in the nutrient concentrations between the two sample periods. Samples collected later in the wet season were invariably lower than those collected at the commencement. In the case of the nitrate ions, this result was probably largely due to the use of a preservative in the water samples collected at this time. For the other elements, the difference may indicate that nutrients released by organic matter decomposition

Table 5.18 Mean concentrations of nutrients in streamwater draining logged and unlogged catchments in the Gogol Valley. Weekly samples collected in the early wet season (October to December, n = 10) and late wet season (March to April, n = 6). The late wet season values are shown in parentheses

Catchment status and name	Catchment Area (km²)	Per cent logged	Concentration (mg/l)					
			NO_3^-	PO_4^{--}	K^+	Ca^{++}	Mg^{++}	pH
1. Not logged								
Sapi	146.0	0	0.30 (tr)	0.53 (0.27)	4.4 (3.1)	60 (46)	12.9 (9.1)	8.1
D1	15.5	0	0.26 (0.45)	0.53 (0.45)	5.0 (4.3)	61 (49)	12.0 (9.7)	8.2
D2	10.6	0	0.22 (0.01)	0.58 (0.43)	4.6 (4.3)	66 (54)	12.7 (10.8)	8.2
2. Three months since logging								
T3	6.9	11	0.16 (0.03)	0.68 (0.61)	5.3 (5.3)	66 (37)	13.1 (8.8)	8.1
T2	6.5	50	2.06 (0.02)	3.03 (1.22)	12.7 (5.3)	53 (45)	16.3 (9.6)	7.6
3. Twelve–eighteen months since logging								
Tun	19.0	23	0.21 (0.05)	1.00 (0.76)	5.5 (5.4)	55 (43)	11.3 (9.1)	7.9
T1	1.1	50	0.20 (0.04)	0.72 (0.56)	6.0 (5.6)	58 (45)	14.5 (10.5)	7.8
4. Two–three years since logging								
G3	1.1	50	0.28 (0.03)	1.01 (0.65)	5.5 (5.0)	61 (54)	14.4 (10.5)	7.9
G5	8.7	70	0.23 (0.02)	0.94 (0.53)	6.5 (5.2)	63 (45)	14.1 (9.0)	7.9
S7	3.1	65	0.34 (0.09)	1.11 (0.56)	6.5 (5.0)	59 (41)	14.8 (10.0)	7.9
S6	4.6	65	0.30 (0.08)	0.95 (0.62)	6.9 (5.4)	64 (53)	13.9 (9.9)	7.9

tr = trace

accumulated in the soil during the dry season and were flushed out with the early rains.

Most of the streamwater nutrient concentrations were high and fall in the upper end of the range of values reported from other tropical rivers (Sioli 1968, Golley *et al.* 1975, Whelan 1977, Viner 1975, Petr 1976). This effect evidently reflects the large concentration of most of these elements in the soil (Table 3.8), the immaturity of these soils, and the geologically recent origin of most of the underlying sediments.

The data suggest that, for most elements, the logging operation caused only a temporary increase in nutrient export from the ecosystem. In the case of phosphorus, the effect may have been longer lasting. This conclusion accords with observations of similar logging operations in temperate forests. Provided these forests were allowed to regenerate immediately, streamwater nutrient levels usually increased slightly after logging but quickly dropped to their former levels or lower once the cycle between soil, plants and microorganism recommenced (Sopper 1975, Patric 1980, Vitousek and Reiners 1975).

There are limitations to the conclusions that can be drawn from measurements of dissolved nutrient levels such as these. Large amounts of nutrients may also be lost from watersheds as suspended sediments originating from topsoil erosion. Streamwater phosphorus is usually soon absorbed on such sediments (Holt *et al.* 1970, Viner 1979). The actual loss of nutrients is, therefore, greater than that indicated by streamwater analyses alone, but such additional losses are also likely to decrease as reforestation occurs and erosion diminishes.

Nutrient losses in relation to ecosystem nutrient reserves

The significance of these losses depends on the total amounts of nutrients originally contained and cycling within the ecosystem. Since there are no quantitative measures of either the total losses (harvesting plus streamwater plus denitrification) or of the total ecosystem nutrient pool (biomass plus soil) such a direct comparison cannot be made. In order to show the relative magnitude of the loss, however, the amount of nutrient exported in logs can be matched against an estimate of the amount of nutrient in the top 50 cm of soil in floodplain and hill forest sites. Except for nitrogen, the soil nutrients have been calculated from the available or exchangeable concentrations of each element. Nitrogen was calculated using the total nitrogen concentration of the soil.

On the basis of this comparison, the most critical element is clearly phosphorus (Table 5.19). In the floodplain soils, 39 kg/ha are removed in logs leaving only 45 kg/ha in the soil. In the hill areas, the difference is even more striking; 33 kg/ha are removed in logs leaving only 13 kg/ha in the soil. For most other elements, the soil reserves contain many times the

Plate 25   Ten-year-old regeneration

amounts removed in pulpwood. A comparison involving just the soil nutrients underestimates the actual nutrient reserves, of course. There is an unquantified amount of phosphorus still present at these sites in the form of logging debris. This amount may be quite substantial since earlier estimates of the timber biomass harvested suggested the process was comparatively inefficient. Further, debarking logs in the forest would reduce the phosphorus loss by 10 kg/ha to 12 kg/ha. Finally, many plant roots undoubtedly grow deeper than 50 cm, and, with their associated mycorrhiza, may be able to exploit more of the soil phosphorus than chemical measures of 'available' phosphorus suggest. This process was well illustrated, for example, in the study by Turner and Lambert (1986). Nevertheless, the proportional loss of phosphorus is high. In the face of these comparisons, the apparently high phosphorus concentrations in streamwater draining logged catchments may be even more significant.

Despite these losses, natural regrowth on logged sites was very rapid and there was no sign of any nutrient limitation to plant growth. Furthermore,

Plate 26 By 1986 logging coupes had increased in size, fewer small trees were left standing and streamside buffer strips were few in number

Table 5.19 Amounts of nutrients in logs removed from the sites in relation to the amounts of nutrients in the soil (to 50 cm)

	Nutrient content kg/ha				
	N	P	K	Ca	Mg
Floodplain					
Logs	98	39	160	520	34
Soil	7460	45	1399	32 365	11 404
Hill					
Logs	85	33	140	452	29
Soil	8040	13	1657	44 640	7811

Note: Soil contents based on total N, available P and exchangeable cations.

there was no evidence of phosphorus deficiency or response to phosphorus fertilizers in plantations of *Eucalyptus deglupta* established after logging debris had been burnt. The only nutrient showing signs of any deficiency in any of these plantations was nitrogen (Lamb 1977b). In this particular case, the site was rather low-lying and could have been particularly subject to denitrification. The subsequent response to fertilizer nitrogen was small and disappeared after 1 year. Otherwise, tree growth in most plantations was rapid, even where nutrients contained in logging debris were not released to the soil surface by burning. In fact, trees in an experimental plantation of *Eucalyptus deglupta* established directly in logging debris grew faster than those planted after the normal pre-planting burn (Lamb 1976).

It is difficult to compare the GTP logging operation with other disturbances to tropical forests where more detailed studies of the effect of the disturbance on nutrient cycling have been carried out. With few exceptions, these studies have concerned changes occurring after clearing forest for some form of agriculture, and have involved fire and a cropping period. Perhaps the most comparable studies are two carried out in caatinga forest on infertile soils in the Amazon region of Venezuela (Jordan 1980, Uhl *et al.* 1982). In both cases, forest was cleared and then allowed to regenerate without fire or cropping. The concentration of various elements in soil leachate was assessed using a series of zero tension lysimeters. In both studies, there were increases after clearing in the concentration of most elements, particularly potassium, magnesium and nitrate nitrogen. The elevated concentrations mostly decreased to their original levels fairly quickly and in all cases returned to the pre-logging level within 3 years as forest regrowth occurred. No assessment was made of the actual amounts of nutrients lost, but Jordan (1980) believed these to have been comparatively unimportant.

An important mechanism limiting nutrient leaching losses in undisturbed forests is the fine root and mycorrhiza layer in the topsoil. After clearing, many roots and mycorrhiza appear to be retained for 12 months or more, even if the site is burned (Ewel *et al.* 1981). If forest regrowth is allowed to develop immediately without cropping, fine root growth is rapid and may match that in undisturbed forest within a year (Raich 1980, Jordan 1980). These reports suggest that mycorrhiza and roots are able to capture much of the nutrient released from decomposing logging debris and retain it within the ecosystem.

Whether original root systems are retained or not, it seems plant growth after a previously undisturbed forest is cleared is often rapid. In fact, trees or crops establishing on newly cleared land may not respond to fertilizer applications (Harcombe 1977b, Clark and Street 1967, Cunningham 1963). That is, losses occurring as a direct result of the clearing operation itself seem to be relatively small compared with the pool of available nutrients remaining in the site.

Taking together the assessment of losses in the Gogol Valley and these observations in other tropical forests, the evidence suggests that there are losses of some elements from the forest ecosystem as a consequence of logging, but that these occur within a fairly short space of time and are unlikely to limit forest regrowth. The magnitude of the apparent loss of phosphorus, however, points to it being a potentially limiting nutrient if plantation crops such as pulpwood are grown in successive short term rotations.

INITIAL EFFECTS ON SOIL PHYSICAL PROPERTIES

Only one measurement has been reported of the extent to which the soils of the area have been disturbed by logging. This was in an area of 14 ha covered by a sampling grid of 20 x 20 m. The study found 20 per cent of the site covered by snig tracks, roads and log loading sites (Vergara 1979). Casual observations throughout the GTP area suggest there may be considerable variation in the extent to which surface soil is disturbed, with some areas being obviously more disturbed than the site survey by Vergara. Experience with selective logging in other parts of the tropics points to values of 30 per cent disturbance being quite common (Ewel and Conde, 1980).

Some soil puddling and soil compaction occurred in parts of this disturbed area, but particularly in the vicinity of the log loading areas. Vergara (1979) reported the bulk density of most surface soils was less than $0.80\,g/cm^3$ but that values exceeding $1.00\,g/cm^3$ could be found within 60 m of many loading sites. Studies elsewhere have shown mechanical clearing of rain forest often causes soil compaction, especially if the soils are wet at the time of clearing. The growth of crop plants can be adversely affected by this (Van der Weert and Lenselink 1972, Van der Weert 1974, Seubert *et al.* 1977). The only place that any obvious restriction on plant growth occurred in the GTP was on the loading sites. On many of these, forest regrowth has been poor and stunted unless the soil was deep ripped by bulldozers at the completion of logging.

The only other obvious effect of logging on soil physical properties was a rise in the watertable in some low lying areas. Many of these sites had always been poorly-drained but it appeared that drainage had worsened, perhaps as a result of greater run-off from cleared hill forest areas. Interestingly, these sites became dominated by *Anthocephalus chinensis*, one of the potential plantation species being tested in the early species trials at the Baku Research Station. In time, forest regrowth and an increase in evapotranspiration appears to have led to a fall in the water table once more. More localized waterlogging and ponding has also occurred in old snig tracks and road construction borrow areas.

A SUMMARY OF THE INITIAL EFFECTS OF LOGGING

Predictably, when the short-term consequences of logging are considered, there are many adverse effects on the forest. Even though detailed ecological monitoring has been incomplete, it is clear that the following changes have occurred.

Plants: mature, reproducing individuals of most plant species have been cleared from large areas; the forest structure has been destroyed.
Birds: species commonly found in the canopy of undisturbed forest are

much less common in young regrowth areas; there is an apparent reduction in both species richness and abundance. Birds more typically present in the forest understorey are also affected.

Other biota: insufficient data to assess changes.

Water: run-off is probably slightly increased, but water quality is sharply decreased as a result of soil erosion in the first wet season after logging.

Nutrients: the loss of nutrients from the ecosystem is accelerated as a consequence of harvesting removals, leaching erosion and possibly, denitrification.

Soil physical properties: soil compaction and puddling leading to adverse changes in many soil physical properties occurs in the vicinity of log landings: some low lying areas become more swampy as a result of reduced evapotranspiration and increased run-off.

With more detailed study, other short-term consequences would almost certainly be evident. It is also obvious, however, that forest regeneration is developing at all the logged-over sites. Many of the adverse changes appear to have been arrested, and, in some cases, reversed. The most important ecological question, therefore, is not what were the immediate effects but what will be the longer-term consequences? For example, how many of the detrimental effects are reversible? To what extent is the forest likely to recover if no further disturbance takes place?

LONG-TERM CONSEQUENCES OF LOGGING

According to the initial land use plan for the Gogol Valley, much of the logged area was to be used for tree plantations and large scale agricultural developments. As already described, this did not happen at the rate and scale expected. Much of the logged forest has simply been abandoned. Some will, of course, be used for small scale agriculture by the landowners, but much is likely to remain undisturbed. Woody regrowth is quickly established on most sites but what is likely to occur in the future?

Ecological theory has not reached the stage where it allows many accurate predictions about the consequences of environmental disturbances. Attempts have been made for the purposes of environmental impact assessment, but, in many cases, these have not been particularly successful (Beanlands and Duinker 1983, Westman 1985). One common explanation of this lack of success is that most ecosystems are just too complex; there are usually a large number of organisms and an even larger number of interactions involving these. It is simply too difficult to make any worthwhile forecast because of the huge number of possible ecosystem responses.

There is, however, an alternative to this view. Some ecologists now believe that, for the purposes of making a forecast about the response of an ecosystem to a disturbance, many of the species and many of the interactions between them are relatively insignificant (Holling 1978,

143

Westoby 1984). Westoby, for example, argues that, for any given species in an ecosystem, most others in the assemblage are unimportant. Further, the main properties of the ecosystem are controlled by a relatively few 'structuring' species that determine the physical nature of the ecosystem and help create a variety of habitats. These structuring species are themselves influenced by a limited number of environmental factors and these are neither obscure nor intricate.

A number of similar arguments have been reviewed by Beanland and Duinker (1983). They found an emerging consensus that environmental impact assessors should concentrate on 'important' or 'key' species. These are species that are either abundant, instrumental in the formation of the habitat, commercially important or valued in some way by society. One way of predicting the response of an ecosystem to disturbance is, therefore, to determine how the disturbance affects the ecological processes sustaining these key species.

Tropical rain forests exemplify complex ecosystems. They contain numerous species and there are various inter-relationships linking many of these. Is it possible to identify key species? If there are 'structuring' or 'key' species present in rain forests, then they are most likely to be the canopy trees. These are the species intercepting most of the incoming energy to the ecosystem and changing it, through photosynthesis, to chemical forms useable by other organisms; they are responsible for exploring the soil for nutrients and for intercepting and redistributing much of the incoming water; they provide a physical support for many organisms such as vines, epiphytes and some animals and they are the primary agents for creating a microclimate suitable for plant and animal species not otherwise able to tolerate the general climate outside the shelter of the forest.

There are a number of critical ecological processes sustaining these trees, but two in particular stand out. One can rather awkwardly be described as the regeneration process. This is the production and dispersal of seed and the establishment of seedlings. The other is the process of nutrient cycling. Clear-felling drastically affects both processes, but, in the short-term at least, does not necessarily destroy them. Prediction of the longer-term consequences of logging depends, therefore, on the extent to which these two processes persist and then recover[7].

Logging and the regeneration process

A plant can become established in a newly created gap from either:

(a) the seedling pool – residual plants previously present on the forest floor prior to gap formation;

(b) the soil seed store – seed present in the soil, either as stored dormant seed or as seed arriving just prior to gap formation;

(c) vegetative regrowth – from damaged plants previously present at the site;

(d) dispersed seed – seed arriving at the gap from a parent tree some distance away after gap creation.

The importance of any one of these sources depends on the size of the gap, the past history of gap formation at the site, and the nature and timing of the disturbance causing the gap. All may have a role in the process of natural regeneration after logging in the GTP area.

Seedling pool
The number of seedlings on the floor of an undisturbed forest is often high, but many are damaged by logging. Fox (1968) described a logging operation in a dipterocarp forest in Sabah in which 27% of the area was covered by tractor tracks and 42% of the seedlings were destroyed. Seedling damage at least as great as this is likely to have occurred in the GTP area. Studies in the Gogol Valley by Saulei (1985) have shown that residual saplings can contribute to the forest regrowth, but, overall, the role of residual seedlings and saplings is probably small.

Soil seed store
It is well known that rain forest soils commonly contain a significant store of seed and that a high proportion of these are secondary tree species (Hopkins and Graham 1983, Liew 1973, Cheke *et al.* 1979, Guevava and Gomez-Pompa 1972). Saulei (1985) measured the soil seed store at several floodplain sites in the Gogol Valley. These soils contained 400–800 seed per m^2 and included up to 76 species. Most of the seeds were of tree or shrub species and most of these were secondary forest rather than primary forest species. The dominant species was the early successional tree *Pipturus argenteus*. These data are broadly comparable with findings elsewhere in the tropics, and suggest that the soil seed store will allow the rapid regeneration of secondary tree species, but few, if any, primary forest species on recently logged sites.

Vegetative regrowth
The occurrence of vegetative regrowth among species in the Gogol Valley has already been described, and it has been widely observed in many other rain forests (Webb *et al.* 1972, Stocker 1981, Kartawinata *et al.* 1980, Uhl 1982). This form of regeneration may play a significant role in the re-establishment of forests on logged sites. Stocker (1981) quotes Symington's (1933) observation in a Malayan forest that 'after felling, coppice growth, if allowed to develop, will within a few years create a stand which, except for the presence of large trees and the presence of a few typical secondary growth species, shows little indication that the rain forest had been so

recently cleared'. Saulei (1985) found the rate of coppice growth in the Gogol Valley was slower than that of competing seedlings. After 2 years, the coppice had reached 3.1 m, but the average height of plants regenerating from seed was 10.7 m. This he attributed to the fact that most of the coppice was from trees that could be classified as 'large secondary' forest species or primary forest species, while most of the trees originating from seed were 'small secondary' species probably emerging from the soil seed store. Many of these are relatively short lived and, in due course, much of the coppice growth will probably occupy part of the canopy.

Dispersal of seed

Seed may reach logged areas from nearby unlogged forest, from intact buffer strips along streams, or from disturbed areas such as nearby regrowth forests. Some seed may also be distributed from the few unlogged residual trees such as *Ficus* and food trees marked for retention by landowners. Apart from vegetative regrowth, such seed dispersal is likely to be the only method by which primary forest species may become re-established in many logged areas.

Saulei (1985) measured the seed rain in a newly logged site in the Gogol Valley over 22 months and found it included 32 species. Most were grasses and herbs; there were no primary tree species and only a few large secondary tree species. Other studies (e.g. Table 5.3) have shown that primary and secondary species were being dispersed into logged sites, and it is possible the five seed traps used in this study were too few to sample what must be a very heterogeneous seed rain.

Little is known about the dispersal capabilities of PNG forest tree seed. In the absence of detailed field records, some indication of these capabilities can be obtained by examining the morphology of the various fruit and seed. J.S. Womersley, long-time director of the PNG Herbarium at Lae, has suggested tree species in the GTP area can be placed into one of the following groups (Womersley 1983).

A: Wind dispersal
'This includes trees with winged fruits e.g. some *Terminalia, Pterocymbium, Kleinhovea* etc. and species with winged seed released from a capsule on the tree (e.g. *Cedrela*)'.

B: Bird dispersal
'most succulent fruits can be presumed eaten and seeds defecated by birds. Terrestrial birds such as cassowary will pick up fallen fruits such as *Spondias, Elaeocarpus, Terminalia* and defecate seeds in heaps'.

C: Bat dispersal
'most succulent fruits are attractive to bats. Small fruits may be ingested whole and the seed defecated (e.g. papaya and *Musa*). Other

fruits are torn apart and seed falls free or may be transported some distance, the pulp removed and the remains fall to the ground (e.g. *Terminalia*). Some arboreal mammals may also assist in fruit and seed distribution in this category'.

D: No special dispersal mechanism, seed or seedling dormant
'The fruit falls entire, dehisces or rots on the ground and the seed remains on the forest floor. This seed may germinate immediately and the seedling remain dormant, possibly a few years awaiting a break in the canopy or the seed may itself remain until light conditions (or perhaps moisture) trigger germination. Terrestrial animals (e.g. pigs) may spread some fruit or seed. Insects, particularly ants, carry small seed. Some fruit and seed are water borne and germinate when flood or tidal conditions recede'.

W: Dispersal by water

X: Unknown

This classification was used to categorize all the tree genera and species recorded during the early Forestry Department timber resource surveys in the Gogol Valley[8], plus those other tree species recorded during the CSIRO survey in the area (Saunders 1976).

Many species are difficult to classify on the basis of morphology alone, and such a classification must be regarded as tentative until actual field evidence is available. Moreover, some genera contain species with a variety of dispersal mechanisms (e.g. *Terminalia*). There is also a particular problem concerning the separation of bird and bat dispersed species. Fleming (1979) has concluded that avian and mammalian frugivores probably seldom compete and that many plants have different types of fruit that attract either bats or birds, but not both[9]. On the other hand, he admitted that not all fruit eaten by bats or birds conformed to these syndromes, and Marshall (1985), in discussing the Old World bats, concluded there was considerable overlap between bats and birds in their choice of food.

Accepting these limitations, Womersley's analysis can be used to indicate the relative importance of the various dispersal methods utilized by the main tree species in the GTP area. This is shown in Figure 5.6. (The classification of individual species, upon which this table is based, is given in Appendix 3.) The data have been arranged to show the overall importance of each dispersal method as well as its importance in the valley forests, hill forests and regrowth forests sampled in the Department of Forests resource surveys.

The main conclusions to be drawn are as follows; first, there is a considerable proportion of genera (24%) with wind dispersed seed. This is slightly higher than the proportion found in a number of other moist tropical forests in the review by Howe and Smallwood (1982), but is well within the range (4–46%) reported. Second, dispersal by birds and bats

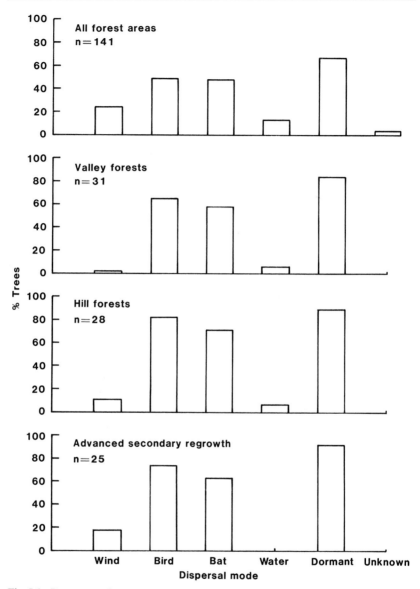

Fig. 5.6 Percentage of tree genera or species having various dispersal modes based on the classification by Womersley (1983). Surveys by Saunders (1976) and the Department of Forests were used to compile a species list for all forest areas while the species lists for valley, hill and secondary forest areas were based on Department of Forests surveys

probably accounts for nearly half of all genera. This proportion may seem high but is, in fact, at the lower end of the range (46–93%) recorded in other tropical forests by Howe and Smallwood. Third, up to 13% of genera may have their seed dispersed by water. This proportion is much higher than the few per cent recorded by Howe and Smallwood, and presumably reflects the fact that a number of species are adapted to the flooding that commonly occurs in many low lying areas of the Gogol Valley. Finally, some 67% of the total genera have no special mechanism and are apparently adapted to some form of dispersal in time, either in a soil seed pool or perhaps even in an above-ground seedling store.

The subset of timber trees recorded during the Department of forests surveys differ slightly in these proportions by containing a much greater proportion of species with seed dispersal by birds and bats (Figure 5.6). This is especially true of the hill forest genera of which 82% are apparently bird dispersed and 71% are apparently bat dispersed. The hill forests also had many fewer genera dispersed by wind in comparison with the larger group. Some areas of advanced secondary regrowth arising out of earlier disturbances in the Gogol Valley were also included in the Forestry Department survey. The genera in these forests are surprisingly similar to the hill and valley forest genera in terms of their dispersal methods, suggesting that vegetative regrowth was especially important in the recovery process in these areas or that sufficient time may have elapsed to allow the normal complement of dispersal methods to be once more represented.

In summary, the analysis points to birds and bats as being critically involved in the dispersal of many tree species, with wind being a common but less important dispersal mode. If Womersley's analysis is correct, the non-dispersed 'dormancy' mode, leading to dispersal only in time, is also common in many genera, although it has already been pointed out that most of the species in the soil seed pool are early secondary species and most of the seedling pool are probably destroyed in logging.

Effectiveness of wind and animals as dispersal agents in logged areas

Wind

Although the fruit or seed of many trees are apparently adapted to dispersal by wind, it is not clear just how effective this mode may be in allowing such species to cover large distances and colonize big gaps. Plants dispersed by wind were the dominant early colonizers of the island of Krakatoa following the volcanic explosion of 1883 (Richards 1979). On the other hand, Whitmore (1984) reported that the seed of *Terminalia calamansanai*, an apparently wind dispersed species, could be poorly dispersed leaving all seedlings close to the parent tree.

Wind dispersal is probably most effective when seeds are small and the crowns of the parent tree are tall and well exposed. Womersley (1983) believed species with wind dispersed seed would be important early colonizers of logged areas in the GTP area, but their actual importance will obviously depend on the orientation of logged and intact forest with respect to wind direction.

Birds

Many PNG tree species are bird dispersed and some may have specialized relationships with particular frugivores[10]. Many of these frugivores are absent or only present in low numbers in young regrowth forests. How likely are bird dispersed plant species to recolonize logged areas?

In the case of tree species dependent on larger birds, such as cassowaries, it is obvious that the chances of recolonization are poor for seed dispersal. The numbers of these birds have already been reduced by hunting whatever the effect of logging may have been. The prospects for other tree species are less clear. The most common frugivore in the regrowth areas noted by Driscoll (1984) was the fruit dove *Ptilinopsus iozonus*. A study of the feeding habits of this species by Frith *et al.* (1976) found it fed mainly on figs but that at least 20 other genera in 18 families were also utilized. These included Arecaceae, Ulmaceae, Moraceae, Menispermaceae, Annonaceae, Myristicaceae, Lauraceae, Leguminaceae, Burseraceae, Euphorbiaceae, Combretaceae, Myrtaceae, Sapotaceae, Symplocaceae, Convolvulaceae, Verbenaceae and Compositae. Frith *et al.* (1976) found the other fruit doves and fruit pigeons observed by Driscoll (1984) in the regrowth forests also had quite varied diets. Thus, *P. perlatus* fed on plants from eight families. Besides those eaten by *P. iozonus*, these families included Vitaceae, Rutaceae and Anacardiaceae. Likewise, *P. magnificus* fed on at least 26 genera from 21 families. In addition to those mentioned, these families included Chysobalanaceae, Erythoxylaceae, Sapindaceae, Sapotaceae and Oleaceae. Figs were a much less important item in the diet than was the case with *P. iozonus* and *P. perlatus*.

Frith *et al.* (1976) believed the diet of these frugivores could be wider than they recorded. In the north-eastern tropics of Australia, these same species fed on an entirely different group of trees. They suggested that the feeding behaviour in an area depended on the availability of food at a particular time. Frith (1976) has also observed that, in some cases, the varied diets of fruit pigeons are made up of trees that fruit sequentially. The removal of one tree species from this sequence can have an adverse effect on the birds. Much less appears to be known of the diet and feeding ecology, including ranging behaviour, of other frugivores present in large numbers in Gogol regrowth forests.

One of the most important features in the regrowth site studied by Driscoll was the presence of residual trees. These were important perching sites and provided food (many were *Ficus*). Driscoll believed they acted as focal points for bird activity and had a considerable effect in the horizontal distribution of the avian populations in these areas. It follows, of course, that such trees may be of considerable importance in determining the pattern of seed dispersal by birds in regrowth forests even though some birds may be seed predators rather than seed dispersers.

Birds may be attracted to these trees because of the food they offer or simply because of their physical presence. An experiment which used artificial structures to simulate saplings in a temperate deciduous hardwood forest region found such structures attracted birds to old fields because they created a structurally more complex habitat. The result was a significant increase in the recruitment of seed to these fields over unmodified fields (McDonnell and Stiles 1983). The same relationship is likely to hold true in logged areas.

From the evidence available it seems probable, therefore, that birds will disperse the seed of many species into clear-felled areas, especially where there are large numbers of residual trees. Whether they do so across large clear-felled areas remains to be seen. It is important to note here that all of the regrowth forests studied by Driscoll (1984) were less than 5 years old. These are changing in structural complexity. As they do so, the differences in bird populations between them and surrounding unlogged forests will diminish and a wider variety of seed will be brought to the disturbed sites. Even so, it is likely that some of the tree species entirely dependent on larger frugivores will be unable to recolonize logged areas for many years.

Bats

Thirteen of the 16 species of bat in the GTP area are fruit eaters and probably play a significant role in seed dispersal. Most of the Old World bats (*Megachiroptera*) feed on a wide variety of plants, although they may show a preference for certain foods if a choice is available (Marshall 1985). Some are capable of eating large fruit although it is doubtful whether such species could entirely compensate for the disappearance of the larger avian frugivores. Interestingly, however, some bats may eat seed from shade intolerant early secondary species and shade tolerant mature-phase forest species in the same night. In doing this, they may, in the words of Heithaus (1982), enhance 'the movement of late successional tree species to sites appropriate to colonization'.

Bats are not seed predators and most seed is either discarded before ingestion or voided, although some small seed may pass through the gut and be expelled in faeces. It seems, therefore, that bats will disperse most seed over small distances although many forage over large distances and some long distance dispersal is also possible (Fleming 1981, Marshall 1985).

There are no observations on the extent to which bats use or fly over regrowth vegetation, but Hall (1986) believes residual trees, especially the figs, may be as important to bats as they obviously are to birds. If this is so, then bats may have a quite significant role in introducing seed to the logged areas.

Other animals

In other tropical rain forests, small animals on the forest floor and pigs (Whitmore 1984) can have a significant role in seed dispersal but the distances involved are probably small. Accounts of such relationships are mostly taken from studies in older forests and not enough is known of how logging affects such animals to be able to say how significant such dispersal might be in the GTP area. It seems likely to be slight.

The regeneration process – conclusions

This review of the available evidence suggests that, in time and under the logging conditions prevalent during the first 10 years of the project, most elements of the regeneration process are likely to continue after logging ceases. That is, it seems probable that many of the original canopy tree species will regenerate on the logged areas. There are, however, several important qualifications that need to be made.

The first of these concerns the pattern of logging. The initial logging operations in the GTP area were characterized by annual logging coupes of 50 ha to 600 ha, significant numbers of unlogged residual trees and adjacent areas of undisturbed forest within about 400 m. In many cases, undisturbed forest surrounded a good deal of each coupe for several years after logging ceased. These conditions may not necessarily continue in the future. In 1980, the Forestry Department adopted a policy that required annual clear-felling areas to be limited to 100 ha when logging was not being followed by a change in land use such as agriculture or plantation establishment. In the Gogol Valley, this should mean that logging coupes in most hill forests are limited to this size. In valley forests where plantation establishment may occur, the new policy allows logging coupes to reach 200 ha. It remains to be seen whether these standards are adopted in practice. Perhaps equally importantly, it remains to be seen whether significant numbers of residual trees remain untouched after logging. In this respect, it is fortunate that *Ficus* is unsuitable for woodchips. That fact should ensure that at least one of the most important animal food trees remains to attract birds and bats into the logged areas. There are a large number of small village reserves, stream side buffer strips and undisturbed patches of hill forest scattered within the GTP area, but there is also an increasing likelihood that successive annual logging coupes will link areas already cleared in previous years. The problem of seed dispersal from undisturbed forest will increase in direct proportion to the extent that this occurs.

A second qualification is the fact that several tree species appear to have no distinct seed or fruit dispersal mechanism. Some of these may regenerate from coppice or root suckers and others may persist after logging as residual seedling or sapling growth. They seem unlikely to recolonize logged areas in any other way.

A third qualification concerns the matter of recovery time. Although the overall operation of the regeneration process appears likely to continue, it is almost impossible to say at what rate the forest will recover[11]. Too little is known of the phenology and amount of seed production by any of the tree species in the area, let alone the rate at which it might be dispersed across large gaps. There is some preliminary evidence from Johns (1976), Whyte (1977) and Saulei (1985) that some of the species representative of the more mature successional phases are already appearing at logged areas, but it is still too early to estimate how long the recovery process will take. This question will be discussed further in a later section.

Finally, any recovery depends on the exclusion of wildfire. Large areas of drying logging debris constitute a significant fire hazard. If burned by wildfire, these could be converted easily to grassland. No such fires had occurred by 1981, but, as the existing grasslands in the Gogol Valley demonstrate, the risk is significant.

The nutrient cycling process

It is one thing for a plant to reach and regenerate at a site after disturbance, but another for it to become established and grow into a reproductive adult. This depends, amongst other things, on there being an adequate level of soil fertility and on the restoration of nutrient cycling. Is nutrient cycling likely to be restored after a disturbance such as pulpwood logging? There appears to be overwhelming evidence that it will (see for example studies by Nye and Greenland 1960, Kellman 1969, Aweto 1981, Jaiyebo and Moore 1964, Bartholomew *et al.* 1953, Toky and Ramakrishan 1983).

Perhaps the clearest demonstration of this process is the success of the practice of shifting cultivation in many parts of the world. In most such situations, nutrient cycling restores soil fertility after 10 to 20 years of forest fallow. Scientific studies of the restoration process have also shown that some elements accumulating in the biomass of such regrowth forests probably reach an equilibrium state after about 20 years (Unesco/UNEP/FAO 1978). Much needs to be done before the restoration process is understood, but there seems little doubt that, in time, nutrient cycling will be established after logging in the GTP area.

Time for recovery

The foregoing review suggests the two key processes necessary for the re-establishment of trees formerly present in the canopy, namely the regeneration process and the nutrient cycling process, will, in all likelihood, recover from the disturbance caused by logging. That is, many of the original forest species will probably come to regenerate in the new forest. A critical question is, however, how long will this take?

There are various opinions and anecdotal evidence concerning recovery times. For example, Bruenig (1985) has described how a site in Sarawak used for rice farming in 1858 had, by 1958, become occupied by forest with 'the status of virgin forest'. He believed it resembled very old secondary forest. Richards (1979) quotes several examples from Africa of primary forest species becoming dominant again 60–100 years after a disturbance. On the other hand, Knight (1975) believed a Panamanian forest was 'still not a climax after 120–150 years'.

The difficulty in extrapolating from observations such as these to other situations is that each is, to some extent, unique. The recovery process is affected by a large number of variables and the circumstances at one site may be quite different at another. If some of the more important variables (e.g. size of disturbance, type of disturbance etc.) can be specified, then the task of extrapolation is made more feasible. However, there are not many old secondary successions where this background information is available. Table 5.20 is a compilation of some of the few, better documented reports.

The first of these is simply an estimate of the age of what is described as 'High Forest' in Nigeria (Jones, 1956). Charcoal and pottery fragments were common in the soils, suggesting most of the forest had been farmlands at some earlier stage. These were thought to have been abandoned some time in the early eighteenth century. Jones (1956) considered the present day forest to be an old secondary forest in the sense that it was still on the way to becoming a floristically and structurally simpler climax forest. The timescale of around 200 years was, therefore, in excess of that needed to reach the maximum forest complexity and floristic diversity possible at this site.

A similar situation has been reported from the Amazon basin near the border of Venezuela and Columbia (Saldarriaga and West 1986). In this case, wildfires arising from lightning or human activity destroyed the original forest. Radio-carbon dates from charcoal indicated these fires had occurred between 250 ± 50 years and 350 ± 70 years earlier. The biomass of these forests varied between 135 t/ha to 326 t/ha and they were regarded as 'mature'. These biomass levels could presumably have been reached at an earlier date.

A much shorter recovery time has been suggested in a dipterocarp forest succession in Malaysia. Kochummen (1966) estimated it could take about 50 years before a large area of cleared agricultural land was 'clothed with primary forest vegetation again'. In this case, the nearest intact forest with primary forest species was 5 km away, but scattered trees from the original forest had been left on the site when the land was cleared and could have assisted in the regeneration process. In another case, a heavily logged dipterocarp forest in Sabah was found to have regained the original complement of canopy tree species 40 years after logging. However, the structural recovery was incomplete and the regrowth forest had only 56%

Table 5.20 A summary of some observations on regrowth of tropical rain forest following disturbance

Location (with latitude)	Type of disturbance	Area disturbed or distance to nearest forest	Current successional status	Estimated recovery time	Other comments	Reference
(a) Large Gaps						
Nigeria 6° N	agriculture	large	'highforest' – described as late secondary forest	200 + years	Archaeological evidence shows area was previously used for agriculture. Current forest is 'overmature' and in process of disintegration leading eventually to a primary forest which, in this area is thought to be structurally and floristically much simpler.	Jones 1956
Venezuela–Colombia 2° N	wildfire	large?	mature	< 250 ± 50	Charcoal found in soil profile and date of fires estimated from radio-carbon dates. Current biomass 135–204 t/ha. Another site burnt 350 ± 70 years before had biomass of 326 t/ha.	Saldarriaga and West 1986
Malaysia 4° N	cleared, burnt and farmed for one year	large; nearest intact forest 4.8 km	17 year old 'late secondary stage', 20 m tall	50 years	Some residual trees left after agriculture. About 12 trees per ha left after logging.	Kochummen 1966
Malaysia 6° N	intensive logging	large	40 year old regrowth	—	Complete floristic recovery but structural recovery incomplete. Standing timber volume now 56% unlogged forest.	Meijer 1970
Malaysia 5° N	storm plus fire (?)	large	70 year old 'storm' forest	—	Floristically simpler than undisturbed forest; fewer large trees and less diverse size class distribution	Wyatt-Smith 1954
Australia 17° S	agriculture	large	40–45 year regrowth	—	Height of regrowth similar to nearby undisturbed forest. Basal area of 55 m²/ha in comparison to 64 m²/ha in undisturbed forest. Some primary forest species entering succession but still dominated by secondary forest species.	Queensland Forestry Dept. 1983

continued

155

Table 5.20 *continued*

Location (with latitude)	Type of disturbance	Area disturbed or distance to nearest forest	Current successional status	Estimated recovery time	Other comments	Reference
(b) Volcanic Disturbance						
Papua New Guinea 9°S	volcano (Mt. Victory)	400 km²	secondary forest; up to 50 m tall	'several centuries'	54 secondary forest tree species and 56 'climax' tree species present 83 years after eruption. This thought to be less than in a comparable stage in garden regrowth.	Taylor 1957
(c) Small Gaps						
Malaysia 3° N	agriculture (multiple crops)	0.8 km	31 year old secondary forest	—	Succession blocked for some years by *Melastoma* and *Gleichenia*; woody species now developing and 51 species present.	Kochummen and Ng 1977
Venezuela 2° N	logging	0.5 ha, 50 m wide	regrowth forest with primary forest species	100 years	Vegetative regrowth common. Soils highly leached and infertile.	Uhl et al. 1982
Australia 27° S	agriculture	200 m	70 year old secondary forest	—	Subtropical forest. Full floristic recovery within 50 years, structural recovery incomplete. Height 25 m while nearby undisturbed forest is 30–40 m.	Hopkins 1975, Lamb (unpublished data)
Australia 31° S	logging	7.8 ha	25 yr old regrowth and secondary forest	140–190 years	Warm temperate rainforest (sub-montane), 90% canopy trees removed. Full floristic recovery, but structural recovery incomplete. Canopy beneath residual trees is 12 m tall while nearby undisturbed forest is 35 m.	King and Chapman 1983
Australia 28° S	logging	3.9 ha	14 yr old regrowth and secondary forest	100–220 years	Subtropical forest. Recovery time is after 70–80% basal removed and is estimated from a growth model using five successive measurements. If only 30% basal area removed the recovery time estimated to be 30–60 years.	Horne and Gwalter 1982

156

of the standing timber volume of a nearby unlogged forest (Meijer 1970).

A contrasting situation was noted in another Malaysian dipterocarp forest by Wyatt-Smith (1954). In this case, a forest believed to have been destroyed in a severe storm some 70 years earlier was found to be floristically simpler than nearby undisturbed forest. It also had a much more uniform tree size class distribution and fewer larger trees. Recovery in this forest was obviously still incomplete.

The final example of successional development on a large area comes from tropical Australia. In this case, the area had been cleared for agriculture and then abandoned some 45 years earlier. Structural recovery was virtually complete. The canopy height of the regrowth forest matched that of nearby undisturbed forest while the basal area was $55\,m^2/ha$ in comparison with $64\,m^2/ha$ in the undisturbed forest. Floristic recovery was still incomplete although many primary forest species had reappeared in the site once more (Queensland Forestry Department 1983).

All the above examples are of successions occurring following severe disturbance over a large area. Another category of large scale disturbance is that caused by volcanoes. In most, if not all, of these, the existing vegetation is destroyed, but the soil is often covered by extensive lava flows or ash deposits. Because of this new soil parent material, successional development can be much slower than that occurring after the sorts of disturbances discussed above. For this reason, the rate of succession development after volcanic eruption is usually no guide to the rate that might be expected after logging. There is, however, one account of a volcanic eruption of the Pelean type at Mount Victory in PNG in which the soil changes were apparently small (Taylor 1957). Since the area affected was large ($400\,km^2$), the account provides a useful perspective on successional development where large colonization distances are involved. In brief, 83-year-old forest was still floristically poorer than adjacent 'climax' forest, but a number of species representative of the undisturbed forest (i.e. mature phase species) had colonized the disturbed area and formed a layer beneath a canopy of early secondary species. Successional development was obviously well underway despite the large colonization distances involved, although Taylor believed 'several centuries' might be needed before it was complete.

Several other reports of successional development in tropical rain forests are worthy of mention. These concern relatively smaller areas. For this reason, it might be expected that the successions were proceeding relatively speedily. In one case in Malaysia, however, the succession had been blocked by *Melastoma* and *Gleichenia* for a number of years. Trees were beginning to dominate the site after 31 years but the forest was stll only at an early secondary stage (Kochummen and Ng 1977). The other report concerns a succession on an infertile caatingan soil in the Amazon Basin. In this case, the early pattern of biomass accumulation suggested recovery could take

100 years before the biomass of nearby undisturbed forest was reached (Uhl *et al.* 1982).

Finally, evidence from several sub-tropical rain forests in Australia suggests floristic recovery might be relatively rapid, but that structural recovery could take considerably longer than 100 years, presumably because of the cooler seasonal conditions. The most tropical of these sites was a 70-year-old regrowth forest that attained its original floristic richness after about 50 years (Hopkins 1975). In terms of height growth, however, structural recovery was still incomplete. Similar observations were made at another sub-tropical site by King and Chapman (1983). In this case, the authors estimated the recovery time could take 140–190 years. At another subtropical forest, Horne and Gwalter (1982) measured the actual growth of trees at five successive times and used a growth model to estimate the time it would take for the regrowth forest to reach the basal area of the original forest. This suggested a recovery time of 100–220 years. The model also suggested there would be no drastic change in the composition of trees in the final canopy.

In all of these cases recovery was estimated in terms of either structure, biomass or floristics. Each may give a quite different estimate of the recovery time. Thus, Riswan *et al.* (1985) estimated the recovery time after disturbance in an Indonesian dipterocarp forest could be 60–70 years if based on the time it took for the numbers of secondary species to stabilize; 150 years if based on the time it took for the numbers of primary forest species to stabilize; or 190–210 years if based on the time it took for the biomass to stabilize.

Accepting these differences, what these various reports collectively suggest is that successions leading to a mature forest ecosystem can occur even after a very drastic disturbance. Depending on how recovery is defined the time required may be as short as 50 years or as long as 200 years. At this point, it is interesting to recall the reports quoted by Cavanaugh (1976) and Johns (1986) referring to large areas of the Gogol Valley being affected by drought and fire earlier this century. If the areas affected were as extensive as these reports suggest, some of the forest now being logged may be 60 years old or less.

A SUMMING UP

The overall conclusion emerging from this analysis is that there are grounds for expecting a forest somewhat similar to the original forest to regenerate on these logged areas at some time in the future; there is no reason to believe that the key ecological processes necessary for the re-establishment of most of the main canopy trees will not persist after logging. Any such second growth forest would not be necessarily identical to the original forest – many of the rare species originally present might be absent; but, in due course, it would probably be similar in composition and structure.

The key element in this is time. As the previous section showed, the recovery process may take a number of years to complete and its success is dependent on there being no further disturbances. Is this likely? In some places in the GTP area it is obviously not. A Government objective since the commencement of the project has been a plantation of pulpwood species. In addition, large areas of regrowth will obviously be used for various agricultural purposes such as cash crops and the more traditional forms of agriculture. The situation could hardly be otherwise given the pattern of land ownership. How much land would be used in this way is difficult to predict because of differences in the areas of land owned by each clan, the numbers in each clan and their present and future attitudes towards agricultural developments. About the best that can be said is that much of the North Coast and Gum Blocks will be converted to agriculture, but that the conversion will not be as nearly widespread in the Gogol and Naru Blocks.

There is an added complication and that is the potential problem of squatters. In many parts of the tropical world, logging roads have been used by immigrant farmers to gain access to new lands. Forest regrowth has been destroyed in the ensuing land clearing. The landowners of the GTP area recognised this risk well before the project commenced and were adamant that such squatters were not wanted. They were particularly concerned about the possibility of migrants from some of the more densely populated highland areas reaching the newly accessible lands of the Gogol and Naru Valleys. The Government agreed to help prevent this immigration occurring and to date the problem has not arisen[12].

The most likely situation is that much of the regrowth forests in the more level and better drained Gogol and Naru Valley lands will be subject to some form of further disturbance well before a complete recovery occurs. This disturbance may take the form of a complete change in land-use (e.g. cash crops, timber plantations) or it may be another temporary disturbance such as that caused by the traditional gardening cycle. The likelihood of future disturbance will probably decrease the further a particular piece of forest is from a main road. Steeper lands are also less likely to be disturbed and may return to something like their original condition.

This prognosis means the two benchmark reserves in the Gogol Valley will have a particular value in preserving areas of valley forest and their constituent biota. It remains to be seen how successful they will be. Theories arising from studies of island biogeography suggest any reserve, irrespective of size, left isolated in a 'sea' of disturbed lands will eventually lose some of the species it once contained when part of a larger 'mainland'. The reason for this is that local extinctions are not replaced by recolonization. As a consequence, those concerned with protecting representative ecosystems have often tended to support a policy favouring only large reserves. This policy obscures the value of smaller reserves. Forest reserves too small for a particular species of bird may be quite a significant haven for small biota such as butterflies (Lovejoy 1982).

Furthermore, there is now increasing recognition that several small reserves may be a useful alternative approach to the unattainable goal of a single large reserve. The reason is that the small reserves may be able to still cover the diversity within a particular region (Simberloff 1982). In this respect, the scattered small village reserves may be even more important than was once thought.

Many of the theories about refuge design assume the reserves are isolated areas surrounded by a completely different type of habitat, a pattern which is unlikely to be the case in the Gogol Valley. Much of the valley is likely to have a considerable area of secondary forest, and, in time, the differences between the reserves and this regrowth will decline. This decline will have benefits and disadvantages. One of the benefits will be that the reserve boundaries will become increasingly blurred and many wildlife species may find the regrowth habitat as suitable as the reserve. On the other hand, the increase in the population density of secondary species may mean that these immigrate and interfere with various ecological processes within the reserve. Janzen (1983), for example, has described how some secondary tree species may invade and colonize gaps created by natural tree falls in an area of pristine forest. The result is that a reserve may gradually change however carefully its boundaries are protected.

In conclusion, the situation can be summarized as follows:

(i)   It seems unlikely that the long-term productive capacity of the lands within the GTP area have been seriously damaged by logging.

(ii)   Many of the short-term impacts are apparently drastic but the disturbance is such that most components of the ecosystem should recover in time. The time required is probably 50–200 years, depending on how recovery is defined.

(iii)   Such a second growth forest would not be identical to the original forest, but it could contain many of the original species and develop a similar structure. The situation with animal species is less clear since many are dependent on particular types of forest.

(iv)   In fact, however, large areas of forest in the GTP will be subject to further disturbance before this recovery is complete. The extent to which this will happen is impossible to predict because of the complex pattern of land ownership.

(v)   The likely long term consequence of logging is, therefore, a disappearance of much of the forest cover in the well-drained valley areas and on gentle slopes. Disturbed forests in other topographic positions will probably recover.

Note 1:   The Purari hydro electric scheme was eventually postponed following a major and

Note 2:   costly feasibility study. The main reason was that its scale and cost was too great for PNG in its present state of development.

Note 2:   The Forestry Department supplied landowners with paint to mark particular trees, especially food trees, they wanted left on their land. The most common trees marked were *Artocarpus attilis, Canarium indicum, Pangium edule, Terminalia* spp. and *Gnetum* spp. Many people also wanted to retain the valuable timber species *Pometia pinnata* and *Intsia bijuga* which necessitated compromises having to be reached between Jant and the landowners.

Note 3:   Intensive logging in the nearby Solomon Islands can result in massive climber development (Neil 1984). The reason for the difference between the Solomon and the Gogol Valley is not clear, but may reflect the frequency of past disturbances at the two places.

Note 4:   Surface wash seems to be more pronounced in lowland forest areas than in montane forests in PNG. It may be due to the small litter and organic matter accumulations in the lowlands in comparison with the montane areas (Löffler 1977).

Note 5:   Such a loss may underestimate the magnitude of the actual nutrient drain from the vicinity of the roots of young seedlings since some is lost from the upper soil profile but is retained in lower soil horizons. On the other hand, some cations in stream water may have originated from deep in the soil at sites of primary weathering (Nye and Greenland 1960).

Note 6:   Duplicate samples were collected in plastic bottles and despatched the following day by air for analysis at the University of Technology at Lae using standard methods (Rand *et al.* 1976). In the second sampling period later in the wet season, one of the samples had a mercuric preservative added and this was used for nitrogen analysis.

Note 7:   This approach neglects the potential importance of certain species that Gilbert (1980) has referred to as keystone mutualists. These are species whose loss precipitates the loss of a large number of other species in a cascade of extinctions. Despite the obvious importance of such species, little is known of the extent to which they may actually occur in PNG forests.

Note 8:   The available summaries of these surveys list only the more important and common trees making up most of the timber resource. Thus in the valley forest 31 genera account for 72% of the total timber volume and in the hill forests 28 genera account for 70% of the timber volume.

Note 9:   'Bird' fruit are coloured red, blue or black; they are relatively small and lack a distinct odour; they are presented in terminal clusters at the tips of branches. In contrast 'bat' fruits are green, relatively large and have a musty odour. They tend to be displayed away from foliage. These differences can occur within a single genus e.g. *Ficus, Eugenia* (Fleming 1979).

Note 10:   For example, by requiring passage through a bird's gut prior to germination. Diamond *et al.* (undated) noted *Campnosperma brevipetiolata* often occurs in seedling clumps under bird or bat perches and foresters have had difficulty in germinating seed collected directly off trees.

Note 11:   As used here, recovery is taken to mean a restoration of the original forest structure and complement of canopy tree species.

Note 12:   Some neighbours from outside the GTP area on the northern boundary of the Gogol Block did move south across the boundary in 1977 after an earthquake apparently destroyed some of their gardens. It seems they have been allowed temporary use of some land.

CHAPTER 6

SOCIAL CONSEQUENCES

INTRODUCTION

Whatever the pattern of forest regrowth, it is obvious that the recovery rate is slow in terms of human lifetimes. The people themselves had cleared forest for agriculture and it had always recovered. Perhaps a belief that forest would also recover in the same way after logging helped persuade them to sell their trees in the first place. But the extent of the areas logged and the recovery process after logging were different to these traditional fellings. More importantly, perhaps, logging brought with it a series of profound changes to village life.

Change was underway throughout PNG as a consequence of the colonial era. New tools, medicines and religious beliefs had reached some of the remotest villages in the country. In this sense, the logging operation was not especially unique. Where it differed from the more general process of change was in the rate at which the new was brought in to confront the old.

To what extent were people aware of the implications of the decision to sell their trees? It is now impossible to say. At the time of each timber rights purchase, numerous patrols by Foresters and Patrol Officers were made to explain what was involved and to seek agreement among the various clans. When the pulpwood logging TRP was being negotiated, a group of clan leaders were taken to the large plymill and *Araucaria* plantations at Bulolo to show them what industrial forestry looked like. But they were few in number and Bulolo was different to the logging planned for the Gogol Valley. It seems likely that most people at the time chose to think mainly of the benefits, such as roads, they were told the project would bring. The Administration, for its part, was keen to believe that the people were in favour of the proposal. Roads were obviously wanted by most people. The lack of roads had been major election issues for local candidates in both House of Assembly elections in the 1960s, and the matter had been raised in the Ambenob Local Government Council on many occasions. People at Jal in one of the more isolated southern

163

parts of the TRP had even tried to build their own road on one occasion. Any project bringing roads to the Gogol Valley would obviously be strongly supported. The Administration was encouraged in this belief when agitation for roads to particular villages increased after logging had commenced and its effects on the forest were obvious.

The Administration may have been paternalistic in its dealings with the landowners, believing as it did in the necessity to utilize the forest wealth of PNG, but it was not authoritarian. The events of 1969 in Bougainville and New Britain were still fresh in peoples' minds and the prospect of self-government in the near future was increasing[1]. One indication of the Administration's attitude is that a small area of land in the Naru Valley was not included in the TRP purchase when the landowners indicated they did not wish to be involved.

As already described, the agreement with Jant was signed in 1971 and the company began constructing a base camp and roads in the Gogol Valley. Wewak Timbers began their logging operations on the North Coast. To coordinate government activities the Madang District Commissioner formed the Madang Timber Working Group (MTWG) in December 1972. This was originally composed of the main government Departments involved in the project but later came to have representatives from the landowners as well. The MTWG began a series of patrols to publicise the development opportunities and to seek views on matters such as methods of royalty payments and future land use in the area. Shortly after, logging began in earnest and with it came a series of irreversible changes.

Some of the social impacts of logging in the Gogol and Naru areas have been described by De'Ath (1980). His account is based on fieldwork in the area between July 1977 and October 1978. This chapter complements De'Ath's more detailed analysis, though it takes a somewhat different view than he does. These differences will be referred to later.

ROYALTIES

Logging of natural forest can only be carried out in PNG after a timber rights purchase, following which the Department of Forests passes on to the landowners a share of the royalties it receives from the logging company. Of all the problems arising out of the GTP, there was probably none more difficult than the size of this royalty payment. It led to considerable hostility amongst landowners, scathing criticism of both the Government and Jant, and, in some cases, to the blocking of roads and a policy of non-co-operation by some clans. There was almost universal agreement amongst landowners that the royalty payments made were very inadequate compensation for the loss of their forests.

At the time of the first TRP in 1963, a single payment of A$50 000 was made. This payment was based on the estimated volume of sawlogs in the area and a 'basic' royalty of 42 c per m^3 [2]. In 1971, the pulpwood purchase was carried out, and a further A$27 930 was paid to landowners.

Although the TRP mechanism was simple, the actual method of payment was not. None of the area was accessible by road in 1963. The numbers of land owning clans, and the clan land boundaries, were not well defined and there was certainly no knowledge of the volume of timber belonging to any particular clan. As a compromise, the MTWG decided to deal with self recognized 'affinity groups'. These were groups of one or more clans willing to be represented by a single agent. The lands of each affinity group were roughly surveyed, and payment was made through the agent in proportion to the amount of land the group owned. It was assumed that the timber volume per hectare was uniform throughout the area. A similar procedure was used again in 1971 at the time of the pulpwood TRP.

In 1972, the procedure for allocating timber royalty payments throughout PNG changed. The Government decided that landowners should get at least 25% of all timber royalties actually received. Therefore any such additional money owing would be paid as a 'flow-on' payment.

The MTWG decided to make these flow-on payments again using the affinity groups. This procedure was administratively simple, and, it was hoped, might lead to the groups acting as investment bodies, thereby preventing the funds from being dissipated amongst too many individuals. However, people wanted to be paid individually. Evidence of this came from the fact that 93 agents for affinity groups came forward in 1963 but 162 agents appeared in 1971. The matter clearly needed to be resolved, and the MTWG decided to carry out a detailed geneaological survey in all TRP areas. This survey was undertaken by Patrol Officer Peter Kraehenbuhl and was completed in 1973. It identified 168 clans in the Gogol TRP, and these clans were subsequently used for all royalty payments. The clan members themselves decided how money was to be distributed within the clan and how to deal with new members not present at the time of the original purchase (e.g. children). Clan leaders acted as agents and received, and then distributed, the funds to clan members. Although it was assumed that all members would share more or less equally, this was not always the case and De'Ath (1980), for example, describes how several clans at Sehan Village had a quite uneven distribution of funds.

The MTWG also decided to map more accurately the land holdings of each clan in all four TRP's (Leet 1976). The survey team were guided by members of each clan claiming land up to a certain boundary and the defined boundary was then marked permanently with concrete markers. This survey was expensive, but was finally completed in 1978.

Sizeable royalty payments to the clans had been made before logging commenced. In theory, no further payments were due until such time as sufficient timber had been harvested to allow the Government to recover this cost. However, the MTWG decided that further payments in anticipation of a sizeable flow-on would be necessary to retain goodwill once logging started. The intention was that these flow-on payments would be paid at a rate below the rate that royalty actually accrued to the Government. In that way, the Government would eventually recoup the earlier pre-payments, but people would continue to receive a regular share. The first payment was made in 1974, after logging had been going on for 9 months. Since logging had been confined to the Gogol TRP, the amount of A$20,084 was distributed amongst the 168 clans in that area. In fact, not all the money was actually given out because of a dispute between several people claiming to be new agents. The average of $120 each clan finally received was very much less than most had expected.

By then, many people had probably forgotten the payment made for the sawlogs 11 years earlier. For those wishing to start a business, the new payment was far too small, and for those whose land had actually been logged it was a trifling amount and an insult. People were even more upset when they were told that the next payment would be made in 6 months time (rather than 9 months) and could, therefore, be even smaller. The situation became further complicated when people in the Naru TRP began demanding that their land be also logged so they too could get roads and a share of the opportunities. Jant had a fixed number of logging teams. If logging started in the Naru Valley, the royalties generated each 6-month period would be similar, but they would be distributed amongst 256 clans rather than 168 clans.

There were several courses of action open to the MTWG. The first option was that payment could be made only to those clans whose land was being logged. This would have the obvious advantage of directness and would avoid any legal problems if, for some reason, the project did not proceed as expected. The disadvantage would be that some clans might have to wait 15–20 years before their timber was logged and roads reached their villages. No one was willing to wait that long, and the older men in particular demanded a share in all flow-on payments. The second option was to arrange some form of prepayment for each clan's timber. The difficulty with this suggestion was that, when discounted back, say 15–20 years, the amounts might be quite small. Further, this would oblige the Government to raise the funds somewhere else. It also assumed there would actually be a significant additional royalty to share. Option three was to raise the people's share of royalty beyond 25%. The disadvantage of this option was that it could lead to similar requests throughout PNG and would reduce Government revenues. It would, therefore, involve a major policy change at the national level.

The MTWG decided to approach the Government and ask it, nonetheless, to consider this last possibility. While waiting for a decision, it could do little but attempt to maintain the current policy and point out to villagers that they were getting considerable indirect economic benefits, such as roads and improved government services.

At about the same time as these decisions were being made, attention was also being given to land-use planning in the Gogol and Naru TRP areas. The proposal to create a series of village and benchmark reserves raised the problem of whether owners of such land should receive a share of the royalty based on these land holdings. Since any further reduction in royalty payments would have been politically impossible, the reserve owners continued to receive payment. In this case, the payment was a *de facto* payment for preservation. When, as happened in several areas, the reserve was cleared for gardening, there was little that could be done.

Complaints and ill-feeling associated with the size of the royalty payment persisted throughout 1974 and 1975. Following Independence, in 1975, the new Government decided to allow a greater share of the royalty to be passed on to the landowners. The situation became complicated, however, because threats of secession in various parts of the country led to a demand for greater regional autonomy. By 1976, the old Madang District had become an Area Authority. In 1978, the Area Authority was made into a Provincial Government. As was to be expected, the various regional political bodies demanded a greater share of the national finances. Against this background, the royalty level was changed in two stages. The first change was made in 1976, when a second 25% of the royalty collected was passed on to the Area Authority to pass on, in turn, to the people. Then, in 1978, the National Government decided to pass on 75% of the total royalty, keeping only 25% for itself to cover its expenses. Of the 75%, 25% went to the landowner and 50% went to the Provincial Government. The Madang Provincial Government then passed on half of its share to the landowner, giving them an effective 50% share of the total royalty (Fig. 6.1).

This compromise did help reduce the problem, although it did not solve it. Many people continued to believe they were being cheated of what was rightfully theirs[3]. The effect of the royalty dispute was to sour relationships between the Government and the landowners at a critical time when the problem of land for reforestation was being discussed.

By 1980, the royalty levels paid by Jant and Wewak Timber were 50 t/m^3 on chips and $K3.95/m^3$ on sawlogs. A total of some K250,000 was being paid each year in royalties, 50% of which went to the landowners. The annual value of timber products (logs, sawn timber chips etc.) was about K6 000 000 (Division of Forestry, Madang 1980).

EMPLOYMENT

One of the expected benefits of the GTP was that it would create substantial employment. One forecast was that this might reach 1500 (Department of Forests 1971/72). By the end of 1980, it was, in fact, about 1135, made up

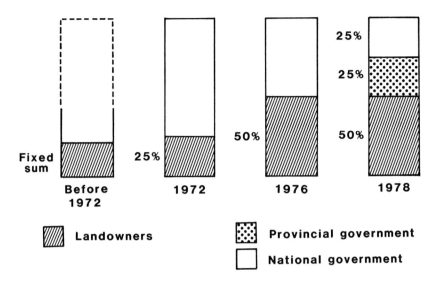

Fig. 6.1 Changes in the distribution of timber royalties over time between the landowners, the Provincial Government and the National Government

of 1090 PNG nationals and 45 expatriates (Table 6.1). Jant was the largest employer, with a workforce of 506, but Wewak Timber was also a significant employer, with 335 persons. The remainder were employed by the Department of Forests and the Gogol Reforestation Company. A large number of the employees with the latter two organizations worked only seasonally on reforestation. The annual plantings at this time were much less than originally expected, but it was anticipated that the workforce would expand when the planting rate increased.

It was the wish of the landowners, and also Government policy, that Jant should preferentially employ people from the GTP area. Jant was agreeable to this policy in principle, but it also wanted to get those with at least some education. This requirement was resented by some of the

Table 6.1 Employment Statistics in December 1980 for the Gogol Timber Project

		PNG Nationals		
Organization	Expatriates	Technical	Labourers	Total
Forestry	3	29	135*	167
Jant	29	10	467	506
Wewak Timbers	12	?	323	335
Gogol Reforestation Company	1	1	125*	127
Total	45	40	1050	1135

*fluctuates with season
Source: Satoh (1980), Department of Madang Province (1980b)

older uneducated men who believed their status in the village gave them precedence. The matter was resolved with time when many village men found that the demands of Jant as an employer conflicted too much with their gardening and other activities in the village. By 1980, about 30% of Jant's employees were from the GTP area, with most of the remainder from elsewhere in the Madang Province.

Most managerial and technical staff positions remained dominated by expatriate employees. The exception was the Department of Forests where a rapid 'localization' programme led to all senior positions being filled by PNG nationals within a few years of Independence. Some expatriates remained, but these were in essentially technical and advisory positions. In Jant and Wewak Timbers, the reverse was the case; all the senior positions were filled by expatriates. By 1980, Jant had recruited 10 Papua New Guineans to technical positions, including several new graduate foresters from the PNG Forestry College at Bulolo and the University of Technology at Lae[4]. Overall, Wewak Timber had a slightly better ratio of national to expatriate employees than Jant.

Jant was keen to retain its staff – especially those who had received any technical training – and gave a special bonus to any achieving 3 years service. By 1980, 20 staff had qualified for the bonus, and three of the original 10 bulldozer operators recruited 9 years earlier were still with the company. Under the circumstances of the time, that record was probably not too bad.

The wages paid to timber workers followed the same two-tiered structure applying throughout PNG. In 1980, the wage was K13.00 for rural labourers and K34.84 for those working in towns. The difference was supposed to take account of the difference in the cost of living in the two situations. These rates were base level pay rates, and higher wages were paid if the worker was full time rather than casual. Jant's workers also received additional payments, depending on the length of service, attendance and productivity. It is probably true to say, however, that many Gogol people failed to qualify for many of these additional payments because clan and village obligations interrupted their attendance.

The GTP created several other forms of direct employment beyond those with the four main employer bodies listed in Table 6.1. Some of these will be described later in this chapter.

NEW AGRICULTURAL DEVELOPMENTS

One of the motives behind many people's willingness to sell their timber was the belief that logging would lead to roads being built into their area. These roads would allow them to join the surge of agricultural development then occurring throughout PNG. Copra had had a long and generally successful history, especially in the Madang region. Coffee growing had been an even greater success, and an oil palm scheme established in 1967 in New Britain looked set to be every bit as profitable. Many people were also growing cocoa, and there was considerable interest in raising cattle in various parts of the country.

While it seems that most people in the GTP area were interested in some form of cash cropping, there were some differences between various landowners in their degree of enthusiasm. Landowners on the North Coast and Gum TRP areas were very keen, but some of those in the Gogol TRP were not quite as impatient or ready to get started. The difference was one of degree and may have reflected a greater knowledge of cash cropping by the landowners closer to the coast because of their nearness to the expatriate-run plantations. The larger number of cargo cultists in the Gogol Valley almost certainly had an effect as well.

In any event, a series of small scale cash cropping projects gradually developed on logged over land. So much so, in fact, that, by 1974, Jant was beginning to worry that most of the land suitable for reforestation was in danger of becoming too fragmented. These projects were in addition to the normal cycle of shifting cultivation. The statistics on these changes are imperfect since the areas were dispersed and not all were necessarily counted on successive visits. The overall pattern, however, was one of a rapid increase in coconut, coffee and cocoa tree plantings. Between 1973 and 1980, the number of coconut trees in the Gogol and Naru TRP's increased from 6400 to 37 900, coffee trees increased from 1400 to 21 000, and cocoa trees increased from 121 to 18 300.

A number of other small projects also commenced in the area. These included a piggery, a chicken farm and several fish farms. By contrast, cattle were taken up less enthusiastically than expected. In 1973, there were eight cattle projects, with 110 animals. In 1978, there were 13 projects, with 306 animals. During this period, some 52 animals had been sold (average price K113). Although cattle raising was still regarded as being somewhat prestigious, villagers had also learnt that it had a comparatively high capital cost (for fences, and pasture establishment) and needed a certain amount of management skill as well. Most of the herds were, for the time being, therefore, allowed to forage along roadsides.

At the time of the development of the 1974 land-use plan, discussions with landowners led the Government to believe there was also some interest in several larger scale agriculture projects in the Gogol and Naru TRP's. As already described, this interest led to a cattle project and a rice project being added to the plan. Jant also expressed interest in being involved, perhaps as a partner with the landowners. Neither project eventuated for the same reason that reforestation has been slow to take place, namely, the problem of land ownership. This experience did not stop the Madang Planters Association (a body dominated by owners of coconut plantations, many of whom were expatriates) berating the Government for being 'deplorably lax' in not having any plans for large scale agriculture to follow logging (Post Courier 28 December 1977). Angmai Bilas who was a member of the association, and also a Madang representative in the National House of Assembly in Port Moresby, moved a motion asking for Government encouragement for Madang-based firms to invest in the area. There is no doubt that such a proposal would have been anathema to virtually all landowners, whatever their agricultural aspirations[5].

Tree farms

One new cash crop not anticipated in the earlier land-use planning stage of the project was tree farming. That is, the planting of trees in small woodlots by individuals or clans for eventual sale to Jant as pulpwood. A small plantation of *Eucalyptus deglupta* had been established in the Naru area in about 1970 by one of the landowners. This was prior to Jant beginning logging and it is not clear what the original motive was behind this planting. However the idea of actually encouraging villagers to grow trees for pulpwood was probably only thought of seriously when news reached PNG of an apparently successful tree planting scheme in the Philippines. This scheme was organized by the Paper Industry Corporation of the Philippines (PICOP) at its operation in Mindanao. Both the PNG Minister for Forests and the regional forest officer at Madang visited the PICOP operation and came back impressed. The scheme worked in the following way. Any farmer could participate, provided he lived within 100 km of the PICOP mill and owned at least 5 ha of land. Up to 80% of

Plate 27   Clear felling using crawler tractors

171

this land was planted with the fast growing species *Eucalyptus deglupta* (which is native to both PNG and the Philippines) or *Albizzia falcataria*. The remaining land was used for growing food crops. The trees were grown on an 8-year rotation, and, once established, an eighth of the plantation was harvested and replanted each year. The company provided seedlings, technical advice and guaranteed to purchase the timber. The scheme was not without problems, not least of which was the tendency of many farmers to plant all of their land at once, leading to an uneven supply situation for the mill. However, by 1981 the scheme had 4000 families participating, covered 30 300 ha, and supplied a third of PICOP's pulpwood (Arnold 1979, Caulfield 1985).

The MTWG were somewhat hesitant to promote the idea because it was new and would necessitate landowners waiting at least 8 years before getting any return. Why grow trees when everyone knew of the highlander's success with coffee? Negotiations over land leasing for reforestation were also at a fairly delicate stage. However, Jant were interested because similar schemes existed in Japan, so a set of specifications for tree farmers were drawn up. The constraints were that the tree farm had to be within 60 km of Madang, be no more than 200 m from a road, be on fertile soil, and be on a site with a slope of less than 20 degrees. It was also recommended to prospective tree farmers that the plantation be no more than 2 ha as this area was thought to be the most any one person could manage to establish and tend each year. The trees were to be planted at a spacing of 4 m x 4 m, and the expected gross return after 10–13 years was in the order of K1000 per ha (based on 200 m^3 of pulpwood at K4.50 m^3).

Two tree farms were started in 1975, and, by 1980, the number had reached 79, covering 137 ha (Table 6.2). The Department of Forests supplied seedlings of *Eucalyptus deglupta* and technical advice free of charge. The whole operation was supervised by a couple of foresters on motorbikes. The scheme was obviously in its infancy and had yet to demonstrate that it could make a significant input to further pulpwood supplies. What was remarkable, however, was that so many landowners were prepared to take the Forestry Department at its word and to plant any trees at all. Six years

Table 6.2 Tree farms of *Eucalyptus deglupta* in the Gogol Valley

Year	Number	Area (ha)
1975	2	—
1976	9	—
1977	31	—
1978	50	60
1979	65	105
1980	79	137

Source: Department of Forests records (Madang)

172

after it started, no one had made a cash return. If and when they do, however, the tree farm idea could suddenly become very attractive and might become as important to Jant as it was to PICOP.

Traditional forms of agriculture continued throughout the GTP. In some cases, small gardens of sweet potato and corn were established on logged over areas immediately following the logging operation. Larger gardens were sometimes also established in these same areas 4 or ·5 years later. However, most people continued to garden in their traditional sites on 10 to 20-year cycles. Few of these sites were touched by the logging operation because they did not contain significant pulpwood timber volumes.

BUSINESS AND OTHER DEVELOPMENTS

Besides employment and agricultural development, another goal of Government planners had been the development of various small business ventures. These, it was hoped, would be based on the logging operation itself or would develop from capital generated by royalties. Some assistance in business development was provided by the Department of Business Development, although, with the large staff turnover in the Department during the period, it is difficult to say exactly how significant its role actually was.

Contract logging

Several businesses did develop in association with the logging operation but none proved to be very successful. The first was a company named Yumi Timbers, formed to carry out sub-contract logging in the Gum TRP. The timber harvested was to be sold to Jant and Wewak Timbers. The company was owned and financed by an expatriate but had some PNG partners as well. Unfortunately, it was seriously undercapitalized. It had $20000, which was spent on two trucks, leaving only $8000 to spend on building roads. This provision was not nearly enough (even a low grade road could cost up to K1200 per km) and the company finally collapsed in August 1976, 6 months after starting. The Gum people had pinned high hopes on Yumi Timbers clearing their land for agricultural development, and Jant was eventually persuaded to divert some of their operations into the area to take its place.

Salvage logging

The second business concerned salvage logging. It was not strictly a business as such, but involved, at various times, up to six small groups totalling perhaps some 20 people. The scheme was based on the fact that a small but significant amount of timber was left behind by Jant after clear-felling. Some estimates put this at $10–20 \, m^3$ per hectare or 1200 tonnes of pulpwood a month. Most of this timber consisted of scattered small logs and branches which Jant believed were uneconomic to collect. Like tree farming, the idea of salvage logging had its origins at the PICOP operation in the Philippines, where teams of sub-contractors used water buffalo to gather scattered timber left behind after logging.

The Forestry Department at Madang persuaded Jant to participate in a trial to develop a similar scheme in the Naru TRP, and this scheme began in May 1976. Certain specifications were established. The logs had to be at least 2 m long and have a diameter greater than 10 cm. They also had to be collected within 3 weeks of felling, before the timber became too dry (and, therefore, harder to chip). Jant agreed to pay K7 per m^3 at the mill door.

The first trials were carried out using manual methods to collect the logs, but the work was too hard, so several water buffaloes were brought to Madang to adopt the Philippines technique. These animals also proved to be unsuccessful. The people did not have sufficient experience in handling water buffalo and productivity was too low. There was also a difficulty in actually loading logs on to the large Jant logging trucks. Jant eventually became unwilling to allow its trucks to be immobilized for the length of time necessary when they could be used much more productively with one of its own logging teams.

To overcome these problems, a truck was hired from the Government vehicle pool in Madang and a crane truck was borrowed from one of the Missions. Subsequently, a small crane truck and several tractors were purchased, using a special fund for rural development financed by the Government and Jant.

Productivity rose to around 300 tonnes per month and it was estimated that the same six groups could probably reach 500 tonnes a month with experience. However, the financial returns to the groups were not especially large. Some idea of the profitability of the operation is shown in Table 6.3 which gives production and costs for two of the better groups. The data suggest a worker in each group might make between K50–K75 a month.

Table 6.3 Nett yield from some salvage logging operations in the Naru Valley in 1977

Logging group	Production K	Costs K	Net profit K
1. Balama (6 persons)			
March	327	80	246
April	184	45	139
June	518	128	390
2. Tingal (4 persons)			
April	224	59	164
June	420	111	309

Source: Department of Forests records (Madang)

This was not much greater than a man could make working on the base rural wage as a casual employee of Jant. That apart, there were a number of other problems with the scheme. First, it was difficult for the teams to travel from their villages to the work site, and, because of this, some groups worked rather irregularly. One group purchased a small truck to solve this problem. Second, fires from gardens being established in logged-over sites occasionally escaped and damaged the logs. Third, the viability of the operation depended on several major subsidies. One was the financial grant for machinery referred to above. The other was the time spent by foresters organizing and co-ordinating the scheme. Finally, the enterprise was just viable while logging was taking place close to Madang at the Naru TRP. It was unlikely to be economic when transport costs increased as more remote areas were logged. By the end of the decade, salvage logging was still being carried out, but its future probably lay more in the logging of plantations than in natural forest operations.

Yumi Timber and the salvage loggers were the only new enterprises to link themselves directly with the timber industry. This may have been because too much capital and management expertise was required. Or it may have been that those with both believed they could work more profitably within the town of Madang or elsewhere in PNG. But in any case Jant was not especially interested in dealing with a large number of sub-contractors, and the Gogol people themselves didn't want outsiders running businesses based on their timber.

Other businesses

All the other new business ventures in the GTP were based on ideas that had been shown to work elsewhere in the Madang area. The most common of these were shops (known locally as trade stores). A large number were built throughout the Gogol and Naru valleys, but many quickly became defunct. In 1976, for example, 31 stores had been built in the TRP and fringe areas, but only 23 were actually operating. Most sold items such as tinned fish, rice, kerosene and tobacco and had very low turnovers. De'Ath (1980) describes one small store at Sehan village, which, after 5 months, cleared a profit of about K400. This result was probably typical of many. The most profitable store was the one established at the Jant base camp at Baku in the middle of the Gogol Valley. This store was originally 30% owned by Gogol people and 70% owned by outsiders. It was highly successful, and the owners subsequently bought several other stores in Madang. Eventually, the store became totally owned by Gogol people. There were then officially 30 shareholders, but many people participated in each share and a large number of clans ended up having an interest in the business. By 1980, the annual turnover probably exceeded K150 000.

The other main business was transport. Most transport groups were

unsuccessful as businesses because few of the trucks were properly maintained. In 1976, only one out of three trucks in the Gogol TRP and five
out of 10 of the trucks in nearby areas were still operating. It seems unlikely
any made a worthwhile profit. On the other hand, they were probably
never strictly a business investment anyway, but bought primarily for social
reasons.

This economic record was not especially promising, given the
Government's hope that the royalties from logging would not be dissipated
but that groups would form and collectively invest the funds. However, the
decade drew to a close with at least 14 formally constituted business groups
registered with the Department of Business Development (De'Ath 1980).
There were, as well, other more informal bodies like the salvage logging
teams. The funds these groups controlled were not large, but the number
of groups was impressive in view of the relatively short time since logging
had commenced. The economic prospects for many of these enterprises
were not bright. After all, there was not a large population in the GTP
area and, therefore, only a limited future for retail activities such as trade
stores. What they did promise, however, was a chance for their owners to
acquire some of the management and financial skills necessary for other,
more productive ventures.

Cargo Cults

It is necessary to digress briefly at this point to discuss traditional attitudes
to goods and economic exchanges. Some have argued that economic growth
in traditonal societies is dependent upon major changes in the norms and
institutions of such societies that may inhibit change – if entrepreneurial
behaviour occurs, it is most likely to be initiated by dissidents or minorities.
Finney (1968) believes this is not the case in most PNG societies, where
materialism is common and the emphasis on individual achievement is so
marked. Ambitious men in traditional PNG societies sought wealth by
managing the use of material goods, and the style of these so-called Big
Men has direct parallels with that of successful entrepreneurs in modern
economic societies. In this sense, the people of the Gogol Valley were well
prepared to take advantage of their new form of wealth. But profit was not
the motive of Big Men – it was prestige. Money was used not as a store
of capital but as a medium of exchange. A consequence of this attitude is
that, throughout PNG, many new businesses have failed, at least by
European standards. A storekeeper, for example, might give unlimited
credit, sell goods below cost or use stock for his own purposes. Such
businesses are failures by strict economic criteria, but may have been quite
successful in the view of the owner. Through a network of exchange and
gift giving, he achieved prestige in the way that his ancestors had done.

Yet, as McSwain (1977) has pointed out, it would be a mistake to presume that such storekeepers were not bewildered by the constant economic problems, and many realized that their stores were not functioning in the way that expatriate owned stores did. Many in the Madang District explained this difference in terms of the old suspicion of the cargo cultist, that the European had access to important deities and rituals, and that complete success would continue to elude them until they, too, knew these secrets.

In 1981, despite a decade of major economic change, Cargo Cults were still persistent in much of the GTP area, and especially in the Gogol Valley. In 1980, for example, a woman from Utu Village, not far from the Jant base camp at Baku, announced she had had a dream in which God had told her she was to take over all the money in the vaults of the Madang branch of the Papua New Guinea Banking Corporation. Three hundred followers joined her in an unsuccessful attempt to do just that. In the same year, Utu Villagers also tied up a meeting of the Madang Provincial Government in demanding a 'key' to the Province's money. There are tree farms near Utu and a successful trade store at the nearby Jant base camp. Neither seem to have counteracted the cultist interpretation of economic changes. McSwain (1975) and Lawrence (1982) both believe people's traditional epistemology has been impervious to change and that the Government is wrong in assuming it will automatically atrophy when socio-economic conditions change. Noah (1980) considered this atrophy will take time and much more significant economic development than has occurred so far.

The issue of cargo cultism in the Gogol Valley is not insignificant because it reveals a major misunderstanding of the real nature of development and the modern world. If economic changes or opportunities are constantly interpreted in magico-religious terms, there is a danger that such opportunities may be put at risk.

INFORMATION

Communication between the various parties involved in the GTP was a problem throughout the life of the project. This was probably not surprising, given the different cultural values and expectations held by each party.

The most critical information exchange was that between the landowners and the Government. In the early days, a good deal of time was spent by foresters, agricultural officers and patrol officers trying to explain exactly what the project was about. In retrospect, it seems that they were only partly successful. Perhaps these explanations tended to highlight the benefits and downplay the costs. Perhaps landowners only wished to hear of the advantages. In any case, by the time Jant began operations in 1972, it was apparent that many people in the area appeared to have only the vaguest idea of the changes the project was likely to bring. Because of this uncertainty, there was little interest in discussing or planning post-logging land-use. It was about this time that the Madang Timber Working Group was formed, and it decided to mount a major patrol through the area early in 1973 to explain Jant's plans, and to determine people's opinions on various matters such as royalty payments, village reserves and future land-use.

The patrol found that, in fact, people did have a number of concerns and opinions. The three main issues were:

(i)   Why should some people have to wait a long time before logging started on their land?
(ii)   Why could not people buy shares in Jant?
(iii) Would landowners lose ownership of the land if it was replanted by someone else, such as the Department of Forests or Jant?

There were a host of other questions related to royalty payments, future development plans and Jant. Some people were concerned about what ecological damage might happen to the land after logging (e.g. would it turn into grasslands?) and whether food trees would be left. Others were concerned about whether clan boundaries would be obliterated by logging. The patrol highlighted the need for a better flow of information between the government and the landowner and led to several representatives of the landowners joining the MTWG.

This undoubtedly helped but communications remained a problem. Part of the difficulty was that the social diversity in the GTP made it difficult for government officers to determine whether there was a common view on any topic. Until the Trans Gogol Local Government Council was formed in 1978, there was no political forum where opinions could be aired and collective decisions made. This lack of a forum necessitated communicating with each clan over each of the multitude of issues that emerged, although the Madang radio was also used to publicise general news items. Visits were made from time to time to various villages, but it was not until 1977 that another major MTWG patrol was again sent out with the express purpose of contacting all villages within a short time. Jant had then been logging for 4 years and the patrol's particular purpose was to publicise the development opportunities becoming available with the building of roads. To help do this, three video films were made. One was a general information film about the project itself, a second dealt with tree farming, and a third covered new forms of technology that could be appropriate in villages. The patrol contacted over 900 persons, and, in that sense, was a success. The films were less successful. The patrol was on foot and the equipment was heavy to carry. It was always difficult to recruit carriers to take it on to the next village. To make matters worse the equipment often failed to work. In retrospect, the films were a good idea, but too sophisticated for the settings in which they were used.

Again, the patrol found a host of questions touching on topics such as royalties, land for reforestation, tree farms, salvage logging and new business opportunities. For the first time, there was interest among some groups in the possibility of forming some kind of Gogol–Naru Cooperative in which to invest some of the royalties. It was also significant that there was no particular criticism of Jant, despite the numerous complaints about royalties and concern over logging damage.

The need for improved communication was obviously as great as ever, but, by 1978, the MTWG was beginning to lose its effectiveness. Many of the original members had gone or been transferred since Independence in 1975, and the replacements were still adjusting to the changes. The group had also become too big because anyone was allowed to attend the meetings. With the advent of a Local Government Council later that year, the MTWG ceased to operate and a smaller body similar in composition to the original MTWG was formed to liaise with the new Council.

Jant had always been concerned with its public image and, from the beginning, had employed a man respected in the Madang District, Mr. Liwai Kolau, to advise it on its dealings with local people. It made a number of donations to schools and hospitals in the district and gave a large donation to the town of Madang to mark Independence Day. It also built a significant number of roads to villages to link these to the main road network, although these were of no immediate benefit to itself for logging. In short, it was fairly aware of the need to be seen as a good corporate citizen. In 1980, concerned that many people still misunderstood what it planned to do or could do, it established a Village Relations Unit in the form of a large tent on the side of one of the main roads. The unit was supposed to handle queries related to Jant's operation. It quickly became seen as a more general information source and began handling questions like 'why is Somare no longer Chief Minister?','how do I get a PMV licence?'[6] 'why are there no longer patrols by agricultural officers?', etc. The problem of communications obviously remained.

VILLAGE LIFE

The GTP had a variety of consequences for village life. One of the most noticeable was the linking up of many villages by the logging road network. The roads reduced the isolation of villages, and, for better or worse, drew them more into the larger economy and society of PNG. The effects of this change are only now slowly becoming evident. At the most obvious level, crops began to be marketed in Madang and at the Jant Base Camp, while goods were imported into villages. Diets changed as more people ate imported foods such as tinned fish and meat, and items like kerosene lamps and aluminium cookingware became more common. Government services such as health care also became more widely available.

179

But perhaps one of the most significant impacts of the project on village life was a reversal in the population drift away from the area. In 1969, the total absentee rate in the Gogol Valley was 25%, but, in 1977, this rate had dropped to 12% (Colton 1976, De'Ath 1980). The comparison is not exact because the 1977 census division did not correspond exactly with the TRP boundaries. However, there is little doubt that the decline is real because a direct comparison of 10 individual villages from within the Gogol TRP shows a similar trend. On average, these villages had absentee levels of 30% in 1969, but this average dropped to 15% by 1977 (De'Ath 1980). Evidently, the changes occurring in the Gogol Valley, and perhaps the new employment prospects, reversed the previous migration trends.

Many villagers worked for Jant at various times. This employment brought cash into the villages, but it also disrupted village work patterns since fewer men were available to do the heavy work. De'Ath (1980) argued that Jant employees should be regarded as absentees and that, in this sense, the situation had not changed much since 1969. However, many such Jant employees continued to live in their villages and to absent themselves from work when the occasion demanded. Many worked only briefly in seasonal jobs such as reforestation.

There are few data on village incomes generated by this employment or by cash cropping. De'Ath (1980) estimated that, in 1977, the village of Sehan had a total income of K6051 and a per capita income of K49.60 or K401 per adult male. These amounts were not great in comparison with the cost of a trade store shirt (K8) or shorts (K5–K10). Money coming into the villages was spent on a variety of items. A 1977 survey found the most common of these were clothes, food and school fees. Other major cost items were council taxes, hospital costs and funds for activities of traditional importance. Many people saved or banked part of their income. Jant's rural employees deposited more in a company run Savings Scheme than its town employees (Leslie, 1980).

The effect of the project on peoples' health is unknown, one of the problems being that no successive health studies were carried out. Roads allowed more health workers to reach previously isolated areas, and the likelihood is, therefore, that overall health standards were improved. Imported food may have also improved children's diet by improving protein intakes. On the other hand, the longer term consequences may be to increase the incidence of chronic degenerative changes in adults, as appears to be happening elsewhere in the south west Pacific. A particular health problem was malaria. The disease is endemic to PNG and it has been suggested logging could make it more serious by leading to the formation of ponds in wheel ruts and other favourable habitats for the mosquito vector (Spencer 1976). There is no evidence to show whether this actually occurred. In any case, malaria control teams were able to visit some of the more remote areas of the Valley using the new roads. It should be noted, however, that the more common chemotherapy techniques used to control malaria have been failing throughout the tropical world, and malaria has been increasing as a health problem.

LOSS OF NATURAL AND CULTURAL RESOURCES

Logging brought various material improvements to many villages, but, at the same time, it also brought many adverse changes. One of these was a reduction in the quality and availability of many traditional natural resources. When logging started, and its impact was first seen, many people became worried that their land would be ruined and the soils would become too infertile for gardening. This concern probably declined over time because traditional gardening areas in existing secondary regrowth forests were not logged and vigorous forest regrowth could be seen occurring on most other areas; but one resource over which concern continued to mount was wildlife. Many people had assumed the system of village reserves would allow animals displaced by logging to survive; the animals would simply move away from the logged areas and into these reserves. This did not happen, and, according to Driscoll (undated), large game such as wallabies, cassowaries, hornbills and Goura pigeons dropped in number throughout the area as logging progressed. The loss was not simply an aesthetic one since animals are important economic resources[7]. A survey in 1978 showed the majority of respondents were worried by the changes underway and doubted that bird populations, in particular, would recover (Table 6.4).

These changes affected most villages in the TRP area, but, by the time they were recognized, there was little that could be done about them short

Table 6.4 Results of a questionnaire (in Pidgin) circulated in 1978 to over 150 people in three villages in the Gogol Valley. Listed are the percentages of replies giving affirmative answers to questions

(a)	Eaten wild birds at least once in the preceding 2 weeks	:	37
(b)	Eaten eggs of wild birds at least once during the preceding 2 weeks	:	37
(c)	Own decorative bird plumes valued at between K1 and K2	:	26
	valued at between K5 and K10	:	60
	valued at between K30 and K100	:	14
(d)	Populations of only a few birds will be decreased by logging	:	41
(e)	Populations of many birds will be decreased by logging	:	59
(f)	Given time for the forest to regenerate		
	– bird populations won't recover	:	41
	– populations of some species will recover	:	38
	– populations of all species will recover	:	21
(g)	Level of concern about the ill effects of loggings		
	– unworried	:	5
	–moderately worried	:	18
	– very worried	:	72

Source: Driscoll (undated)

of stopping the project. A particular form of environmental damage that occurred at one village, however, was so bitterly resented that it eventually led to court action. It concerned the loss of a piece of ground used for making clay pots and became known as the Clay Pot Dispute.

The Clay Pot Dispute

The Clay Pot Dispute centred on Wezip Alaloum who lived at Jobto Village, a small hamlet about 4 km south west of the Jant base camp in the Gogol TRP. In order to understand the significance of the incident, it is necessary to describe some of the proceeding events.

Like many people in the Gogol Valley, the landowners of Jobto Village were upset at what they believed were insufficient royalty payments. Clans in the village had only small areas of land in proportion to the number of clan members. The per capita royalty payments were low. Many people considered they were being cheated and complained vigorously to the MTWG. Perhaps as a consequence of this, a senior member of one of the clans, Wezip Aloloum, refused Jant permission to come and log his clan's land. Following the decision by the Government in 1976 to pay a second 25% of the royalties to landowners, he agreed to allow the land to be logged, but only after a reserve had been excluded and his food trees had been marked for retention. When, as was usual, foresters came to inspect these boundaries prior to logging, they found the land actually marked by Wezip as a reserve for his clan was very large and exceeded the size of the area usually reserved for all clans in a village. The MTWG advised Jant not to proceed with logging until the matter had been resolved. In the meantime, Wezip's brother Kiligaum and another clan member Nanal Kaum marked boundary trees around another area containing the clay used for making clay pots. They neglected, however, to tell Forestry Department staff or Jant that the marked trees represented a second reserve boundary. While foresters were trying to find out what the marked trees meant, and who had painted them, Jant decided to rearrange its logging schedule and move into an area behind the reserve marked by Wezip. In doing so, several machines passed through the clay pot ground and damaged it. While this was bad enough, the trespass was made worse because the villagers believed the guardian spirit of the ground had been disturbed.

In the view of the Jobto villagers, they deserved compensation and the matter was obviously one to be settled in the newly established Village Court[8]. The Magistrate of the Court summoned Jant and government representatives to appear before him at his house on 3 December 1976 in Jobto Village. The Magistrate was Namal Kaum, the man who had helped Wezip's brother mark out the boundary for the clay ground.

Neither Jant nor the Government attended the hearing, apparently out of ignorance of the significance of the still new Village Court system. This

182

failure to attend caused considerable ill feeling in the village. Wezip then discussed with government foresters the possibility of an out-of-court settlement, but was subsequently persuaded against this course of action by his friends. On 17 December 1976, the court was reconvened and the Magistrate fined Jant and the Government K5000 each[9]. Jant was willing to pay some compensation, but was upset at the size of the fine, and told the Government it was not interested in proceeding with reforestation until the matter was settled more equitably. Jant wanted to publicise the case to emphasize what it believed to be the absurdity of trying to operate within the jurisdiction of the Village Court system. The Department of Forests' view was that this approach might have the opposite effect to that intended. Besides, the Magistrate had clearly exceeded his legal authority in imposing such a large fine. An appeal was heard on 24 December 1976, this time in the charge of a Provincial Supervisory Magistrate and the fine was quashed. Jant offered to pay damages in compensation, but the villagers insisted on the full K10000 fine and wanted the case taken to the National Court in Port Moresby. At one stage, Law students at the University of Papua New Guinea were interested in pursuing the case in this way, but the matter was eventually dropped. By September 1977, Wezip said he was willing to settle for between K2000 and 4000 rather than the K10000 which had been pressed on him by others. In July 1978, a meeting was held to try to settle the matter. The clan owning the grounds estimated that about 10 men and women could have made up to 60 pots worth K130–240 a week. The clan offered to drop its claim of K10000 if instead it could get a trade store, a liquor licence or a truck. The Department of Forests offered to build a trade store using timber supplied by Jant, but negotiations continued until 1980 without a settlement being reached.

The whole dispute seems to have arisen out of a series of misunderstandings on both sides, compounded by the belief amongst some villagers that the new Village Court system might be a way in which landowners could control Jant's activities. This was not the first expression of such a belief. The Village Court magistrate at Bemal, a village not far from Jobto and in the same language group, had earlier tried unsuccessfully to intervene in a labour dispute at Jant's base camp in the Gogol Valley.

In the Government's view, the Jobto villagers had always been a rather 'difficult' group. Besides having a history of cargo cult involvement, they had been among the more vociferous of those complaining about royalty payments[10]. The alternative viewpoint, of course, is that the Jobto villagers in general, and Wezip Aloloum in particular, had suffered a wrong, and had been dealt with unjustly. This viewpoint was represented by De'Ath (1978a), who portrayed Wezip not as an avaricious troublemaker but as an articulate spokesman for his people. De'Ath subsequently helped Wezip Aloloum to attend a national conference in Port Moresby in 1980 on traditional forms of conservation in PNG at which he presented his account of the problems logging had brought to the area[11].

It is difficult to know, in fact, the extent to which Wezip Alaloum's views on the overall project represented those of other landowners in the Gogol Valley. As mentioned earlier, Driscoll's informal survey in 1978 showed that many people were concerned about the impact of logging on birds. However, Wezip Aloloum was apparently unable to get anyone to come to meetings he arranged in 1980 to discuss the subject prior to him attending the Port Moresby conference. This may have been because some form of forest regrowth was then seen to be underway on logged areas and people's fears were gradually being allayed. Alternatively, it may have been because Wezip Aloloum was not seen as a spokesman for his people, but rather as a self-interested individual concerned only with extracting the maximum compensation for himself from Jant and the Government. Whatever the case, there is little doubt that logging caused more damage than most people expected. The sense of injury was, of course, worsened by the concurrent dissatisfaction over royalty payments.

POLITICS

From the very beginning of the project, a major problem for the government was the social diversity within the TRP. The large number of clans, and the tradition of clan centred activity, meant it was virtually impossible for the Government to persuade people to agree on any single objective or viewpoint. This diversity hamstrung attempts at land-use planning. It also prevented royalties being pooled for some collective purpose. The same problem faced the people themselves. There was no way they could deal collectively with the Government on matters of common concern such as the level of royalty payments, the problem of employment for their children, or the matter of road building and maintenance. The MTWG had been established to try to act as a focal point, but it could only receive separate viewpoints.

In theory, the people of the Gogol and Naru areas had the Ambenob Local Government Council to represent them. They had joined the Council in 1967 when it covered most of the hinterland around Madang. From its beginning, however, the Council was dominated by councillors from areas close to Madang. Although the people of the GTP area may have made up about 15% of the Council's electorate, they were effectively ignored. The only time the Ambenob Council seems to have taken an interest in the Gogol Valley was when it once asked to be given shares in Jant. In time, the Council came to be seen by most Gogol and Naru people as an organization to which they paid tax and received nothing in return. By 1976, most people had ceased paying tax.

In 1978, 5 years after Jant began logging, a new Trans-Gogol Local Government Council was formed to represent the affairs of people in the

GTP area. The Government suggested the new Council might be an appropriate body to receive the second 25% royalty share, but this idea was universally rejected. People claimed that the earlier Ambenob Council had 'stolen' their funds and were not prepared to give the new Council the benefit of the doubt. The matter was not pursued because a dispute involving the new Council early in its life would have ruined it.

The Council's first budget totalled K13 000 and was made up of K6000 from taxes (based on a 'head' tax of K5 per adult male), K1000 from store licences, K3000 from a donation from Jant, K1000 from a grant from the Provincial Government and K2000 from the Ambenob Council. Within a few years, the budget nearly doubled, with further grants from Jant, the Provincial Government and various National Government programmes. The Government disbanded the old MTWG and formed a new committee made up of representatives of relevant Departments to work with the new Council. The Council itself began to take on some of the social welfare operations such as bridge maintenance formerly carried out by Jant or the government. By 1981, the new Council had not acquired the status and authority necessary to represent all landowners in the area in their dealings with the government or Jant, but some progress had been made, however, towards that end.

CONCLUSION

It is obvious that the project had a mixed reception. Landowners in the Gum TRP, the North Coast TRP and in some of the more remote villages of the Gogol TRP were eager for logging to proceed. Other people such as Wezip and the Jobto villagers were much less enthusiastic. It is ironical that the MTWG occasionally found itself being pressured to have logging carried out by clans from isolated villages while at the same time having to deal with attempts by others to stop logging because of disputes over royalty.

The project brought some beneficial changes to most villages. A road network was established linking some of the more remote villages in the area to Madang, opportunities to participate in new forms of agriculture increased, and access to government services such as health care and education was improved. There was a flow of capital into the area from royalties; many people gained employment and the opportunities for business development increased. On the whole, the range of choices available to people probably improved and the societies that Colton (1976) once believed to be endangered by emigration remained threatened no longer.

It as equally true, however, that the costs of all these benefits were high and that many of these costs were unforeseen by the early planners except, perhaps, in the most general of terms. The forest environment was transformed, leading to a significant material loss, as well as a cultural and aesthetic one. Village work patterns and value systems were altered and there was a lessening in self-sufficiency and independence as the villagers became more involved in new economic and political systems. Where the balance between these benefits and costs lies is impossible for an outsider to judge.

De'Ath (1980) argues that the project has had an essentially negative effect and portrays the Gogol people as betrayed and downtrodden, they were misled when they sold their timber and gained little from the project subsequently. He believes their views were ignored and that they were powerless in the face of the Government and the Companies' desire to make a quick financial gain. This is a somewhat extreme view and one that is unfair to all parties. It is almost certainly true that, at the time the original TRP's took place, few landowners anticipated the changes that actually occurred when logging commenced; but it is equally true that government officers genuinely tried to explain what these changes might be. There is no evidence that any intentional deception took place. Some landowners were upset at the limited financial benefits they received from logging, but it is certainly not the case that the landowners were a passive and inarticulate set of victims. Villagers retained ownership of their land and had a predominant role in determining its future use, including the extent to which plantation reforestation occurred. They determined the boundaries of benchmark and village reserves and were instrumental in persuading the Government to change its policy on royalty distribution to give themselves a higher share of the total receipts. Far from being powerless victims, villagers had a significant influence on events once logging started.

Indeed, in the eyes of many fellow Papua New Guineans living in Madang, Gogol landowners were in danger of becoming a pampered group always demanding handouts of various kinds from the Government and the Company. This may be an unfair criticism. If the GTP prospered then they stood to be major beneficiaries, but, if it failed, they were the ones who would bear the brunt of the costs.

Note 1: Another indication of this unwillingness to override landowners came a few years later when, in 1974, the potentially large Ioma timber project was cancelled. In that case, the House of Assembly member representing the area had been in favour and negotiations were underway with a large American timber company. The project was eventually cancelled when it became clear most landowners were against the proposal (Waiko 1977).

Note 2: This was estimated to be the minimum amount, discounted at 5%, that the Government itself would get when the timber was eventually logged (Ross, 1980).

Note 3: On one occasion, a patrol officer visiting a village was told the people wanted to tell him a story. He was asked to sit in front of three small grass huts, specially made for the occasion and set up in the middle of the village. One hut was labelled with a sign marked 'Japan', another was marked 'Port Moresby' and the third was marked 'Madang'. A man emerged from the 'Japan' hut with a large copra sack. The weight of the sack almost bent him double and the patrol officer was told this was full of money. The carrier staggered across the ground and disappeared into the hut marked 'Port Moresby'. A short time later another man emerged from this hut also carrying a sack, but this time it was a much smaller sack and he walked quickly over to the 'Madang' hut and disappeared inside. After a brief interval a third man emerged from the 'Madang' hut. He had no money sack but sauntered over to where a group of villagers were sitting and threw a handful of coins on the ground in front of them. That was their share of the original royalty. The play was good theatre and over-acted with great gusto but the political message was clear. The patrol officer went away impressed.

Note 4: A major coup for Jant was to employ a highly skilled Papua New Guinean driving instructor from Bougainville. Unfortunately, through no fault of his, a truck he was driving struck and killed a young girl in one of the villages on the road back into Madang. A road block was set up by the villagers to prevent all traffic movement and he was threatened with death as a 'pay-back'. Such 'pay-back' killings are widespread throughout PNG and are often carried on between clans arising from some real or imagined injury. Several expatriates have been killed as 'pay-backs' following traffic accidents near Port Moresby. As a result of the accident, the driving instructor resigned from Jant.

Note 5: The Madang Planters Association had previously tried earlier, in 1977, to get the Government to 'release' 20 000 ha of land to overseas investors.

Note 6: Mr. Michael Somare the former Chief Minister had recently lost government in the House of Assembly in Port Moresby. A PMV or public motor vehicle licence was the equivalent of a bus driver's licence.

Note 7: In 1978, cassowaries were worth up to K140 each in some places in the highlands and highlanders were visiting the Gogol Valley specifically to buy these birds (Liem 1978c).

Note 8: The Village Court Act had been passed in 1973, but it was not until 1975 that the first court was actually established. The role of the Village Courts was to deal with local problems according to local customary laws and procedures. The Act declared that 'The primary function of a Village Court is to ensure peace and harmony in the area for which it is established by mediating in and endeavouring to obtain just and amicable settlements of disputes' (Section 19 of the Act). The courts were given powers to adjudicate in disputes, make orders for compensation, to impose fines or demand the performance of community work (Bayne 1981). In the case of compensation for civil offences, this was originally set at K100 but later (1977) raised to K300. Typical matters dealt with by the courts are stealing, sorcery, trespass, property damage and adultery. Areas specifically excluded from the courts jurisdiction are murders, land matters and traffic offences. No formal qualifications are required of magistrates and in most areas magistrates are chosen by election although the Government is usually able to exert some influence on the type of person chosen (Paliwala 1982).

Note 9: The court case was a serious matter and feelings in Jobto ran high. The Magistrate made it clear he gave little credence to the testimony of the defendants. Yet events later in the day say something about the people and the general atmosphere in the Gogol Valley at the time. At the conclusion of the hearing, after two K5,000 fines had been imposed, the villagers invited the government and company representatives to sit down in the shade and share some watermelons with them.

Note 10: In fact most of the land owned by Jobto village clans was covered by secondary regrowth forest and was, consequently, not logged. Despite this, the clans of Jobto Village did share in all royalties and did have a road constructed past their village.

Note 11: These included a reduction in soil fertility, a loss of natural resources, including wildlife, and the destruction of his clay pot ground. He believed some of these problems might be resolved if the forest was allowed to regenerate but that others might not (Alaloum 1982).

CHAPTER 7

AN ASSESSMENT

INTRODUCTION

By 1981, 10 years had elapsed since Jant first took up the timber concession in the Gogol Valley. What could one then say about the project? Had it been a success? Was it a model for utilizing other lowland forests? These are difficult questions to answer because they raise a series of other questions such as: Who is entitled to judge? How should they form a judgement? How much time should pass before they can fairly do so? The three main parties to the project – the Government, the landowners and the companies — were all entitled to some say in the matter, but each had a different set of social, economic or environmental priorities and each had a different perspective of time. The approach taken in this chapter, therefore, has been to assess what the three main parties might justifiably have taken into account when weighing the benefits and costs of the project in 1981. The 10-year time scale is necessarily quite arbitrary but is probably sufficient. Some more complex ecological and social changes may take longer to become apparent, but the direction of change in most of these issues was reasonably clear.

THE PROJECT – A GOVERNMENT VIEW

The colonial Administration's objectives for the project had been simple. These were to utilize a natural resource, thereby increasing national revenues, to develop an integrated timber industry, to provide rural employment, and to foster rural development in the region. The new Papua New Guinean Government of 1973 came to power with a somewhat different view of development from its colonial predecessor. Rather than just creating growth and employment, the new government was also concerned that more of the economy should come under the control of Papua New Guineans, that there should be a greater degree of self-reliance, and that there should be a more equitable distribution of the benefits of development. These objectives were formalized in what became known as

189

the National Eight Point Improvement Plan, or the Eight aims. Each Government Department was requested to translate these aims into a set of policies specific to its function. The Eight Aims and their forestry equivalent are shown in Table 7.1. The original objectives referred to above, plus the Eight Aims, therefore constitute a convenient set of criteria by which to judge the project from a governmental perspective.

Both the colonial Administration and the new Government wanted the project to generate revenue, and early financial forecasts by Administration officers and external assessors suggested additional income would be readily forthcoming (Overseas Development Group 1973, Davidson 1983). The external assessors, for example, believed the Government would achieve a 25 per cent return on its capital investment. However, many of the assumptions on which these analyses were based were not subsequently fulfilled. For example, the rates of logging were different from those anticipated and the expected veneer mill was never built. The effect of this failure on actual government revenues is not known. De'Ath (1980)

Table 7.1 National eight point improvement plan translated in a national forest policy

1. A rapid increase in the proportion of the economy under the control of Papua New Guineans.
    Increase opportunities for local participation in forest activities and encourage the development of locally owned or predominantly locally owned forest enterprises.
2. Equal distribution of economic benefits including a move towards equalizing incomes.
    Direct a greater share of the benefits from forest development towards the landowners and other nationals involved in the industry.
3. Decentralized economic activity planning and government spending, with emphasis on agricultural development and village industry.
    Forestry is a rural industry – promote forest industries in rural areas, stimulate village participation – involve forest owners and local government in all phases of forest development.
4. An emphasis on small scale artisan services and business activity.
    Create opportunities for local businessmen and artisans to participate in transport, logging and all other activities related to forest industry.
5. A more self-reliant economy less dependent for its needs on imported goods and services.
    Promote the use of local forest products to replace imported goods.
6. An increase in capacity for meeting government spending needs from locally raised revenue.
    Promote the development of profitable forest industries to improve revenue returns through royalties and taxes.
7. A rapid increase in the active participation of women in both economic and social activities.
    Explore ways of increasing opportunities for women to participate in forest activities.
8. Government control and involvement in those sectors of the industry where control is necessary to achieve the desired kind of development.
    Forests are a national asset and must be managed in the national interest.
    To ensure the people of Papua New Guinea both now and in the future receive maximum benefits from the management of the forests the National Government will formulate and regulate policies governing the use of forest resources.

Source: Department of Forests (1972–73)

attempted a simple comparison of benefits and costs for the first $3\frac{1}{2}$ years of the project. This showed the Government received K1.76 million and expended K1.40 million over the same period, but De'Ath himself admitted the analysis was incomplete.

In the absence of such an analysis, one can only highlight some of the more obvious and public items. According to Jant (quoted by Seddon 1984) the annual cash benefits to PNG by 1981 included:

(i)	woodchips sold	K6 001 000
(ii)	electricity purchased from Electricity Commission	K128 000
(iii)	royalties	K221 000
(iv)	levy	K10 000
(v)	employees wages	K1 035 000
(vi)	taxes on these wages	K132 000
(vii)	reforestation	K250 000
	Total	K7 777 000

Other payments to the Government included harbour charges, road maintenance charges and import duties on fuel, machinery and spare parts.

One anticipated benefit noticeably absent from this list was company tax owing to the fact that Jant had not up till then declared a profit. De'Ath (1980) and Richardson (1981) both expressed some scepticism about this omission and suggested it indicated transfer pricing was taking place. Transfer pricing can take a variety of forms. One of the most common is for a subsidiary company to sell products to an overseas parent at a price lower than the cost of production, thereby ensuring the subsidiary never makes a profit. Jant was prevented from doing this, however, by the regulatory guideline chip price. Another form of transfer pricing is to allow the subsidiary to borrow funds from the parent company and build up a large debt to equity ratio. A high interest burden can then limit the profitability of the subsidiary because of the need to service the loan. Jant did borrow heavily to become established rather than get its capital directly from Honshu, but the rates of interest on these loans were monitored by the Government to ensure they were comparable with international rates at the time (Gardner 1980). The extent of the loans did lengthen the period of unprofitability for Jant, but it is not clear that this constituted a case of transfer pricing, since most of the loans were made by institutions other than Honshu[1].

There are other forms of inter company accounting that can reduce the profit of a subsidiary, such as those described by Barnet and Muller (1974) and Weinstein (1976), but there are also other less cynical explanations of Jant's unprofitability. One obvious problem was that the yen appreciated significantly against the Kina making loan repayments more expensive. In 1971, for example, K1 = 383 yen but in 1978 K1 = 281 yen. Another problem was that the project was the first of its kind in PNG and that

Jant had some early difficulties with its chipmill design which limited productivity. Many of the logs were crooked and the conveyor system carrying these to the chipper failed to work as well as expected. There were also difficulties in dealing with a variety of woods having different basic densities. Finally, Jant had little experience in tropical conditions and was making its way by trial and error. The most obvious example of this was the large amount of money initially spent on road construction before it was realized that less expensive roads would suffice.

Whatever the cause, Jant's period of unprofitability apparently ended towards the end of the decade. By then, the annual operating profit, before loan repayments were taken into account, had reached K1.9 million, while the accumulated deficit had fallen from a maximum of K4.8 million in 1978 to about K1.5 million in 1980 (Table 7.2). Jant's management expected the company to clear this deficit and start paying tax early in the new decade (Satoh, 1980). This did, in fact, occur[2].

There are many examples of creative accounting by transnational corporations, but there is, in Jant's case, some independent evidence that these company returns probably did represent the true financial position and were not a contrived understatement of the Company's real profitability. The evidence comes from an analysis of the woodchip industry which formed part of a larger input–output analysis of the PNG timber industry (Fraser 1981). In this analysis, financial outputs in the form of woodchip sales were matched against financial inputs needed to generate these sales. These included estimates of the costs of labour, capital, energy and other items such as consumable materials. They did not include royalties which were considered as being deducted from the operating surplus because they represented a cash item and not the cost of a resource. The analysis found that, for the years 1978–1980, the average annual financial input to the woodchip industry was K4.15 million and the output was K4.84 million, i.e. there was a surplus but it was small (Table 7.3). This surplus was not

Table 7.2 Jant's operating profit and accumulated losses between 1974 and 1980

Year ending	Operating Profit (Loss) before tax and loan repayments K	Accumulated losses K
June 1974	(419 277)	135 292
June 1975	(1 631 497)	1 766 789
June 1976	(329 627)	2 821 351
June 1977	31 391	3 464 115
July–Dec 1977	23 173	4 034 331
Dec. 1978	698 625	4 808 585
Dec. 1979	240 118	2 840 714
Dec. 1980	1 949 166	1 521 296

Source: Jant Company return File Local C 3545, Registrar General's Office, Port Moresby.

Table 7.3 Estimation of Total Annual Value of Output and Input of Woodchip Industry and Total Forest Industry in PNG based on years 1978–1980.

		Woodchip	Total forest industry
Output			
1.	*Production* (000 m³)	205	1180
2.	Domestic Sales		
	Quantity (x 1000 m³)	—	127
	Value K (x 1000)	—	18110
3.	Export Sales		
	Quantity (x 1000 m³)	205	
	Value K (x 1000)	4840	29110
4.	Total Output K (x 1000)	4840	47220
Input			
5.	Labour		
	km³	7	
	K (x 1000)	1439	9810
6.	Capital		
	km³	10	
	K (x 1000)	2050	12165
7.	Energy		
	km³	4	
	K (x 1000)	820	5406
8.	Other		
	km³	1	
	K (x 1000)	205	767
9.	Total Inputs		
	km³	22	
	K (x 1000)	4510	28148

Source: Fraser (1981)

nearly as great as for the timber industry as a whole but it did suggest Jant was then beginning to operate profitably.

Wewak Timbers is a much smaller enterprise than Jant and has a log intake of perhaps one tenth of the larger company. Unlike Jant, most of its production was sold on the domestic market, so it made no direct contribution to foreign exchange earnings. On the other hand, of course, it was important in reducing the need for imports of sawn timber. Like Jant, it made direct payments to the Government for such things as timber royalties, electricity and employee tax. Wewak Timbers traded at a loss for several years, but gradually became profitable and began to reduce its accumulated deficit. In 1977, this deficit was K700 000, but in 1981 it had declined to K186 393 (Table 7.4). No tax had been paid before this period, but, in 1980, tax of K11 397 was paid and this tax payment increased in 1981 to K56 230. In 1980, the company also paid its shareholders a dividend of K94 757, the first such payment for many years. Most of the shares were held in PNG[3].

These various economic gains were matched by some significant government expenses. Besides day to day administration and monitoring, these

Table 7.4 Wewak Timbers operating profit and accumulated losses between 1977 and 1981

Year ending Dec.	Operating profit (loss) before tax and loan repayments	Accumulated losses
K	K	K
1977	(41 758)	700 000
1978	114 957	585 103
1979	222 691	371 382
1980	313 946	163 590
1981	30 975	186 393

Source: Wewak Timber returns File Local C1235, Registrar General's Office.

included the early timber resource surveys and the detailed clan land boundary surveys. Some government expenditure, such as reforestation research, had benefits that could be passed on to other areas of PNG. Other expenditure such as health care and agricultural extension might have been made whether the project went ahead or not. The matter is obviously complex and an assessment of the overall cost to the Government is beyond the scope of this book.

A second objective of the Government, after economic gain, was the establishment of an integrated wood processing industry at Madang. This was only partially achieved, with a chip mill and sawmill being built, but not a plymill or a pulpmill. With the benefit of hindsight the absence of the latter two facilities may have been no bad thing. Earlier expectations of good markets for veneer and ply were not fulfilled, and, by the late 1970's, the international market was greatly oversupplied[4]. In these circumstances, a veneer or plymill at Madang would most likely have been unprofitable and would have limited the profitability of the Wewak Timber's sawmill. The pulpmill was probably never a short-term possibility. Modern pulpmills need to operate on a large scale to be economic and the technology is now such as to be virtually confined to the industrialized world (Leslie and Kyrklund 1980).

Although the chipmill was installed and eventually ran successfully, reforestation did not take place at anywhere near the rate necessary to allow a change-over to a plantation resource once the original forests were logged. By 1981, the total plantation area was only 2900 ha compared with the eventual target of 20 000 ha (Skelton 1981). In the short-term, it was obvious that the industry could only be sustained by moving to additional natural forests further from the chipmill at Madang. One area that interested Jant was a large forest resource in the Ramu Valley to the west of the Gogol Valley. The Provincial Government were also interested in building a road through the area to provide a link to Aiome on the Ramu River and were looking to the timber industry to help finance the road. However, the distance of the timber from Madang meant the profitability of the operation was low. Wewak Timber was also hoping for a similar concession on the north coast. If granted, these extra concessions might allow time for sufficient plantations to be established to enable an eventual transfer to a wholly plantation resource. But, in 1981, no decision had been made, and the whole matter of the future resource base remained uncertain.

In the matter of opportunities for Papua New Guinea control of forest based enterprises, the project could be counted a partial success. After passing through several owners, Wewak Timbers eventually became predominantly owned by PNG shareholders[3]. The Gogol Reforestation Company was jointly owned by the Government (49% and Jant 51%), while Jant remained wholly owned by Honshu. The Government retained an option to take up a 20% share of Jant but had not done so by 1981. Some economists have argued against the Government exercising such options, suggesting that it is an inefficient use of scarce Government capital and that the benefits, such as sharing in profits and influencing company policy, can be achieved in other ways (Goodman *et al.* 1985).

Other locally owned businesses based on the timber resource were slow to develop. Jant and Wewak Timber both preferred to carry out road making and felling themselves rather than use contractors. The logging group Yumi Timber was short lived and the tree farmers and salvage loggers were still to become fully established. Some new businesses unconnected with the timber industry commenced in the Gogol Valley, and existing businesses in Madang benefited from the companies' need for various goods and services, plus the substantial wages bill paid to their employees. Overall, however, progress in this direction was slight.

If these various economic objectives were only partially met, what of the Government's social objectives? The results for these seem rather better, at least from the Government's viewpoint. There is no doubt that the project contributed to the policy of decentralization at a time when elsewhere in PNG large numbers of people were drifting towards the larger towns. In fact, the project seemed to have reversed this trend in the Gogol Valley area. The road network helped foster cash cropping and a substantial number of jobs were created in an area with few other employment possibilities. Most of the jobs were for unskilled or semi-skilled labourers, and, with the exception of some new graduate foresters, relatively few were in the senior technical or managerial classes. However, both the National and Provincial Governments believed the landowners were receiving an appropriate share of the royalties coming from logging and, comparatively speaking, had received financial and other benefits well in excess of many of their fellow citizens elsewhere in the country.

The weight given to these various government objectives did not remain constant over the time period. As already mentioned, the first National Government was initially more inclined to give greater weight to developments leading to a larger control of the economy by its citizens, more self-reliance, and to a more equitable distribution of benefits. As the international economic slump of the 1970s deepened, however, employment creation and economic growth again became uppermost in the Government's view.

To summarize, by 1981, and from the government's viewpoint, it seems that the project was neither a clear cut success nor an obvious failure. There had been a number of short term financial gains, although there was a suspicion amongst some that these were not as great as they might have been. Some benefits had also flowed to many landowners, though perhaps these too had not been as great as hoped. To varying degrees, decentralization had been fostered, and opportunities for local participation and local business development had been created. In short, many of the objectives in the Eight Aims had been at least partially achieved. The problem lay with the longer-term prospects and whether these short-term gains could be sustained and amplified. The key factor here was the forest resource. The original forest had been sacrificed at a significant environmental and social cost in the expectation that this natural asset would be replaced by one of greater economic value (i.e. a plantation and road network). Ten years after the project was agreed upon, and 7 years after the chipmill opened, this replacement process was still only in its earliest stages.

THE PROJECT – THE LANDOWNER'S VIEW

It is less easy to discuss 'the' landowner's viewpoint since the societal heterogeneity of the population means there were probably as many such viewpoints as there were landowners. Each clan entered into a TRP agreement with the former Administration with its own expectations and wishes, and their perspective of the project in 1981 probably depended on the extent to which these had been satisfied.

That said, it is also true that there seem to have been at least several commonly held views. One of these was that the road network was beneficial. A desire for roads was one of few universally shared objectives among landowners prior to the commencement of the project. Long after logging started, Jant continued to receive requests to link particular villages into the expanding road network. A second common view was that royalty payments were too low. Some disgruntled landowners even began claiming they had been tricked by the Government and Jant. It should be mentioned, however, that the more vociferous of these complaints tended to come from villages that had already been linked into the road network. A third common view was a concern over the decline in natural resource availability. This concern was widespread and only partly allayed by evidence that regrowth was occurring in logged areas.

Other benefits and costs seem to be less generally agreed upon. Some people shared the Government's view that the project had increased their opportunities for cash cropping, business and employment. Those on the North Coast and Gum areas in particular seemed to regard cash cropping as a distinct benefit arising out of logging. In contrast, others were slow to take advantage of such opportunities and apparently discounted these as benefits. It is probably not surprising that some of the older men in particular had misgivings about the passing of the old ways and were concerned about the changes taking place in village life. It should be said, however, that this view is probably common amongst men of their age group throughout PNG.

The views of many landowners changed with time and will probably continue to change. Some clans who were particularly vocal in demanding that Jant build a road to their village subsequently gave the impression that they had entirely discounted the value of the road when they later demanded higher royalties from the felling of their forest. Other clans with strong misgivings shortly after the felling of their forests seemed to become interested in cash cropping and tree farming once the opportunities became more obvious.

By 1981, complaints about royalty payments had diminished (but not ceased). There were increasing areas under cash crops and a rising number of tree farmers. More groups were becoming involved in business enterprises of one kind or another and the new Local Government Council showed signs of becoming a political focal point. Much of this economic development was heavily dependent on the financial input from the timber industry. If this industry is sustained, then, in time, most landowners will probably come to agree that, on balance, they have benefited from logging. If on the other hand, the industry collapses, then most people will rightly judge they have paid much of the cost for whatever short term benefit PNG will have gained from the project.

THE PROJECT – JANT'S VIEW

Compared with the Government and the landowners, Jant's objectives were far simpler. In essence, the company wanted to make a profit. Profits can be made in the short-term or in the long-term and there is no reason to believe Jant's parent company, Honshu, was interested in anything other than the long-term when it began negotiations with the colonial Administration in the late 1960s. At that time, domestic suppliers of woodchips in Japan were limited and the Ministry of International Trade and Industry had just abandoned the 'co-operative reorganization' it commenced in 1962 to control the establishment of new paper making facilities in Japan. As a result, the industry had been plunged into 'completely free competition' (Anon. 1969b). The USA then began restricting log exports to Japan, so Honshu, like a number of other Japanese pulp and paper companies, started looking elsewhere for a supply of raw materials. Pulp made from a mixture of tropical tree species represented a completely new resource. If this mix proved to be commercially feasible, and if Honshu could negotiate long term supplies of this material, its competitive position would be enhanced.

For some in Honshu, a sizeable investment in PNG just before self government must have seemed a rather risky proposition. As it was, Jant had to deal with a group of new politicians and an administration in which experienced staff were rapidly being replaced by younger, less experienced officers. On the whole, Jant managed to maintain good relations with both. There were some early problems with the chipmill design and with pulpmaking but these were solved. The company also had to make a number of concessions to the Government on matters not covered in the original agreement. But, by 1981, it was clear that the species-rich rain forest could supply chips suitable for pulp and that the operation was commercially feasible. Furthermore, Jant had been built into a company with assets of over K10 million (Table 7.5). Honshu might have received a better return on its capital investment elsewhere. On the other hand, it had established a presence in PNG, a country with large timber resources, and in this sense could be reasonably satisfied with the way the GTP had developed.

But what of the matter of a long-term supply of chips? The whole basis

Table 7.5 Jant's balance sheet at 31 December, 1980

1979			*1980*
5 255 922	Fixed assets		4 988 112
638 137	Intangible assets		499 147
830 841	Investments in subsidiaries		1 105 104
6 724 900			6 592 363
4 983 307	Current assets	5 490 997	
1 482 020	Current liabilities	1 876 245	
3 501 287	Nett current assets		3 614 752
10 226 187			10 207 115
	Capital employed		
5 700 000	Issued capital		5 700 000
	less:		
	Accumulated losses		
2 173 571	– from operation	544 244	
	– from unrealised		
667 143	exchange fluctuations	977 052	
2 840 714			1 521 296
2 859 286	Capital less accumulated losses		4 178 704
	Non current liabilities		
7 340 020	– unsecured loan to		
	parent company	5 999 956	
26 881	– provision for long	28 455	
7 366 901	service leave		6 028 411
10 226 187			10 207 115

Source: Registrar General Office, Local File C3545

of the GTP had always been that, in time, the woodchips from the natural forest would be replaced by those from plantations. But, by 1981, Jant had still not made a full scale commitment to plantation reforestation. The company apparently preferred to seek further concessions of natural forest further away from its mill at Madang, even though these would be very expensive to log. This option also meant using a low quality species-rich woodchip mix rather than higher quality single species woodchips from a plantation. Further, by delaying large-scale reforestation, Jant began to lose much of the goodwill that existed between it and the Government, thereby diminishing Honshu's prospects of getting access to PNG forests in the longer term.

Two factors seem to have been responsible for the company's apparent indecision. One was almost certainly the problem of land ownership. Having seen some of the problems at first hand, and heard of others involving the Government's own plantations elsewhere in PNG, (e.g. Table 4.6), Jant's reluctance to commit large sums of money to reforestation is understandable.

The second factor may have been the downturn in the Japanese pulp and paper industry that occurred not long after Jant began operations in PNG. This downturn was serious, and, after late 1974, caused many plants to operate at only 60–70% of their capacity. Its effects on the industry were compounded by a tightening of Japanese pollution laws which forced many companies to spend large sums on pollution control[5]. The combined effect of these two events caused a number of companies to stand down workers, an unusual practice in Japan. In 1976, the *Industrial Review of Japan* referred to the situation as the worst recession in the history of the Japanese pulp and paper industry (Junro Sato 1976). In 1977, the Japan Paper Association revised its estimates of growth in paper brands sharply downwards from 5% to 2.7% as the revalued yen dampened industrial demand. Companies relying on paperboard, such as Honshu, were seriously hurt (Toshihisa Komaki 1978). In the following year, many kraft mills began shutting down for a week each month. At the same time, however, imports of kraft paper into Japan increased strongly because of the stronger yen. In 1978, a number of kraft paper producers formed a cartel to try to control prices and began to reduce plant capacity (Anon 1979/80).

The year 1980 was the year of the so-called 'chip shock'. As a result of chip shortages in North America, the price of Douglas Fir chips (the main chip import to Japan) increased from US$55 per BDU in July–December 1979 to US$92 per BDU in early 1980. In April–June 1980, the US company Wyerhauser set the staggering price of US$130 per BDU.

In late 1980 and early 1981, the pulp and paper companies Otake Shigyo and Idemizu Seishi went bankrupt and Toyo Pulp and Daishowa Paper faced serious financial difficulties. Many facilities were working at half capacity (Anon 1981/82). By September 1981, Honshu had joined with three other leading paper-pulp companies (Oji Paper Co., Juju Paper Co.,

Kanzaki Paper Manufacturing Co.) in exploring the possibility of setting up a joint company for purchasing raw materials and unifying their research divisions (Hirogami 1981).

In summary, the years following the establishment of the Jant chipmill in PNG were difficult ones for Honshu. Its total sales grew over the period, but its earnings never reached the level achieved in 1974 and were always a small proportion of sales (Table 7.6). The year 1978 in particular was a very poor year for the company when earnings declined 92% from the previous year. In 1981, profits were only US$1.9 million in comparison with US$8 million in 1974[6].

Jant's operations were comparatively unaffected by these events, at least initially. Production was maintained, although four shiploads of chips were sold to Taiwan in 1979, and a further two shiploads sold in 1980, to offset the poorer market conditions in Japan. In August 1980, however, the company decided to reduce production and the number of logging teams was reduced from eight to five. In 1981, chip exports fell to 103 000 dry tonnes, down from 121 000 dry tonnes the previous year. At the same time, Honshu began paying Jant more for woodchips than specified by the guideline price. In effect, it was giving Jant an interest-free loan (Gardner, 1980)[7]. As already described, the result of this loan was to take Jant into a position where it was soon to start paying company tax.

Just what effect these changed economic circumstances had on Honshu's investment decision making is difficult to say. After all, the company was one of Japan's largest paper companies and was almost entirely dependent on wood imports to run its mills. One might have expected such a company to take a long-term viewpoint when it came to ensuring pulpwood supplies, especially if it had access to cheap loan funds.

In contrast to Jant and Honshu, Wewak Timbers probably took a rather

Table 7.6 Sales and earnings of Jant's parent company Honshu Paper over period 1974–1981

Year	Sales US $ million	Per cent* change from previous year	Earnings US $ million	Per cent* change from previous year
1974	561.9	−3.7	8.0	
1975	525.7	12.7	3.0	−56.9
1976	592.9	0.8	2.6	−14.4
1977	660.2	1.0	3.1	11.2
1978	850.6	25.8	0.3	−92.0
1979	1027.6	8.9	2.1	552.8
1980	1081.2	−2.4	2.1	3.9
1981	1086.0	1.7	1.9	−12.1

*Based on values in Japanese Yen
Source: Surveys of Top 100 Paper Companies in September Issues of *Pulp and Paper International* Volumes 17 (1975) to Volume 24 (1982).

shorter term view of the GTP. Once the original forest containing sawlogs had been logged, its future in the area was over. There had been some enrichment planting trials at one stage to test whether sawlog species could be established in regrowth areas, but no large scale plantings were ever carried out. Wewak Timber was a much smaller company than Jant. By 1981, its fixed assets totalled K1.26 million and its nett assets were only K0.63 million. Amongst its intangible assets were several years worth of logging in its concession at the North Coast TRP. It had also been promised another TRP area of 10 900 ha known as the Far North Coast Block to use when the original area was completed. This Far North Coast Block was to be selectively logged only, and Wewak Timber would then be operating independently of Jant. For Wewak Timbers, therefore, the GTP was mainly a temporary source of high quality sawlogs acquired through its association with Jant. It was a short-term operation without serious prospects of a long-term future.

There is, therefore, no simple answer to the question asked at the beginning of this chapter about the success of the project. In the short-term, all parties gained certain benefits and all incurred costs. However, with the exception of Wewak Timbers, any real success depended on the future of the plantation scheme and, in 1981, the likelihood of that eventuating rested, it seemed, on a solution to the problem of land availability and on the future state of the Japanese pulp and paper industry.

SOME ALTERNATIVES

It must be clear from this account that, by 1981, there were a number of ecological and social reasons for questioning the desirability of projects such as the GTP. But what alternative courses of action might have been taken instead? Some possible alternatives to the woodchipping industry were –

Alternative 1: To exclude logging and provide no major Government inputs

This alternative would have been essentially a continuation of the *status quo* that applied before any logging took place in the various TRP areas. The advantage of this option would be that, compared with woodchipping, it would minimise the rate of change to village social life and to the environment. Some such changes would have been inevitable, but, under this alternative, their impact would have been gradual and thus easier to accommodate.

The disadvantage of this alternative would have been that it provided few opportunities for villagers who wished to improve their standard of living. Shifting cultivation is a functionally sound agricultural system under certain circumstances, but at best it generally limits people to affluent subsistence. The option would have precluded roads, and without roads there would have been few opportunities for cash cropping. Government services such as health care and education would also have been limited for the same reason. The extent of absenteeism revealed by the 1969 census (Table 3.14) suggests people were not happy with the *status quo* and that this alternative would not have appealed to many. Nor, of course, is it an alternative that would have contributed to the Government's national economic objectives.

Alternative 2: To exclude logging but provide modest Government inputs

This alternative is similar to the first, the main difference being that the Government would have provided certain facilities such as roads, agricultural advice, health care etc. The advantages are obvious and it reflects the course of action being attempted to varying degrees in much of rural PNG. The disadvantage, is that it would be an expensive course of action for the Government, and, in the short-term, do nothing to improve Government revenues. By the late 1960s, Madang and its surrounds was regarded as being a comparatively developed area and accordingly, was ranked lower in the Administration's priorities than more isolated areas such as the Western District or the West Sepik District. The Gogol Valley did not have a large population and was not especially different from any other inland area in the Madang district. There was no reason, therefore, why it should deserve any special consideration over other rural areas in PNG in terms of Government expenditure.

Alternative 3: To allow selective logging by commercial enterprises

Under this option, forest resources would have been utilized to improve Government revenues and help finance rural development. The logs could have been simply exported overseas or, more preferably, sawn locally. Both approaches would have provided a road network, royalties to Government and landowners as well as some employment. The scale of operations would have been less than woodchipping so the immediate impact on the forest environment would have been less. Likewise, the social impacts would have been significantly smaller. Since the output from such a sawmilling operation would contain a high proportion of the well-known *Intsia bijuga*, its overseas marketing problems might not have been as difficult as those of other mills in PNG, and, by increasing the volumes of PNG timber in the international market place, the overall long-term prospects of other species might have been expected to improve.

This alternative had, in fact, been the Government's initial first choice and it had built the road to Mawan and the bridge across the Gogol River primarily for this purpose. But, despite the resource being widely advertised on several occasions, no suitable companies had been attracted.

The other difficulty with this alternative is that it would have done little to develop a permanent forest reserve or national forest estate. Many landowners in the North Coast and Gum TRP's were apparently keen to convert their forest to agriculture. Any trees remaining after selective logging would probably have been wasted by being felled and burnt. In areas where this did not occur, it is uncertain what effect selective logging would have had on the future productivity of the forest. The same could be said, of course, about many other selective logging operations elsewhere in PNG, and that is the national dilemma. The single difference in the Gogol Valley was that the chipmill option offered the prospect of a plantation.

Alternative 4: To allow selective logging by village based sawmills

In this case, the forest would have been exploited by the landowners themselves. This option would have necessitated less expensive and more easily managed sawmilling equipment but such equipment was readily available (Gardner 1978). Small mills could have left exploitation of the forests in the hands of Papua New Guineans rather than outsiders, helped make the communities more self reliant and provided them with sawn timber. Environmentally and socially, the impacts could have been relatively small. There were a large number of small mills like these already operating throughout rural PNG and the Forestry Department had several extension officers to help service them. Further mills in the GTP would have simply extended this network.

Despite the apparent advantages there were several considerable disadvantages with this alternative. From a national viewpoint, it would have done nothing to help government revenue and the export trade. Small sawmills may be useful to supply isolated communities, but they are a quite inappropriate technology for any large scale export industry. At the local level, it was also unlikely small sawmills would have been desirable. The communities of the Gogol TRP had few financial resources and would have been unable to purchase the smallest of portable sawmills. Government funds would have been difficult to obtain for reasons already outlined. A bank loan might have been possible, but the loan would have needed to include funds for road building equipment to allow some of the output to be marketed in order to repay the loan. Some expatriate technical advice would have also been necessary. Since there was already a small sawmill run by the Catholic Mission at Utu just outside the northern boundary of the Gogol TRP, it is unlikely a bank loan for another mill in the area would have been forthcoming. Finally, and perhaps most significantly, it was not an option which any landowners had ever evinced any interest, despite the example of the Utu mill.

203

Alternative 5: Delay any decision

In its short-term effects, this alternative is identical to alternative 1. The difference is that the area would have been recognized as a significant timber resource to be marketed at a time when there was more interest by buyers. With hindsight, the alternative may have had some merit, but it required an assumption on the part of the Administration at the time that the market would improve in PNG's favour in due course. While a country with a robust and diverse economy might have been able to make such an assumption, it was a much more difficult one for a colonial Administration in charge of an economy such as Papua New Guinea's, especially when the country's forest area was so large. In any case, the alternative still leaves the choice of an appropriate form of forest exploitation undecided.

There were of course, other alternatives beyond these few. For example, a central resaw mill and maintenance shop might have been supplied with timber from a number of portable flitch mills owned by villagers or individual contractors. These could have used 7–15 tonne trucks for logging and timber transport patterned after the Malaysian San Tai Wong winch lorry. The cost of these trucks is considerably less than the normal combination in PNG of skidder or bulldozer plus logging truck. Perhaps the small Wewak Timbers operating in the Gogol Valley before the Jant agreement was signed could have evolved in this way. Perhaps, at a larger scale, some form of wood panel manufacturing using wood residues and veneer might have been combined with a sawmilling operation. Whatever the merits of these alternatives, the PNG timber industry of the late 1960s was not especially interested and the Administration lacked the funds and expertise to sponsor them itself[8].

There might also have been scope for commercially exploiting some of the non-timber products of the forest. Myers (1983) has outlined the economic value of some of these products and argued that their harvesting can be done in a sustained and non-destructive manner, unlike many other forms of rain forest exploitation such as logging or small scale cultivation. The products discussed by Myers (1983) mostly fall into two groups. One group includes products such as canes, rattans, gums, exudates, volatile oils etc. The second group is what might be referred to as genetic resources. This includes plant and animal species of importance or potential importance to international agricultural, medical or chemical industries. Both groups are difficult for a small country like PNG to exploit commercially. Products such as rattans or gums have to be found in significant concentrations to make the cost of collection reasonable and this was not the case in the Gogol Valley, although commercially usable quantities of many of these products do occur elsewhere in PNG[9].

The genetic resources of the second group are usually only valuable after the germ plasm has been taken overseas and reproduced on a large scale or introduced into an existing technology. In these circumstances, the owners of the land from which the germ plasm originates rarely receive a share of any profits. In most cases, the material is generally regarded as a 'free' good. For these sorts of reasons, non-timber products did not attract the attention they undoubtedly deserve. In the context of a land use decision in the late 1960s, the best that might have been expected would have been that they could have been a supplementary product to some other primary land use.

CONSEQUENCES FOR FOREST POLICY IN PAPUA NEW GUINEA

Events in the Gogol Valley did not occur in isolation, of course. As already mentioned, Jant's chipmill opened the year after Papua New Guinea achieved self-government, and 1 year before the country became independent. The end of the colonial era was a time of dramatic change. It was also a period when many long-held Administration policies began to change or were replaced by completely new policies. One of the most important legacies of the GTP was the effect it had on a number of these policies.

The most immediate effect was to alter the way the Department of Forests dealt with foreign companies wishing to exploit PNG's forests. The negotiations leading to the agreement with Jant had been a major learning experience for the Department of Forests. To build on this experience, the Department obtained the services of an FAO consultant to review the final agreement and advise on how it could have been improved. At the same time, the new Government replacing the old colonial Administration established a National Investment and Development Authority (NIDA) to regulate the activities of all overseas companies in PNG. One of the first actions of NIDA was to issue, in conjunction with the Department of Forests,'Guidelines for Forestry Development Proposals'. This document contained an extensive list of information required from new investors (Appendix 4), much of which was a direct result of the lessons learned from the GTP.

A second area in which the GTP affected government policy was environmental protection. The Department of Forests itself began to demand certain minimum environmental standards be maintained by Jant soon after logging commenced. It also began including these in the conditions demanded of all new investors. But, at the same time, criticism of the environmental effects of logging in the Gogol Valley and reports, particularly that of Webb (1977), reinforced the desire of the newly created Office of Environment and Conservation to introduce strong environmental protection legislation in PNG. This was duly carried out in 1978 with the passage of the Environmental Planning Act.

Both of these changes were reflected in a major review of forest policy that took place in 1979 (Ministry of Forests 1979). The review was undertaken because it was clear that the earlier World Bank objective of fostering a national timber industry based on large integrated operations had failed. Many timber areas had been acquired by the Government through timber rights purchases, but few of these had been taken up by industry (Table 7.7). Little of the money advanced by the Government to carry out the purchases had been recouped in royalties.

The review concluded that the previous insistence on integrated industries that processed timber for export should be relaxed and recommended that log exports be allowed under carefully prescribed conditions. This would provide some financial return to PNG and could lead to improved markets for some of the country's lesser known species.

The new policy arising from the review incorporated some of the lessons of the GTP. One of these was the matter of environmental protection during logging operations. The new policy declared that 'ground rules' would be specified in as much detail as possible prior to the issue of a permit to log. Prospective protective measures would be explained to representatives of the people from the forest areas and their comments sought so that the implications of the logging operation could be more clearly understood and their views taken into account. A forest working plan which included details of areas to be excluded from logging would also have to be submitted prior to the commencement of operations. Land-use planning was also to be strengthened with provision for better

Table 7.7 The state of negotiations over some major forest resource areas in Papua New Guinea by the end of 1980

Resource location	Size (000 ha)	First advertised	Progress
Tonelei	44	1963	Agreement signed and logging started 1966. Company subsequently failed.
Gogol	83	1964	Agreement signed 1971.
Kulu Dagi	33	1966	Selective logging from 1969.
Vanimo	287	1968	Advertised on several occasions; inconclusive negotiations with various companies.
Open Bay	183	1970	Agreement signed 1973.
Sagarai-Gadaisu	160	1971	Agreement signed in 1975 but terminated shortly afterwards.
Kumusi	64	1971	Initial interest but no agreement, consortium disbanded.
Kapiura	85	1974	Some interest but no agreement.
Kapaluk	181	1974	No agreement.
Ioma	182	—	Negotiations with a company reached an advanced stage but landowners changed minds in 1974 and withdrew. See Waiko (1976).

integration of post-logging forestry and agriculture development. Another change was that the Government would defer the allocation of forest concessions where land for agreed-upon post-logging uses could not be obtained. Conversely, no further timber rights would be acquired unless there were good prospects for an industry because these could raise the expectations of landowners. Finally, the new policy gave greater emphasis to the creation of PNG businesses in association with large overseas enterprises. Many of these changes were a direct result of experiences in the GTP.

The new policy was not especially radical. In fact, it was the sort of policy one might expect to find in any western industrialized country. It soon became evident, however, that the policy was not attractive to the international timber industry. In 1981, the PNG Institute for National Affairs commissioned a study of the new forest policy by Dr D.A. Fraser. The Institute's Director of Research also contacted a number of 'the world's better known companies with experience in tropical timber' and asked them to comment on the reason for their absence from PNG in the light of the new policy. Their comments, included in Fraser (1981), are instructive:

Company A: 'We feel that the current approach (of Government), although of laudable intent, will in certain cases result in the 'cut and run' syndrome and the serious investor will be repelled'.

Company B: 'There is growing disenchantment in the industry today with requests for detailed proposals and studies. These are expensive exercises – when properly conducted – and today fewer companies are as willing to conduct them than was the case 10 years ago'.

Company C: 'Simply stated, we have concluded that operations in Papua New Guinea would cost more to produce less. That officialdom, although perhaps recognizing this, does not appear to have been influenced accordingly. I suggest that the technique of inviting proposals is not really appropriate since the prospects are not attractive enough to induce competitive tenders by the more experienced investors'.

Company D: 'The forests of Papua New Guinea are not such an attractive proposition to many, whereas the expectations from and the demands made upon the foreign investor tend to be disproportionately high. That really sums it up'.

Company E: 'Companies in Europe would not normally invest in Papua New Guinea as a means of supplying a home industry. They would do so mainly to develop profits. Moreover the Western investor is conceivably more conscious of the obligation to respect the niceties of the regulatory processes. Which is why ('X'), along with some others, feels that the investment equation is unequal'.

Company E: 'I would repeat that we do not understand the reason for protective legislation. We have here a developing nation desirous of introducing a modern forestry industry which will result in irreversible change. I would however suggest that interest would be encouraged if, for instance, a Government were to say to potential investors that they wished to develop a forest industry and discuss with them their fears and hopes, and the safeguards they seek'.

These replies suggested the Government's attempts to foster utilization of its forests on its own terms might have failed.

Meanwhile, the GTP continued, but in the context of the responses above, it had acquired an additional significance. If the new regulations governing the utilization of PNG's forests were to be shown to be viable, then GTP was the obvious test case.

CONCLUSIONS

By 1981, the project was 10 years old and not even half way through its projected first stage. Many mistakes had come to light and major changes had been made to the original project design. The Government and the two companies had reason to be moderately satisfied with progress, given the political and economic events of the time. Not all expectations had been fulfilled but there was reason for optimism. The results as far as the landowners were concerned were less satisfactory. Their environment had been changed more than they had expected and the financial compensation had been too small, but the project had created new opportunities and there were signs that these were being increasingly utilized. The greatest single problem was reforestation. If the project was to have any chance of ultimate success, a rapid acceleration in the plantation programme was essential.

Note 1: In 1975, Jant's creditors were the Japan International Co-operation Agency, the Overseas Economic Co-operation Agency, the Overseas Co-operation Fund of Japan, the Commercial Bank of Japan and the Papua New Guinea Development Bank (De'Ath 1980).

Note 2: In 1983, Jant paid tax of K34 039 and this rose in 1984 to K104 218. (File Local C3545 Registrar General's Office, Port Moresby.)

Note 3: Major shareholders of Wewak Timbers in 1981 included Sepik Timbers (32%), the PNG Investment Corporation (26%), Madang Development Corporation (17%), and the East Sepik Development Corporation (17%). The latter two groups were owned by their respective Provincial Governments.

Note 4: The international market for ply and veneer had been growing at around 5% annually in the 1960s and was expected to continue at around 4.5% until 1980 (Takeuchi 1974). However, the ply market was seriously oversupplied by the late

1970s and many Japanese mills were becoming bankrupt. The situation continued to worsen in the 1980s. Indonesia, which had invested heavily in the ply industry was also hit by over production and rising costs (Habir 1984).

Note 5: The ratio of antipollution spending to total capital expenditure within the industry in Japan increased from 5.7% in 1970 to 31% in 1974 (Sato 1976).

Note 6: James (1981) has suggested this was a deliberate company strategy. Honshu had originally been part of the Oji Seishi company which accounted for 90 per cent of all paper produced in Japan in the mid 1930s. Following World War II, Oji Seishi was forcibly split into three companies (Honshu Seishi, Jujo Seishi and Tomakomai Seishi – later renamed Oji Seishi). These three companies continued to maintain close relationships although each occupied a different segment of the pulp and paper market. In 1979, Honshu had the smallest profit of the three but the largest assets. James suggested that 'as the group integrates its operations closely, it seems reasonable to infer that the split up of assets and profits is carefully planned' to mask the real situation. An equally plausible explanation is that the differences in profitability were due to the state of the market segment occupied by each company.

Note 7: This practice has continued. In 1984, Jant received K61 per BDU when the guideline price was K52 per BDU (A. Ross, letter – 24 December 1984). A somewhat similar situation occurred in 1977 in Australia and New Zealand when producers negotiated a 10 per cent reduction in export volumes. American chip producers on that occasion preferred to maintain their export volumes but agreed to decrease the price per BDU (Komaki 1978).

Note 8: By the late 1970s, the Government had established a Timber Industry Training Centre at Lae. Part of its purpose was to explore appropriate technologies for the PNG timber industry.

Note 9: Elsewhere in PNG, at this time, efforts were made to develop small industries based on rattan, copal resin from *Agathis labillardieri*, resin from *Vatica papuana* essential oil from *Cryptocarya massoy*, candlenut oil, plant dyes and vegetable tannins. Some sales of rattan and copal resin were made but both required considerable Forestry Department organisation inputs and the industries collapsed when this support was withdrawn. Not all forest areas in PNG were equally endowed with these resources (e.g. Department of Forests 1972/73).

CHAPTER 8

A POSTSCRIPT

INTRODUCTION

In 1986, I had an opportunity to return to PNG. A number of changes had occurred. The most surprising of these was that a second woodchip mill had been built in the early 1980s by a Korean company at Kapuluk in New Britain. This seemed a direct contradiction of the attitudes being expressed by various international timber companies towards PNG not so many years earlier. But all was not as it seemed; the mill had not operated since it had been completed. The company claimed it was unable to find a market for mixed tropical hardwood chips. So, while the mill stood idle, the company simply exported unprocessed logs. Sceptics suggested that this had been the company's intention from the beginning.

At Madang, routine management was in the hands of the Provincial Government's Division of Forests; the National Government's Department of Forests' involvement was then essentially just silvicultural research. A number of the original staff in the two organizations had left and been replaced by newcomers, but procedures had been established and management was more settled than in the earlier days when decisions had to be made in the face of continuously changing circumstances. Financial constraints were more difficult and vehicles were in short supply limiting the ability of staff to get into the field.

As for the GTP in particular, prospects seemed distinctly poorer. In 1981, the project had been neither a success nor a failure. Some things had not developed as planned but there was still a fair chance of success. In 1986, that success was still possible but it seemed increasingly unlikely. In this Postscript, I shall describe some of the events since 1981 that led me to this more pessimistic prognosis. I shall begin by describing the socio-economic situation and then consider progress towards creating a plantation to replace the original forest resource.

SOCIO-ECONOMIC MATTERS

In 1986, most people in the GTP seemed to take the project rather for granted, at least that was the view of many government staff. The benefits such as roads and employment appeared to have been accepted and disputes over matters such as royalty payments to have declined. At the same time, the earlier concern over the loss of natural resources also seemed to have diminished as forest regrowth developed and experience showed that gardens could be successfully established on these lands. Another explanation, of course, might be that landowners had reluctantly accepted the inevitable and realized it was finally too late to do anything. This seems unlikely, since the Gogol people have never been reluctant to voice an opinion. In this respect, it is also interesting that Wezip Alaloum of Jobto Village, one of the most vocal critics of the environmental consequences of the project, stood in the 1982 Provincial Government elections but lost. This result lends support to the suggestion above that most people were less concerned about environmental matters. Interestingly, Wezip became much less prominent after this defeat[1].

Unlike the situation in many other tropical countries, the logging road network had not led to an influx of squatters. The pattern of land ownership and the Government's concern to limit immigration had prevented this. Instead, the roads seemed to have helped draw many Gogol people into the wider society of the Madang Province. One sign of this was the large number of candidates from the Gogol Valley, besides Wezip Alaloum, standing in the 1982 Provincial Government elections referred to above. Interestingly, the main issue of the campaign was not the timber project but 'development' and all candidates were firmly in favour of more rapid development for their electorates.

Development in the Gogol Valley had been fostered by a fund established in 1980, the Madang Timber Permit Area Development Fund. The fund amounted to K90 000 and was made up of contributions from the National Government, the Provincial Government, Wewak Timbers and Jant. Most of the money was spent on health aid posts, small agricultural projects and the like. The fund stopped in 1984 when other regions in the Province complained that the Gogol people were getting favoured treatment. By then, however, a survey had shown that 80% of all people in the GTP area were in favour of their second 25% share of the timber royalty being pooled instead of being distributed. The second 25% of royalty was therefore used to establish a new Development Fund. This change in the community's attitude was a remarkable turnabout from the views being expressed only a few years earlier when angry clan leaders had demanded that all royalties should be returned to them and had felled trees to set up road blocks to press their case.

With the increase in the importance of the Provincial Government, the prestige and significance of Local Government councils had declined. Consequently, the Gogol Local Government Council had never achieved much power or become the centralized representative body for people in the valley it might once have been. It is somewhat ironic that this decline in the role of Councils coincided with the changing community attitude towards royalty distribution and the apparent recognition of the benefits of joint action.

But, despite the various development funds and enthusiasm for development, there were disappointingly few signs of much economic progress since 1981. Cash cropping had increased but not especially rapidly and the large scale agricultural project proposed in the earlier land-use plan had not eventuated[2]. Only one cattle project remained of the several commenced and the pasture in that showed signs of being overrun by weed species. The small groups running the salvage logging operations had gradually ceased after the government foresters stopped providing an administrative input, and the various business associations had either broken up or remained inactive. In short, there was little sign of an economic multiplier effect arising from the project.

This slow rate of economic development in what are essentially materialistic societies apparently interested in development is surprising. Roads have always been assumed to be the primary limitation on economic activity in the Gogol Valley. Why had not economic growth followed the road network? Why had not the same level of rapid entrepreneurial activity taken place that occurred, for example, after the introduction of roads and coffee into the area around Goroka in the highlands of PNG in the 1950s and 1960s?

Part of the reason may have been the differing levels of malaria in the two regions; malaria was widely prevalent in the coastal lowlands, but was much less of a problem in the highlands. However, there may have also been other factors at work. Finney (1968, 1973) believed the particular success of highland coffee growers at Goroka was due to two sets of circumstances. One of these he referred to as *preadaptions*. These are 'factors internal to the make-up of a society which, although they have evolved independently from the cash economy, prove adaptive to new economic activities once the society becomes linked to the cash economy'. Such factors include an emphasis on individual achievement, a cultural focus on wealth and its exchange and an achieved-status system (i.e. the Big Man system) linked intimately to the accumulation of wealth and exchange. The other set of circumstances he described as economic *preconditions* which were 'factors external to a society which make the adoption of new economic activities feasible, attractive and profitable to the people concerned'. In the case of the highland people, such *preconditions* included fertile and well-watered soil suitable for growing high-value arabica coffee, a non-disruptive colonial experience that allowed people to retain their pre-contact social integrity, a transport and marketing system and an extension service providing technical advice.

How well do these concepts apply to the Gogol Valley? It is obvious that many of the *preadaptions* among Goroka people were also common among the clans of the Gogol Valley. However, not all the *preconditions* postulated by Finney have been fulfilled. In the first place, the prospects for rapid cash returns from many of the planned economic activities have been poorer. This certainly applied to salvage logging in which profits were modest in proportion to the physical effort involved. It also applied to many trade stores for the reasons described earlier (Chapter 7). Exportable cash crops such as copra, cocoa and coffee grow reasonably well in the Gogol Valley but have been subject to major price fluctuations since the GTP commenced[3]. Thus, the average price of cocoa was K919 per tonne in 1975, it soared to K2938 per tonne in 1977, but fell to K1113 per tonne in 1982. Similar price fluctuations have occurred for copra products and coffee over the same period (Goodman *et al.* 1985). Industry stabilization schemes helped protect growers from such fluctuations, but many new farmers or prospective farmers unfamiliar with the idea of international commodity pricing must have been confused and discouraged by these changes. By contrast, the prices received by the early highlands coffee growers were far more stable, and, as production grew, they experienced constantly increasing cash rewards (Finney 1973).

Second, the availability of technical advice to Gogol landowners interested in cash cropping was probably less than was the case for the new coffee growers in the highlands. Not only did the latter have a number of government agricultural extension officers, but there were also expatriate-owned plantation acting as models from which advice could be sought. With the possible exception of copra, this was not the case in the Gogol Valley.

Third, the colonial history in the two areas has been different. Finney (1973) argues that, for the Madang district generally, the long colonial history was not as conducive to good relations between local people and expatriates as was the case in the highlands. Social and economic relations were especially poor during the German colonial era in Madang, but, even after that time, little attempt was made to foster indigenous economic development. Overall, therefore, the preconditions for economic growth in the Gogol Valley were less favourable than was the case in the highlands.

There is one final factor that must be referred to at this point and that is the role of cargo cults. There seems little doubt that many people in the Gogol Valley continued to be influenced by cultist explanations of how economic success might be achieved. When logging was not followed, as expected, by a rapid improvement in material welfare, such people were predisposed to seek an explanation from cult beliefs rather than persist with the methods recommended by expatriates. This sort of response has been observed before elsewhere in the Madang Province among people influenced by cult activities. Thus, McSwain (1977) noted –

'At a certain temporarily static level of achievement the Kar Kar began to question the usefulness of their experiments with the Western concept of hard work for modest return in favour of traditional expectations of achieving wealth through divine intervention. Their expectation of finite and instantaneous rather than preplanned and evolutionary achievement threatened the consolidation and expansion of changes so far, possibly by the replacement of secular with ritual methods'.

What this suggests is that modest economic progress has not eradicated cargo cult beliefs. On the contrary, it has helped perpetuate them. Significantly, a new cult movement appeared to be developing in 1986, centred about the son of Yali Singina, the most influential of the post war cult leaders of the Madang area (Noah, 1986). These developments do not mean that economic progress in the Gogol Valley is impossible. Rather, they imply that any progress will be more difficult and take longer simply because there is a widespread misconception in the area about how such progress is achieved. This misconception is certain to be strengthened when royalties cease after Jant completes logging the natural forest in a few years' time.

In summary, the socio-economic progress following logging has been much slower than anticipated by the early planners of the project. Many changes have taken place and some have been beneficial, but it is clear that the original assumption that economic benefits would automatically follow the creation of roads and the distribution of royalties was simplistic and misplaced. Similarly, the expectations of landowners have not been realised. Perhaps these were unintentionally raised too high by government foresters trying to 'sell' the project and unite the various clans in a single TRP. Or perhaps people's expectation of the project were unavoidably affected by the cargo cult beliefs common in the area. Whatever the reason, any development that does finally take place will occur more gradually than once hoped. This might not matter, perhaps, if the long term future of the timber industry in the Gogol Valley were assured. Unfortunately, this is not the case. The reason is the reduction in the forest resource.

THE FOREST RESOURCE

In 1986, it appeared that most of the accessible natural forest would be completely logged out within a few years. There was a strong likelihood that Jant could be awarded a further small concession on a TRP to the south of the original Naru TRP which would extend the companies operations for a few more years. The question is, however, what will happen then?

From the very beginning of the project, it was always assumed that Jant would switch to plantations of fast growing trees once the original forest was felled. In 1986, the state of this plantation was as follows:-

PNG Forestry Department plantations	1500 ha
Gogol Reforestation Co. plantations	4800 ha
	6300 ha

This total was referred to as the gross plantation area and it included roads, compartment boundaries and buffer strips to limit the spread of any fire, so that the actual nett area was nearer 5500 ha (Skelton, 1986). If one assumes the 1986 planting rate of about 450 ha is maintained each year, and that it takes Jant another 5 years to complete logging its original concession plus any new areas allocated to it, then the total gross plantation area in 1991 could reach about 8000 ha. This is less than half the plantation area originally hoped for by the Government and is not nearly enough to sustain the industry into the future, at least at its present scale of operations.

How has this situation developed? One factor involved is availability of land. Despite efforts by the Provincial Government to arrange for leasehold land to be planted by the GRC, the amount of such land becoming available each year has been small. This may be because timber growing is regarded by many Gogol landowners as an activity surrounded by too much uncertainty. It doesn't have the economic record of other cash crops and, consequently, contributes little towards enhancing a landowner's status. Moreover, as in many parts of PNG, the planting of trees by someone on a particular piece of land can sometimes be construed as the first step by that person to establishing an ownership claim over the land. Until it can be demonstrated that timber growing is a worthwhile economic activity that does not threaten land ownership, these sorts of attitudes will probably continue to limit the availability of plantation land[4].

A second factor is that provincial authorities appear to have missed several opportunities to popularize tree growing and, hence, make land leasing for reforestation easier. The first was in 1981 when a villager from the Naru River area named Yegas harvested a small plantation of *E. deglupta* that he had planted on his clan's land in 1970 or 1971. The timber was sold to Jant for pulpwood, and, with more publicity, the sale could have been a public relations coup. Another missed opportunity was the tree farming movement. It, too, might have popularized and legitimised reforestation, but, after a promising start, the provincial forestry authorities allowed the scheme to languish and, eventually, cease.

A third factor limiting plantation development concerns land leasing arrangements. The leasing procedure is extremely slow, and, in 1986, it was taking up to 5 years for some leases to be registered with the National Government. Consequently, planting by the GRC was usually carried out well before the legal niceties were finalized, a practice causing the auditors of GRC's annual accounts to regularly qualify their report by pointing out that the company's rights to harvest these plantations and recover its investment were not secure[5].

A fourth factor responsible for limiting plantation development is Jant's reluctance to commit much money to the project. Jant, the major shareholder in the GRC, was of course, well aware of the problems of land tenure in PNG and of the Government's apparent inability to solve many land ownership disputes involving its own forest plantations. Its public stance had long been one of favouring reforestation to sustain the project into the longer term. At the same time, its approach had always been understandably cautious but this caution never seemed to lessen, despite the availability of low interest loans for reforestation from JICA, evidence of satisfactory growth rates in the existing plantation and of the ability of the government to acquire and register leasehold land in the Gogol Valley, albeit at a slow rate. Perhaps the rate was too slow? Anyway, Jant's caution persisted despite increasingly favourable market conditions in Japan for hardwood chips of a type that could be supplied from the Gogol plantations. Indeed, one market analyst believed these had the brightest market future of all forest product commodities because Japanese demand was rising while local and overseas supplies were static or declining (FEER, 1985).

Then, in mid 1985, something odd happened. A report appeared in the English language Japan Lumber Journal (20 July 1985) entitled 'Honshu Paper's Planted Eucalypts in PNG Enters Harvesting Period'. The report announced that *E. deglupta* woodchips were regarded by Honshu as being good for high quality printing paper and not just kraft pulp and that Honshu was going to take more hardwood from PNG instead of softwood from Canada or eucalypt chips from Brazil. Honshu was said to have undertaken 'substantial afforestation since 1975 and to control plantations totalling 33 500 ha' (sic). It seemed that Jant's parent company, Honshu, had finally decided that time was running out for the GTP and that a commitment to a full-scale plantation scheme would be made.

The source of this report and the reasons for it, especially the inflated plantation area, are not clear. It may have been based on trade gossip, or it may have been that a company decision was made, but was reversed a short time later. Whatever the background, the report was wrong; there was still no evidence 6 months later of any change in Honshu's attitude or that Jant's long-term future in the Gogol Valley was any closer to being resolved. In fact, the situation from PNG's viewpoint was beginning to look even more unsatisfactory. One reason for this was that Japan was being pressured by the USA to redress the huge trade balance in Japan's favour by taking more USA exports, including woodpulp. A second was that Japan itself was recycling a greater proportion of its paper in an attempt to reduce its dependency on imports. Such recycled pulp needs to be blended with long-fibred coniferous wood pulp rather than short-fibred hardwood pulp, and the very large *Pinus radiata* plantations of New Zealand and Chile were well placed to supply this material. The optimistic forecast for hardwood chips of only a few years earlier was, apparently, premature (Ross 1986).

The lack of a viable plantation scheme to replace the original forest is, therefore, due to a combination of problems with land availability, land leasing arrangements and inaction on the part of Jant. Whether Jant's inaction was simply excessive caution by a commercially conservative management or whether it was caused by some other motive, I cannot say. What can be said, however, is that recent trade conditions are not of the kind to make plantation establishment in PNG more attractive to Jant, and the situation, in 1986, may be beyond the point of no return.

Wewak Timber's role in all this was minor. By 1986, it was still logging in the North Coast TRP area, but the Company had also acquired a TRP of 10,900 ha known as the Far North Coast block. This TRP was too distant from Madang to make chipwood logging viable and Wewak Timber was simply selectively logging the area and sawing its timber in the Madang sawmill.

ENVIRONMENTAL CONDITIONS

Finally, what of the forest itself? In early 1986, nearly 40 000 ha of a total of 73 000 ha in the Gogol, Naru and Gum TRPs had been logged, leaving some 45 per cent as unlogged forest. This 40 000 ha represented most of the easily accessible land in these three TRPs and is close to the estimate made in the original land-use plan of the amount of forest that would remain unlogged as protection forest. Forest regrowth occupied all the logged areas and appeared to be growing rapidly.

One particular concern from the start of the project had always been that wildfires might escape from people's garden sites and burn accumulated logging debris. The inevitable result of this would have been an invasion of grassland. In fact, no such fires had occurred, and, with the exception of a few sites where cattle projects had been attempted, there was no sign of any new grassland areas.

Rather disturbingly, however, it seemed that many of the logging standards established in earlier years had been abandoned. The logging coupes were much larger than before and tended to form long continuous swathes. No buffer strips were being left along streamsides and no particular care was being taken to keep logging debris out of the streams. In fact, some of the earlier streamside buffer strips had been revisited and logged. The overwhelming impression was that provincial authorities had ceased to police environmental safeguards and that Jant had abandoned its former standards. The effect of this can only be to slow even further any recovery process.

SOME CONCLUDING COMMENTS

Supposing the GTP plantations do not reach their targeted size and the project ultimately fails; what will have been the result? Not all the ecological or social consequences of the project have been identified, but certain matters are obvious. The project will have provided some modest financial gains to PNG in the form of wages and taxes and royalties, some infrastructure and a road network will have been established and employment and training will have been provided for a mainly rural population. At the same time, the forest resource will have been exhausted without generating the long-term industry necessary for permanent economic and social advancement. The dream of a development node for Madang will have evaporated. Instead, the GTP will have become just another statistic in the long list of promising forestry ventures in the third world that failed to contribute in any significant way to socio-economic development. A cynic might note that one of the chief beneficiaries of the project that will have received perhaps 15 years supply of woodchips, was a multinational company based in one of the world's richest countries. Such a cynic might also say that, in this respect, the GTP simply conformed to a well-established pattern.

But is this right? Was the GTP just another case of a rich country exploiting a poorer country? Or like other forestry projects elsewhere, did the scheme fail instead because of a lack of technical skills? Or was it because of an overdependence on a limited market? Or behind-the-scenes manipulation by a political elite? Or corruption? Or was failure caused by rural poverty and, hence, competition for land?

As should be clear from my account earlier in this book, most of these factors have had little or no role to play in the events in Gogol Valley. Rather the fundamental difficulty seems to have been that neither the landowners nor Honshu were willing to take the final step upon which the whole project depended. For different reasons, both seem to have decided the risks of proceeding were too high.

The source of these differences is that both parties perceived the forest in quite different ways. The landowners viewed the forest as a source of foods and materials as well as part of their cultural heritage. It helped sustain traditional values and allowed for economic self-sufficiency. By contrast, the forest for Honshu was simply a raw material, a commodity to be bought, processed and sold. The two views necessarily generated two approaches towards how the forests and lands should be used. By selling the rights to harvest their trees, the landowners showed they were willing to temporarily join Honshu in the market place. However, they also wished to remain on their lands once logging commenced and remain land managers as they had always been.

The National Government (and its colonial predecessor) was different again. It sought to form a bridge between the landowners and the two timber companies, but, of course, it had different priorities to both groups. It recognised the importance of the forests to the landowners but believed they should be utilized and sold in the international market place. By doing so, national objectives that it, the Government, had decided upon could be financed. It might once have been able to resolve the stalemate between the landowners and Jant but its power to do so was seriously weakened by the advent of provincial governments in PNG. This emasculated the national Department of Forests and created a number of small and separate forestry administrations in many of the 19 provincial governments. Unfortunately, the new forestry authority in Madang appeared to have neither the resources nor the competence for the task required of it.

Hence, the reason for the project developing the way it did, and for any failure that may finally occur, can be found within the forest, in the government bureaucracies and in the boardrooms of the international financial world. It involves a lack of understanding by villagers of the value placed on their trees by the international market place, as well as a lack of sympathy by government and industry over the villagers' concerns and aspirations. It also involves a lack of effective government action, perhaps even political will, at a critical moment in the project's life. A consequence of this is that, the more any explanation lies in this socio-economic and political context, the less direct and more unpredictable is the impact of any national forest policy likely to be. That is, the harder it is to formulate policies to avoid such outcomes in future.

Are there any lessons that can be learnt from the GTP? The first and most obvious lesson is that in any similar large timber project, whether involving clear-felling or selective logging, some way must be found to resolve or diminish these differences in perception and attitude between the various parties. It goes without saying that this is likely to be extremely difficult to do. Before the pulpwood TRP was done in the Gogol Valley, foresters and patrol officers did attempt to explain just what pulpwood logging would entail. In hindsight, their efforts were not enough. Furthermore, the landowners were unwilling or unable to see much beyond the village, let alone consider the national objectives of an Administration of whose existence or purpose they were only vaguely aware. In such situations, it is too easy for government planners to decide that they know what is best and to proceed accordingly. But this can only aggravate and perpetuate the differences in attitude and expectations between the various parties involved. Perhaps a committee or council representing landowners should have been formed at the time of the pulpwood purchase to act as a counterpart to the Administration's MTWG.

A second lesson follows from the first and concerns post-logging land use. If the success of a project depends on reforestation following the initial logging, then it must be clear from the day the first tree is felled just how reforestation is to be carried out, who will do it and on what land it shall be done? Again, the problem is more easily stated than solved, especially in areas with complex patterns of land ownership like the Gogol Valley. In the case of the GTP, the Department of Forests was led to believe that land would be available when required. Because of the political changes then underway throughout the country, it concerned itself more with the question of whether it or Jant should carry out the reforestation, but evidence of logging damage and dissatisfaction over royalty payments evidently caused people to change their minds over committing their land to further government schemes. This might not have been the case if reforestation had started immediately.

A third lesson is that the spread of economic benefits cannot be left to chance. In the case of the GTP, it was assumed that the economic gains would follow more or less automatically. But they didn't. While the GTP was not exactly an economic enclave, the desired multiplier effect was much smaller than originally hoped for. This is a matter of judgement, of course. By any standard, the Gogol people have adapted to remarkable changes over a comparatively short time, but the spread of economic benefits might have been improved by guaranteeing certain sub-contracting opportunities at particular stages as the project developed or more effort might have been made explaining economic opportunities to social leaders such as the 'Big Men' who, in other parts of PNG, have often become the economic entrepreneurs.

The final lesson from the GRP concerns the need to have environmental safeguards form an integral part of the overall management programme and not be simply added on once a project starts. In one sense, it is almost irrelevant whether or not a forest can recover after some long time period because the short-term damage can be severe, and it is the short-term that is of most concern to villagers. Hence, protection forests and other reserves should be identified before logging commences; if clear-felling is to be carried out, coupe limits and a dispersal mosaic should be defined; environmental controls such as streamside buffer strips should be unambiguous and logging and roading plans should be established well enough in advance such that a monitoring programme can be established to detect if environmental standards are being maintained or not. Given the uncertainties of fulfilling all post logging land-use plans, logging operations involving clear felling should be carried out in such a way as to help facilitate the recovery of natural ecological processes if these land use plans do not eventuate.

Are these 'lessons' confined to Papua New Guinea, or might they also apply elsewhere? Some might argue that PNG is too much of a special case and that its land laws in particular prevent any lessons being applied more widely. But evidence is mounting that the land – people relationship in PNG is also common elsewhere in the region among traditional landowners, irrespective of current national laws. So, for example, the largest timber company in the Solomon Islands was forced to cease its operations and withdraw from the country because of continuous disputes and sabotage by local landowners. This occurred despite the fact it had a legal permit from the central government which allowed it to carry out logging. At the time, the company accounted for 25 per cent of the national export income (Wright, 1987). In Sarawak, tribal people have complained to the government over damage caused to their traditional lands by logging. When the Government took no action, the people began blockading the roads (Sterba 1987, Borneo Bulletin 8 August 1987). In Thailand, villagers' protests forced an indefinite suspension of the removal of logs from one forest area (Sricharavatchanya 1987) and in Australia, action by Aborigines in Arnhem Land forced the government to close the whole of its forestry operations in the area (Haynes 1978). The legal situation and form of land ownership was different in each example but in each it was clear that, as in the GTP, people actually living on the land should have been much more involved in the planning and decision making than had been the case.

What, finally, is the consequence of the GTP for Papua New Guinea? Was it an appropriate way to attempt to manage these forests? In the absence of a developed plantation area to replace the original forest it appears not. If the plantations had been established, if environmental safeguards had been better, if economic benefits had gone further, then it may have been. But it now seems that PNG is back where it was 20 years earlier and the problem of how to manage its forests remains. Some form of natural forest silviculture seems the only alternative if it hopes to exploit its forests and, at the same time, conserve them in a productive state.

This will require that the earlier silvicultural research be re-examined and that detailed ecological knowledge of the more valuable species be acquired. It will also necessitate a new form of management being developed which accommodates both long-term silvicultural prescriptions and the aspirations of the villagers who live in the forest and own the land. The same efforts will also be required if areas of these forests are to be preserved, as they should be, in reserves or natural parks. At the present time, there is no certainty that such a management system can be developed. In which case, forest-rich Papua New Guinea may find itself in the paradoxical situation of having to build a forest based industry out of plantations developed wherever land can be acquired.

Note 1:   The claypot ground dispute of 1980 involving Wezip Alaloum appeared to have been forgotten by 1986. Despite the earlier compensation offers, the matter was never resolved and no compensation was ever paid.

Note 2:   In commenting on the slow rate of agricultural development, one disappointed

Forest Officer instanced the case where a small cocoa plot had been established as a trial under a *E. deglupta* plantation. Once it was clear the cocoa grew well, the owner of the land from whom the plantation area had been leased was offered the cocoa plot as an ongoing concern. Although he harvested it for several seasons, it was gradually allowed to degenerate and was finally abandoned.

Note 3: The coffee grown in the Gogol Valley is robusta coffee. In the highlands, the more valuable arabica coffee can be grown.

Note 4: In 1986, the land leasing arrangements were that land could be leased at an annual rental of K0.50 per ha with the first 5 years paid in advance. The landowner would also receive 2.5% royalty on the timber harvested from the plantation. Thus, the owners of 10 ha of land planted with *E. deglupta* could conservatively expect K50 from land rent plus K225 from the final harvest (based on a final harvest of 200 m^3 per ha priced at K4.50 per m^3 every 10 years).

Note 5: The 1985 auditor's report, for example, stated 'As mentioned .... the company has not obtained leases for areas of customary owned and Government leased land upon which reforestation expenditure has been incurred. The right to ultimately utilize these forested areas commercially, and thus the company's continuation as a going concern is dependent upon the ratification by the government of the company's title to the area of land and allocation of formal leases. Further, the capitalised value of K3 200 533 (1983-K2 668 669) is dependent upon the eventual commencement of commercial production at a level which will recover these costs'. Auditor's report for Gogol Reforestation Co., File Local C 3545, Registrar General's Office.

APPENDICES

---

1. Summary of events
2. Establishment of woodchip price
3. Seed dispersal modes
4. Guidelines for investment in forestry after 1975

APPENDIX 1

SUMMARY OF EVENTS

Year	PNG General	PNG Forests	Gogol Valley
1949	UN General Assembly approves administrative union of Papua and New Guinea.		
1951	Australia: P. Hasluck appointed Minister for Territories in Australian Parliament.		
1957		Hasluck's forest policy announced.	Land survey of an area including the Gogol Valley carried out by CSIRO.
1959			Forest Dept. reconnaisance survey
1962		Five Year Forestry Plan	Forestry Dept. timber survey
1963	Australia: C. Barnes appointed Minister for Territories in Australian Parliament.	Tenders invited for Tonelei TRP, Bougainville.	Sawlog TRP completed.
1964	World Bank submits report to Minister for Territories. First elected PNG House of Assembly		Tenders invited for sawlog resource in Gogol TRP.
1965			Small sawmill opens at Catholic Mission at Utu.
1966		Tenders invited for Kulu-Dagi TRP (New Britain).	Gogol TRP re-advertised.
1967	New Britain: Tolai people occupy alienated but unused land on Gazelle Peninsular; are evicted. First indigenous political party (Pangu Party) formed with policy of early self-government.		Road to centre of valley at Mawan completed.

Year	PNG General	PNG Forests	Gogol Valley
1968	Second House of Assembly elections. Colonial Administration announces first Five Year Plan	Tenders invited for Vanimo TRP (287000 ha).	Gogol TRP re-advertised. Honshu begin pulping feasibility trials. Cargo cultists active in House of Assembly election campaign.
1969	Bougainville: riots during compulsory land acquisition for copper mine townsite. Subsequently pro secession nationalist group formed. New Britain: unrest on Gazelle Peninsular, troops placed on alert. Mataungan Association confronts new Multi-racial Local Government Council.	Role of Indonesia as a major timber exporter and competitor becomes more evident.	Forestry Dept. begins reforestation trials at Baku. Wewak Timber begins small-scale logging. Negotiations between Administration, Honshu subsidiary and Wewak Timbers.
1970	Land Bills introduced to PNG House of Assembly but then withdrawn after opposition. New Britain: further unrest involving Mataungan Association and police. Bougainville: unofficial 'referendum' finds in favour of secession. Australia: Leader of Opposition in Parliament promises self-government for PNG when elected.	Tenders invited for Open Bay TRP (183 000 ha).	Pulpwood survey. Negotiations over Gogol Valley timber resources continue.
1971	Land Bills re-introduced to PNG House of Assembly but withdrawn again. Papua: secession threats by some Papuan House of Assembly members. New Britain: District Commissioner assassinated on Gazelle Peninsular.	Tenders invited for Sagarai-Gadaisu TRP (160 000 ha), and Kumusi TRP (64 000 ha).	Pulpwood TRP completed. Agreement on harvesting timber reached between Administration and Honshu subsidiary. Jant formed and takes up concession.

Year	PNG General	PNG Forests	Gogol Valley
1972	Third House of Assembly elections (March); Pangu Party wins office in a coalition with several other groups. Australia: change of government (December); Australian Labour Party gains office, promises early self-government for PNG. Bougainville: copper mine begins production. Government announces Eight Point Improvement Plan.		Madang Timber Working Group formed. Government's National Executive Council decides to allow landowners 25 per cent of timber royalty.
1973	Papua New Guinea achieves Self Government.	Tenders invited for Kapiura TRP (83 000 ha). Open Bay TRP area negotiations completed.	Jant begins road and chipmill construction; first logging commences (December). Genealogical survey completed.
1974		Tenders invited for Kapaluk TRP (181 000 ha). Negotiations over Ioma Timber Area (182 000 ha) cease when landowners refuse to sell timber rights.	Jant chipmill opens, first chip exports. Land-use plan (Scenario 3B) approved by Government. Preliminary reforestation study by Japan International Co-operation Agency. First royalty payments made. Dept. of Forests seeks foreign aid for pilot reforestation scheme.
1975	Papua: nationalist group Papua Besana proclaims independence for Papua (March). Bougainville: nationalist group Napidokoe Navita proclaims independence for Bougainville (August). Papua New Guinea gains full independence (September).	Dept. of Forests and National Investment and Development Authority issue Guidelines for Forestry Development Proposals.	

Year	PNG General	PNG Forests	Gogol Valley
1976			Reforestation feasibility study undertaken by Japan International Co-operation Agency. Yumi timbers formed but goes bankrupt. National and Provincial Government change method of allocating timber royalties – people to receive 50 per cent. Salvage logging begins.
1977	Laws establishing Provincial Governments passed.		Gogol Reforestation Company formed.
1978	Madang Provincial Government formed.	Environmental Planning Act passed. Regional forestry authorities split off from National Dept. of Forests.	Trans Gogol Local Government Council formed. Detailed survey of clan boundaries completed.
1979		New National Forest Policy announced.	
1980			Jant establishes a Village Relations Unit.

APPENDIX 2

ESTABLISHMENT OF WOODCHIP PRICE

The factors influencing the price of a new source of woodchip have been extensively reviewed by Higgins and Philips (1973c). The price of chips from a new project in $ per bone dry unit (BDU) is given by

$$Pn = Pe + \Delta P$$

$$= Pe + \Delta Pw + \Delta Pf + \Delta Py + \Delta Pq + \Delta Pc$$

where Pn and Pe are the fob prices of new and established resources respectively and ΔPw, ΔPf, ΔPy, ΔPq and ΔPc are the differences in $ per BDU in the value of chips from the new resource compared to the established resource due respectively to the factors, wood quality, freight costs, pulp yield, pulp quality, processing costs.

The quantity Pe is not constant but may be expressed as:

$$Pe = B + tE$$

where E is an escalation factor in $ per BDU per year and t is the number of years elapsing since the base price of B per BDU was fixed.

Thus

$$Pn = B + tE + \Delta Pw + \Delta Pf + \Delta Py + \Delta Pq + \Delta Pc$$

The significance of the various resource factions is as follows:

(a) Wood quality Pw.
     The most important differences between the new and existing resource can be expressed in terms of basic density, extractives and variability. Woodchips from the GTP were estimated to have a basic density of around 430 kg/m³ while an average Australian eucalypt hardwood woodchip basic density is generally higher at about 540 kg/m³ (though values higher and lower than these are common – Higgins and Philips

231

1973c). The most significant effects of the difference are in relation to pulp yield, freight, pulp quality and processing costs and are therefore included in the price differences arising from these factors. Variability was expected to be greater in the PNG chips due to the heterogeneous nature of the forests and changing species composition. Overall the PNG chips were thought to be lower in quality.

(b) Freight Pf.
This factor is a function of basic density and shipping distance. The lower the basic density, the lower the weight of chips that can be carried in a particular cargo hold. In this respect, therefore, the PNG chips were at a disadvantage compared with the eucalypt chips. On the other hand, shipping distance is a major factor. The more round trips a year a vessel can make, the greater the weight of chips carried and the lower the transport costs. In this respect the PNG chips had a major advantage over the Australian chips.

(c) Pulp yield Py.
Different pulp yields may be obtained from the same weight of wood of the two resources. The difference in the value of the wood can be shown to be

$$\Delta Py = (3U/280)\,(Yn{-}Ye)$$

where U is the market value of the pulp in $ per ton of oven dried pulp and Yn and Ye are the percentage yields of pulp from the new and established sources of wood. Average quality eucalypt chips have a pulp yield around 45.6 per cent while chips from the Gogol Valley have a pulp yield of 42.8 per cent. The PNG chips are therefore at a slight disadvantage.

(d) Pulp quality Pq.
The significance of this term depends on the use to which the pulp is put; the treatments to which the pulp is subjected and the facilities at the mill. Calculations can then be made of Pq on the basis of the cost of upgrading the inferior pulp to produce paper of comparable quality to that produced from the superior pulp. The range of products for which the pulp is suitable may also be relevant in assessing pulp quality.

(e) Processing costs Pc.
Different woods may require more chemicals than others to reach a given Kappa number (a measure of the amount of potassium permanganate required to oxidise lignin remaining in pulp) under specified pulping conditions. High chemical requirements reduce the value of the wood and are usually accompanied by lower pulp yields. These and other processing costs can only be determined at a particular mill in the light of prevailing conditions. It may be hard to determine

some of them accurately and to relate differences between pulps of different woods to a price differential per BDU. In any case, their contribution to the overall cost differences is likely to be low in comparison with differences in pulp yield and freight.

APPENDIX 3

SEED DISPERSAL MODES

A tentative classification of dispersal modes of seed of some of the main tree species from the Gogol Valley and nearby regions based on Womersley (1983).

A: wind
B: bird
C: bat and arboreal mammal
D: dormant as seed or seedlings or dispersed by terrestrial mammals or insects
X: unknown

1.	*Ackama*	A
2.	*Adenanthera pavonina*	D
3.	*Adinandra*	B
4.	*Aglaia*	B, C and D
5.	*Ailanthus*	A
6.	*Albizzia falcataria*	A and D
7.	*Alseodaphne*	B or C
8.	*Alstonia scholaris*	A
9.	*Alstonia* spp.	A
10.	*Althoffia*	A
11.	*Althoffia pleiostigma*	A
12.	*Anthocephalus chinensis*	A
13.	*Alphananmyxis*	B and C, possibly D
14.	*Archidendron*	B or possibly C
15.	*Artocarpus* spp.	? B,C
16.	*Baccaurea papuana*	D,C
17.	*Barringtonia* spp.	C, most float in water
18.	*Bischofia javanica*	D
19.	*Boerlagiodendron*	B or D
20.	*Buchanania*	D
21.	*Calophyllum* spp.	D or B, cassowary
22.	*Campnosperma brevipetiolata*	D, possibly water carried
23.	*Cananga*	B, C and D
24.	*Cananga odorata*	B or C
25.	*Canarium*	? B,D
26.	*Casearia*	D

27.	*Castanopsis acuminatissima*	C and D, possibly B, Cockatoo
28.	*Cedrela*	A
29.	*Celtis* spp.	B,C and D
30.	*Celtis* (hard)	B,C and D
31.	*Cerbera floribunda*	D, water carried
32.	*Chisocheton*	B and C, possibly D
33.	*Chrysophyllum*	C and D
34.	*Cinnamomum* spp.	possibly C,D
35.	*Cordia*	B or C, possibly D
36.	*Cryptocarya*	B, C, probably D
37.	*Dillenia* spp.	D, some water carried
38.	*Diopyros* spp.	B and C, possibly D
39.	*Dracontomelum*	B,C,D
40.	*Duabanga moluccana*	A
41.	*Dysoxylum*	B,C, and D
42.	*Elaeocarpus* spp.	B,C and D
43.	*Elmerrillia papuana*	D
44.	*Endospermum*	B,D
45.	*Erythrina*	D, water carried
46.	*Erythrospermum candidum*	X
47.	*Erythroxylon ecarinatum*	probably D
48.	*Eugenia*	B,C
49.	*Euodia*	D
50.	*Euroschinus papuanus*	B,C or D
51.	*Eurya*	B
52.	*Fagraea*	B,C
53.	*Ficus*	B,C and D
54.	*Firmiana papuana*	A (or B)
55.	*Flindersia* spp.	A
56.	*Galbulimima belgraveana*	B, C and D
57.	*Garcinia* spp.	B,C and D
58.	*Garuga*	B,D
59.	*Garuga floribunda*	B,C and D
60.	*Gigasiphon schlechteri*	D, possibly waterborne
61.	*Glochidion*	D
62.	*Gonocaryum*	possibly B and C,D
63.	*Gossampinus*	A
64.	*Gymnaeranthera*	B,C and D
65.	*Gyrocarpus*	A and D
66.	*Harpullia*	possibly C,D
67.	*Helicia*	D
68.	*Hernandia*	possibly B, ? water or wind
69.	*Homalium*	A,D
70.	*Homonoia javensis*	X
71.	*Horsfieldia*	B,C
72.	*Inocarpus fagiferus*	C,D water
73.	*Intsia palembanica*	D
74.	*Intsia bijuga*	D
75.	*Kingiodendron alternifolium*	D, possibly C
76.	*Kleinhovia hospita*	A, waterborne
77.	*Lagerstroemia*	A
78.	*Laportea*	D
79.	*Linociera*	B,C and D

236

80.	*Lithocarpus* spp.	B (cockatoo), D
81.	*Litsea*	B,C and D
82.	*Macaranga*	A and D
83.	*Mangifera*	D
84.	*Maniltoa*	C and D
85.	*Maranthes corymbosa*	D and water
86.	*Mastixiodendron*	? B and C, probably D
87.	*Mastixiodendron pachyclados*	B,C and D
88.	*Meliosma*	probably A
89.	*Microcos*	B,C and D
90.	*Myristica* spp.	B,C and D
91.	*Nauclea*	A, possibly B and C
92.	*Neonauclea*	A
93.	*Neoscortechinia*	X
94.	*Neuburgia*	B,C and D, ? waterborne
95.	*Octomeles sumatrana*	A
96.	*Opocunonia nymanii*	A
97.	*Palaquium* spp.	? B,C and D
98.	*Pangium edule*	D, also planted
99.	*Parartocarpus venenosus*	C,D
100.	*Parinari* (see also *Maranthes*)	D
101.	*Pimeleodendron amboinicum*	B,C, possibly D
102.	*Pisonia*	B (? exclusively)
103.	*Planchonella* spp.	B,C and D (some may be planted)
104.	*Planchonia papuana*	C,D waterborne
105.	*Platea*	X
106.	*Podocarpus* spp.	? B, ? C, D
107.	*Polyalthia* spp.	B,C, possibly D
108.	*Polyosma*	? A,B
109.	*Pometia pinnata*	? B,C and D
110.	*Pometia tormentosa*	? B,C,D
111.	*Prunus* spp.	B,C and D
112.	*Pterocarpus inducus*	A and D, possibly waterborne
113.	*Pterocumbium beccarii*	A and D
114.	*Pullea*	A
115.	*Quintinia*	A
116.	*Randia*	C,D and waterborne
117.	*Rhus taitensis*	B, possibly D
118.	*Saurauia*	B,D
119.	*Schizomeria*	B,C and D
120.	*Serianthes*	? C,D
121.	*Sloanea*	? B and C, D, possibly waterborne
122.	*Solenospermum torricellense*	A
123.	*Spondias cytherea*	B (cassowary) C and D waterborne
124.	*Steganthera*	B, ? C and D
125.	*Sterculia* spp.	B,C and D
126.	*Syzygium*	B,C and D, some waterborne
127.	*Terminalia* – succulent and semi-succulent fruit types	D
128.	*Terminalia* – wing fruited types e.g. *T. brassii* and *T. calamansanai*	A
129.	*Tetrameles nudiflora*	A
130.	*Teysmanniodendron bogoriense*	B,C and D

131.	*Thespesia*	D, some waterborne
132.	*Timonius*	B,C
133.	*Trichadenia*	probably A
134.	*Tristiropsis* spp.	D, maybe waterborne
135.	*Turpinia*	X
136.	*Urandra umbellata*	B or C
137.	*Vatica papuana*	D, waterborne
138.	*Vitex cofassus*	B,C and D
139.	*Weinmannia*	A
140.	*Wrightia*	A
141.	*Xanthophyllum papuanum*	B,C or D
142.	*Xylopia*	B,C or D

APPENDIX 4

GUIDELINES FOR INVESTMENT IN FORESTRY
AFTER 1975

In 1975, following the commencement of the Gogol Timber Project the Department of Forests and the National Investment and Development Authority developed a set of guidelines for prospective investors in Papua New Guinea's timber industry showing the sort of information required in all new investment proposals. This was summarized as follows:

1. PROJECT TITLE

2. COMPANY SUBMITTING PROPOSAL
    a. Name
    b. Origin (country of incorporation)
    c. Current major business concerns
    d. Paid-up capital

3. PROJECT LOCATION
    a. Industrial site
    b. Town site
    c. Wharf and port site

4. FOREST RESOURCES TO BE UTILIZED
    a. Location
    b. Total area
    c. Estimated total merchantable log volume in resource area
        i.   Pulpwood
        ii. Saw/Veneer log

5. PROJECT FINANCING
    a. Companies or persons contributing equity.
        For each major shareholding company –
        i.   Name
        ii.   Origin
        iii. Percentage of total equity

    b.   Institutions providing loan finance.
        For each institution –
        i.   Name
        ii. Origin
        iii. Total funds provided
        iv. (Average) interest rate
        v.   Percentage of total borrowed funds
    c.   i.   Total equity
        ii. Total loans
    d.   Gearing ratio (Loan:Equity)

6.   **MARKETING AND SHIPPING**
    a.   For each major product list
        i.   Product
        ii. Major countries of destination
        iii. Volume of sales at full production
        iv. Value of sales at full production
        v.   Average price (c.i.f.)
            Average price (f.o.b.)
    b.   Total value of sales at full production (f.o.b.)

7.   **LOGGING AND ROAD CONSTRUCTION**
    a.   Investment in logging and roading equipment (excluding replacements) (over 10 years)
    b.   Annual log harvest at full production
        i.   Saw/Veneer logs
        ii. Pulpwood
    c.   Employment in logging and roading at full production
        i.   Foreign
        ii. Papua New Guinean
    d.   Estimated average mill door log cost at full production

8.   **PROCESSING FACILITIES**
    For each processing facility (sawmill, veneermill, plywood mill, particle board factory, chipmill, pulpmill, etc.) indicate:
    a.   Production facility
    b.   Capital investment
    c.   Annual capacity (log intake)
    d.   1 shift, 2 shifts or 3 shifts basis?
    e.   Employment at full production
        i.   Foreign
        ii. Papua New Guinean
    f.   Estimated average costs of conversion
        i.   Per cubic metre of log intake
        ii. Per cubic metre (or tonne) output
    g.   Estimated recovery rate

9.   INFRASTRUCTURE
     Indicate estimated capital investment for each major item of
     infrastructure, e.g.:
     a.   Roads
          i.   Main roads (investment over 10 years and kilometres to
                be constructed)
          ii.   Other (over 10 years)
     b.   Industrial infrastructure
          i.   Administrative facilities
          ii.   Wharf and harbour facilities
          iii. Power supply (showing kilowatts)
          iv.   Telecommunications
          v.   Airstrip
          vi.   Industrial water supply
          vii. Fuel storage
          viii. Fire station
          ix.   Other (specify)
          x.   Sub-total
     c.   Community and social facilities
          i.   Housing, showing number housed for families and single
                men
          ii.   Town development (subdivision, roading, sewerage, etc.)
          iii. Education facilities
          iv.   Law enforcement facilities
          v.   Medical facilities
          v.   Recreation facilities
          vii. Shopping facilities
          viii. Government administration offices
          ix.   Other (specify)
          x.   Sub-total

10. REFORESTATION
     a.   Total area planned for reforestation
     b.   Employment at full planting –
               Papua New Guinean
               Foreign
     c.   Estimated total expenditure on reforestation prior to first
          harvest

11. EMPLOYMENT, TRAINING AND LOCALIZATION
     a.   Employment for Year 1, Year 5, Year 10 and Year 15,
          showing Papua New Guinean, foreign and Totals
     b.   Training staff to be employed by company
     c.   Cadetships and sponsorships offered

12. **PARTICIPATION BY PAPUA NEW GUINEA BUSINESS GROUPS**
Provide a brief summary of measures to encourage and assist participation by Papua New Guineans into businesses connected with the enterprise, e.g. personnel to be employed by company, finance to be provided, type of business enterprise that will be assisted.

13. **ESTIMATED MAJOR FINANCIAL BENEFIT TO PAPUA NEW GUINEA GOVERNMENT**
    a. Log royalties
       i. Pulpwood royalty rate
       ii. Saw/veneer log royalty rate
    b. Discounted present value of major financial benefits:
       Discounted at 10% per year
       Over 10 years.   Over 20 years
       Pulpwood royalties
       Saw/Veneer log royalties
       Company taxes
       Dividend withholding taxes
       Import duties and Tariffs
       Other (specify)
       Wages and salaries to Papua New Guineans
    c. Estimated net contribution to balance of payment at first full production year

14. **ENVIRONMENT MANAGEMENT AND POLLUTION CONTROL**
A brief summary of the impact of the development on the environment should be provided and the main preventive measures stated.

15. **ASSOCIATED NON-FORESTRY PROJECTS**
Make brief comment on any non-forestry projects (agricultural, industrial) that may or will be associated with or flow on from this project, and in which the company will be involved.

REFERENCES

Anonymous (1969a) Gogol area to be market tested. *Australian Timber Journal*, **35**(5), 100.

Anonymous (1969b) *Japan Economic Yearbook*. The Oriental Economist, Tokyo.

Anonymous (1979/80) Pulp and Paper, p. 83. In *Japan Economic Yearbook*. The Oriental Economist, Tokyo.

Anonymous (1981/82) Pulp and Paper, p. 68. In *Japan Economic Yearbook*. The Oriental Economist, Tokyo.

Alaloum, W. (1982) Problems with Jant clear-felling in Madang, In Morauto, L., Pernetta, J. and Heaney, W. (eds) *Traditional Conservation in Papua New Guinea: Implications for Today*. Monograph 16, pp. 217–220. Institute of Applied Social and Economic Research, Port Moresby.

Anderson, J.A.R. (1964) Observations on climatic damage in peat swamp forests in Sarawak. *Commonwealth Forestry Review*, **43**, 145–58

Arnold, M. (1979) New approaches to tropical forestry: a habitat for more than just trees. *Ceres*, **12**(5), 32–7

Aubertin, G.M. and Patric, J.H. (1974) Water quality after clear cutting a small watershed in West Virginia. *Journal of Environmental Quality*, **3**, 243–9

Aweto, A.O. (1981) Secondary succession and soil fertility restoration in south-western Nigeria. *Journal of Ecology*, **69**, 609–14

Barnet, R.J. and Müller, R.E. (1974) *Global Reach: The Power of the Multinational Corporations*. (Simon and Schuster: New York)

Bartholomew, W.V., Meyer, J. and Laudelot, H. (1953) *Mineral nutrient immobilization under forest and grass fallow in the Yangambi (Belgian Congo) region*. Publications de L'Institut National pour L'etude agronomique du Congo Belge, Serie Scientifique **57**.

Bayne, P. (1981) Legal policy making, In Ballard, J.A. (ed.) *Policy making in a New State: Papua New Guinea 1972–77*. pp. 132–156. (University of Queensland Press)

Beanlands, G. and Duinker, P. (1983) *An ecological framework for environmental impact assessment in Canada*. Institute for Resource and Environmental Studies, Dalhousie University and Federal Environmental Assessment Review Office, Canada.

Bleeker, P. (1983) *Soils of Papua New Guinea*. (Australian National University Press: Canberra)

Blong, R. (1982) *The Time of Darkness – Local Legends and Volcanic Reality in Papua New Guinea*. (Australian National University Press: Canberra)

Brown, M. and Powell, J.M. (1974) Frost and drought in the highlands of Papua New Guinea. *Journal of Tropical Geography*, **38**, 1–6

Bruenig, E.F. (1983) Vegetation structure and growth, In Golley, F.B. (ed.) *Tropical Rain Forest Ecosystem: Structure and Function. Ecosystem of the World*, 14A. p. 49–75. (Elsevier Scientific Publishing Co.: Amsterdam).

Bruenig, E.F. (1985) Deforestation and its ecological implications for the rain forests in South East Asia. *The Environmentalist*, **5** (10), 17–26

Budowski, G. (1982) The socio-economic effects of forest management on the lives of people living in the area. The case of Central America and some Caribbean countries, In Hallsworth, E.G. (ed.) *Socio-Economic Effects and Constraints in Tropical Forest Management*. pp. 87–102. (J. Wiley and Sons: New York)

Bulmer, R.N.H. (1982) Traditional conservation practices in Papua New Guinea, In Morauta, L., Pernetta, J. and Heaney, W. (eds) *Traditional Conservation in Papua New Guinea*:

Implications for Today. Monograph 16, pp. 59–78. Institute of Applied Social and Economic Research, Port Moresby.

Bureau of Water Resources (1973) Unpublished records.

Burton-Bradley, B.G. (1973) The psychological dimension, In Sack, P.G. (ed.) *Problem of Choice, Land in Papua New Guinea's Future.* pp. 32–39. (Australian National University Press: Canberra)

Carrier, J. (1982) Conservation and conceptions of the environment: a Manus case study, In Morauta, L., Pernetta, J. and Heaney, W. (eds) *Traditional Conservation in Papua New Guinea: Implications for Today.* pp. 39–44. Monograph 16, Institute of Applied Social and Economic Research, Port Moresby.

Carton de Colombia (1985) *Forest research in the Bajo Calima Concession.* Ninth Annual Report, Cali, Colombia.

Carson, G.L. (1974) *Forestry and forest policy in Papua New Guinea.* Consultant's report to the Papua New Guinea Government's Department of Forests from the Commonwealth Fund for Technical Aid, Department of Forests, Port Moresby.

Caulfield, C. (1985) *In the Rainforest.* (A. Knopf: New York)

Cavanaugh, L.G. (1976) The Gogol wood chip project, In *Ecological Effects of Increasing Human Activities on Tropical and Subtropical Forest Ecosystems.* Australian Unesco Committee for Man and the Biosphere, Publication No. 3, pp. 175–184. (Australian Government Publishing Service: Canberra)

Chapman, M.D. (1985) Environmental influences on the development of traditional conservation in the South Pacific region. *Environmental Conservation,* **12,** 217–30

Cheke, A.S., Nanakorn, W. and Yankoses, C. (1979) Dormancy and dispersal of secondary forest species under the canopy of a primary tropical rainforest in northern Thailand. *Biotropica,* **11,** 88–95

Chudnoff, M. (1976) Density of tropical timbers as influenced by climatic life zones. *Commonwealth Forestry Review,* **55,** 203–17

Clarke, W.L. and Street, J.M. (1967) Soil fertility and cultivation practices in New Guinea. *Journal of Tropical Geography,* **24,** 7–11

Colton, P. (1976) Some social implication of the Madang Timber Project, In *Ecological effects of increasing human activities on tropical and subtropical forest ecosystems.* Aust. Unesco Committee for Man and the Biosphere, Publication No. 3, pp. 192–194. (Australian Government Publishing Service: Canberra)

Cook, R.J.S., McKee, C.O., Dent, V.J., Wallace, D.A. (1976). Striking sequence of volcanic eruptions in the Bismark volcanic arc, Papua New Guinea in 1972–75, In Johnson, R.W. (ed.) *Volcanism in Australasia.* pp. 149–172. (Elsevier Scientific Publishing Co.: Amsterdam)

Cunningham, R.K. (1963) The effect of clearing a tropical forest soil. *Journal of Soil Science,* **14**; 334–45

Davidson, J. (1983) Forestry in Papua New Guinea: a case study of the Gogol woodchip project near Madang, In Hamilton, L.S. (ed.) *Forest and Watershed Development and Conservation in Asia and the Pacific* pp. 19–138. (Westview Press: Colorado)

De'Ath, C. (1978a). *Pots, power and progress in the Trans-Gogol of Papua New Guinea.* The Second International Symposium on the Art of Oceania Victoria, University of Wellington, Wellington, New Zealand.

De'Ath, C. (1978b) The story of the great Masalai (spirit) Fipi. Mimeograph notes, 2 pages (unpublished).

De'Ath, C. (1980) *The Throwaway People: Social impact of the Gogol timber project, Madang Province.* Monograph 13, Institute of Applied Social and Economic Research, Papua New Guinea.

Denoon, D. (1985) Capitalism in Papua New Guinea. *Journal of Pacific History* **20,** 119–34

Department of External Territories (1971) Trade and Investment in Papua New Guinea. Australian Government Publishing Service, Canberra.

Department of Forests (1970–71) Annual Report. Port Moresby, Papua New Guinea.

Department of Forests (1971–72) Annual Report. Port Moresby, Papua New Guinea.

Department of Forests (1972–73) Annual Report. Port Moresby, Papua New Guinea.

Department of Madang Province (1980a) Madang Provincial Forests Policy. Division of Forests, Madang, Papua New Guinea.

Department of Madang Province (1980b) Report on Division of Forests activities (mimeographed). Division of Forests, Madang, Papua New Guinea.

Diamond, J.M. (1975) The island dilemma: lessons of modern biogeographic studies for the design of nature reserves. *Biological Conservation*, **7**, 129–46

Diamond, J., Raga, M., Wiakabu, J., Maru, T. and Feni, S. (undated) *Fruit consumption and seed dispersal by New Guinea birds.* Typescript, Department of Forests, Papua New Guinea.

Dittus, W.P.J. (1985) The influence of cyclones on the dry evergreen forest of Sri Lanka. *Biotropica*, **17**, 1–14

Downs, I. (1980) *The Australian Trusteeship Papua New Guinea 1945–1975.* (Australian Government Publishing Service: Canberra)

Driscoll, P.V. (1984) *The effects of logging on bird populations in lowland New Guinea rainforest.* Ph.D. Thesis, University of Queensland.

Driscoll, P. (undated) *The sale of timber rights in the Gogol Valley and the outcome for local people.* Unpublished Manuscript, Zoology Department, University of Queensland, Australia.

Dun, D. and Fenton, R.T. (1974) *Some aspects of reforestation in Papua New Guinea.* Project report, FO:PAP/73/007-W/F 1490. Food and Agriculture Organization of the United Nations, Rome.

Dwyer, P.D. (1982) Wildlife conservation and tradition in the highlands of Papua New Guinea, pp. 173–190. In: Morauta, L., Pernetta, J. and Heaney, W. (eds) *Traditional Conservation in Papua New Guinea: Implications for Today.* Monograph 16, Institute of Applied Social and Economic Research, Port Moresby.

Earhart, H.G. (1984) Monitoring total suspended solids by using nephelometry. *Journal of Environmental Management*, **8**, 81–6

Edwards, P.J. and Grubb, P.J. (1977). Studies of mineral cycling in a montane rain forest in New Guinea. I. The distribution of organic matter in the vegetation and soil. *Journal of Ecology*, **65**, 943–69

Endacott, N.D. (1971) Implications of the woodchip industry as it affects the New Guinea scene. *Australian Timber Journal*, **37** (May), 54–61

Ewel, J., Berish, C., Brown, B., Price, N. and Raich, J. (1981) Slash and burn impacts on a Costa Rican wet forest site. *Ecology*, **62**, 816–29

Ewel, J. and Conde, L.F. (1980) *Potential ecological impact of increased intensity of tropical forest utilization.* Biotrop Special Publication No. 11, SEAMEO Regional Center for Tropical Biology, Bogor.

FAO/UNEP (1981) *Tropical Forest Resources Assessment Project: Forest resources of tropical Asia.* FAO, Rome.

FEER (1985) Forest products, In *Asia 1985 Yearbook* pp. 72–73. Far Eastern Economic Review, Hong Kong.

Finney, B.R. (1968). Bigfellow man belong business in New Guinea. *Ethnology*, **7**(4), 394–410

Finney, B.R. (1973). *Big Men and Business.* (Australian National University Press: Canberra)

Fleming, T.H. (1979) Do tropical frugwores compete for food? *American Zoologist*, **19**, 1157–72

Fleming, T.H. (1981) Fecundity, fruiting pattern and seed dispersal in *Piper amalago* (Piperaceae) a bat dispersed tropical shrub. *Oecologia*, **51**, 42–6

Fraser, A.I. (1981) *Issues in Papua New Guinea forest policy.* Institute of National Affairs Discussion Paper No. 7, Port Moresby.

Frisk, T. (1978) Harvesting mixed tropical timber for pulp. *Unasylva*, **39**(122), 14–24

Frith, H.J. (1976) The wildlife, In Monroe, R. and Stevens, N.C. (eds) *The Border Ranges: A Land Use Conflict in Regional Perspective.* pp. 13–20. (Royal Society of Queensland: Brisbane)

Frith, H.J., Crome, F.H. and Wolfe, T. (1976) Food of fruit pigeons in New Guinea. *The Emu*, **76**, 49–58

Gaigo, B. (1977) Present day fishing practices in Tatana Village, In Winslow, J.H. (ed.) *The Melanesian Environment.* pp. 176–181. (Australian National University Press: Canberra)

Gardner, M.J. (1978). *The use of small sawmills in Papua New Guinea – history and description.* Eighth World Forestry Congress, Jakarta. October 1978.

Gardner, M.J. (1980) Assistant Director, Department of Forests. Personal communication, Port Moresby.

Gilbert, L.E. (1980) Food web organization and the conservation of neotropical diversity, In Soule, M. and Wilcox, B. (eds) *Conservation Biology* pp. 11–13. (Sinauer Associates,

Sunderland: Massachusetts)

Gilmour, D. (1977) *Effect of rainfall, logging and clearing on water yield and quality in a high rainfall zone of north east Queensland.* Hydrology Symposium, 28–30 June 1977, Institution of Engineers of Australia, Brisbane.

Golley, F.B. McGinnis, J., Clements, R., Child, G. and Duever, M. (1975) *Mineral Cycling in a Tropical Moist Forest Ecosystem* (University of Georgia Press: Athens)

Golson, J. (1977) The making of the New Guinea highlands, In Winslow, J.H. (ed.) *The Melanesian Environment.* pp. 45–56. (Australian National University Press: Canberra)

Goodman, R., Lepani, C. and Morawetz, D. (1985) *The economy of Papua New Guinea: an Independent Review.* Development Studies Centre, Australian National University, Canberra.

Grubb, P.J. and Edwards, P.J. (1982) Studies of mineral cycling in a montane rain forest in New Guinea. III. The distribution of mineral elements in the above-ground material. *Journal of Ecology,* **70**, 623–48

Guevara, S. and Gomez-Pompa, A. (1972) Seed from surface soils in a tropical region of Veracruz, Mexico. *Journal of Arnold Arboretum, Harvard University,* **53**, 312–29

Habir, Manggi (1984) *Waterlogged timber* Far Eastern Economic Review, 6 Sept. pp. 112–113

Hall, L. (1986) Anatomy Department, University of Queensland, personal communication.

Harcombe, P.A. (1977a) Nutrient accumulation by vegetation during the first year of recovery of a tropical forest ecosytem, In Cairns, J., Dickson, K. and Herricks, E. (eds) *Recovery and Restoration of Damaged Ecosystems.* pp. 347–378. (University Press of Virginia: Charlottesville)

Harcombe, P.A. (1977b) The influence of fertilization on some aspects of succession in a humid tropical forest. *Ecology,* **58**, 1375–83

Harding, T.G. (1972) Land tenure, In Ryan, P. (ed.) *Encyclopaedia of Papua New Guinea.* pp. 604–610. (Melbourne University Press: Melbourne)

Harding, T.G. and Lawrence, P. (1971) Cash crops or cargo, In Epstein, A.L., Parker, R.S. and Reay, M. (eds) *The Politics of Independence.* pp. 162–217. (Australian National University Press: Canberra)

Harrison, J.L. (1969) The abundance and population density of mammals in Malayan lowland forests. *Malayan Nature Journal,* **22**, 174–8

Hasluck, P. (1976) *A Time for Building: Australian Administration in Papua New Guinea 1951–1963.* (Melbourne University Press: Melbourne)

Hatch, T. and Tie, Y.L. (1979) *Shifting cultivation in Sarawak and its effect on soil fertility.* Seminar on the Fertility and Management of Deforested Land, Kota Kinabalu, Sabah, 17–20 May 1979.

Haynes, C. (1978) Land, trees and man (Gunret, Gundulk, Dja Bining). *Commonwealth Forestry Review,* **57**, 99–106

Heithaus, E.R. (1982) Coevolution between bats and plant, In Kunz, T. (ed.) *Ecology of Bats.* pp. 327–362. (Plenum Press: New York)

Higgins, H.G. and Phillips, F.H. (1973) Technical and economic factors in the exports of woodchips from Australia and Papua New Guinea, Pt III. *Australian Forest Industry Journal,* **39**(3), 33–40

Hirogami, S. (1981) Four leading paper pulp makers eye close tie up. *The Japan Economic Journal* Vol. 19 No. 974, September 29, p. 1.

Holling, C.S. (1978) *Adaptive Environmental Assessment and Management.* (John Wiley and Sons: New York)

Holt, R.F., Timmons, D.R. and Latterall, J.J. (1970) Accumulation of phosphorus in water. *Journal of Agriculture and Food Chemistry,* **18**, 781–4

Hopkins, M. (1975). *Species patterns and diversity in the subtropical rain forest.* Ph.D. Thesis, University of Queensland.

Hopkins, M.S. and Graham, A. (1983) The species composition of soil seed banks beneath lowland tropical rain forests in North Queensland, Australia. *Biotropica,* **15**, 90–9

Horne, R. and Gwalter, J. (1982) The recovery of rain forest overstorey following logging. I. Subtropical rain forest. *Australian Forest Research,* **13**, 29–44

Howe, H. and Smallwood, J. (1982) Ecology of seed dispersal. *Annual Review of Ecology and Systematics,* **13**, 201–28

Humphreys, N. (1977) Logging coupe size reduced at Eden. *Australian Forest Industry Journal,* **43**(8), 39–45

International Bank for Reconstruction and Development (1965) *The Economic Development of the Territory of Papua New Guinea.* (John Hopkins Press: Baltimore)

Jaiyebo, E.O. and Moore, A.W. (1964) Soil fertility and nutrient storage in different soil-vegetation systems in a tropical rain forest environment. *Tropical Agriculture, Trinidad*, **41**, 129–39

James, R. (1981) The Pacific Economic Community at work: Japanese paper companies come to Papua New Guinea. *AMPO: Japan-Asia Quarterly Review*, **13**(4), 64–72

Janzen, D. (1983) No park is an island; increase in interference from outside as park size decreases. *Oikos*, **41**, 402–10

Johns, R.J. (1976) Natural regeneration following chip logging in the lowland tropical rain forest: a case study from the Gogol River Valley. Paper presented at Third Meeting, Botany Society of Papua New Guinea, Lae, May 1976.

Johns, R. (1986) The instability of the tropical ecosystem in New Guinea. *Blumea*, **31**, 341–71

Johnson, L.W. (1983) *Colonial Sunset: Australia and Papua New Guinea, 1970–74.* (University of Queensland Press: Brisbane)

Jonas, W. (1976) The forest ecosystem and the development process in less developed countries, In *Ecological Effects of Increasing Human Activities on Tropical and Subtropical Forest Ecosystems.* Australian Unesco Committee for Man and the Biosphere, Publication No. 3. pp. 159–171. (Australian Government Publishing Service: Canberra)

Jones, E.W. (1956) Ecological studies on the rain forest of southern Nigeria. IV. The plateau forest of the Okamu Forest Reserve. *Journal of Ecology*, **44**, 83–117

Jordan, C.F. (1980) Nutrient leaching from agro-ecosystems in the Amazon basin, and implications for the recovery of the forest, In Furtado, J.I. (ed.) *Tropical Ecology and Development.* pp. 553–559. Proceedings of Vth International Symposium of Tropical Ecology, Kuala Lumpur 1979.

Jordan, C. and Kline, J. (1972) Mineral cycling: some basic concept and their application in a tropical rain forest. *Annual Review of Ecology and Systematics*, **3**, 33–50

Kartawinata, K., Riswan, S. and Soedjito, H. (1980) The floristic change after disturbances in lowland Dipterocarp forest in East Kalimantan, Indonesia, In Furtado, J. (ed.) *Tropical Ecology and Development.* pp. 47–54. Proceedings of the Vth International Symposium of Tropical Ecology, Kuala Lumpur, 1979.

Kellman, M.C. (1969) Some environmental components of shifting cultivation in upland Mindanao. *Journal of Tropical Geography*, **28**, 40–56

King, G. and Chapman, W. (1983) Floristic composition and structure of a rain forest area 25 years after logging. *Australian Journal of Ecology*, **8**, 415–23

King, K.F.S. (1975) Its time to make paper in the tropics. *Unasylva*, **27**(109), 2–5

Knight, D.H. (1975) A phytosociological analysis of species-rich tropical rain forest on Barro Colorado Island, Panama. *Ecological Monographs*, **45**, 259–84

Kochummen, K. (1966) Natural plant succession after farming in Sg. Kroh. *Malayan Forester*, **29**, 170–81

Kochummen, K. and Ng, F.S.P. (1977) Natural plant succession after farming at Kepong. *Malayan Forester*, **40**, 61–78

Komaki, T. (1978) Increase in low-priced imports exacerbate makers falling profitability. *Industrial Review of Japan* pp. 116–117.

Kunz, T.H. (1982) Roosting ecology, In Kunz, T.H. (ed.) *Ecology of Bats.* pp. 1–55. (Plenum Press: New York)

Ladrach, W. and Mazuera, H. (1985) Source and characteristics of the natural regeneration in a humid tropical rain forest after clear cutting, In *Carton de Colombia, Forest Research in the Bajo Calima Concession*, Ninth Annual Report, pp. 117–143. (Cali: Colombia)

Lamb, D. (1976a) *Reforestation following chipwood logging: a review of silvicultural research at the Gogol Valley.* Tropical Forestry Research Note No. 34, Office of Forests, Papua New Guinea.

Lamb, D. (1976b) *Changes in nutrient availability following clearing of tropical rain forest.* Tropical Forest Research Note 30, Office of Forests, Papua New Guinea.

Lamb, D. (1977a) Conservation and management of tropical rain forest: a dilemma of development in Papua New Guinea. *Environmental Conservation*, **4**, 121–9

Lamb, D. (1977b) Relationships between growth and foliar nutrient concentrations in

Eucalyptus deglupta. Plant and Soil, **47**, 495–508

Lamb, D. and Beibi, F. (1977) *The effect of logging on stream turbidity levels in the rain forests of the Gogol Valley.* Tropical Forest Research Note 36, Office of Forests, Papua New Guinea.

Lane-Pool, C.E. (1925) *The forest resources of the Territories of Papua and New Guinea.* Report to Parliament of the Commonwealth of Australia.

Lawrence, P. (1964) *Road Belong Cargo.* (Melbourne University Press: Melbourne).

Lawrence, P. (1970) The widening political arena in the Southern Madang District, In Ward, M.W. (ed.) *The Politics of Melanesia.* Fourth Waigani Seminar, pp. 85–99. Research School of Pacific Science, Australian National University and University of Papua New Guinea.

Lawrence, P. (1982) Madang and beyond, In May, R.J. and Nelson, H. (eds) *Melanesia: Beyond Diversity.* Research School of Pacific Studies, pp. 57–72. Australian National University.

Lea, D.A.M. (1976) Human sustenance and the tropical forest, In *Ecological Effects of Increasing Human Activities on Tropical and Subtropical Forest Ecosystems.* Australian Unesco Committee for Man and the Biosphere. pp. 83–102. (Australian Government Publishing Service: Canberra)

Leet, N. (1976) Survey work in the Madang Timber Project, In *Ecological Effects of Increasing Human Activities on Tropical and Subtropical Forest Ecosystems.* Australian Unesco Committee for Man and the Biosphere, Publication No. 3, pp. 204–205. (Australian Government Publishing Service: Canberra)

Lembke, C.A. (1974) New era for PNG Forest Industries. *Australian Forest Industries Journal,* **33**(7), 6–31

Leslie, L. (1977) Where contradictory theory and practice co-exist. *Unasylva,* **28**(115), 2–17

Leslie, A. and Kyrkland, B. (1980) Small scale mills for developing countries. *Unasylva,* **32**(128), 13–15

Leslie, S. (1980). Public relations manager, Jant Pty. Ltd., personal communication, 12 December 1980.

Lewis, W.M. and Grant, M.C. (1979) Relationships between stream discharge and yield of dissolved substances from a Colorado mountain watershed. *Soil Science,* **128**, 353–63

Liem, D.S. (1978a) *Results of Wildlife Division faunal surveys in the Gogol timber area, Madang Province,* Papua New Guinea. Paper presented at Man and Biosphere Workshop, Madang, 17–20 March 1978.

Liem, D.S. (1978b) *Ethno-zoological survey of the Gogol timber area, Madang Province, Papua New Guinea.* Paper presented at Man and Biosphere Workshop, Madang, 17–20 March 1978.

Liem, D.S. (1978c) Wildlife Officer, Department of Lands and Environment, Personal communication, Port Moresby.

Liew, T.C. (1973) Occurrence of seed in virgin topsoil with particular reference to secondary species in Sabah. *Malayan Forester,* **36**, 185–93

Likens, G., Borman, F.H., Johnson, N. (1969) Nitrification: importance to nutrient losses from a cutover forested ecosystem. *Science,* **163**, 1205–6

Likens, G., Borman, F.H., Johnson, N., Fisher, D., Pierce, R. (1970) Effects of forest cutting and herbicide treatment on nutrient budgets in the Hubbard Brook watershed-ecosystem. *Ecological Monographs,* **40**, 23–47

Loffler, E. (1977) *Geomorphology of Papua New Guinea.* (Australian National University Press: Canberra)

Lovejoy, T.E. (1975) Bird diversity and abundance in Amazon forest communities. *Living Bird,* **13**, 127–91

Lovejoy, T.E. (1982) Designing refugia for tomorrow, In Prance, G. (ed.), *Biological Diversity in the Tropics.* pp. 673–680 (Columbia University Press)

Lugo, A., Applefield, M., Pool, D.J. and McDonald, R. (1983) The impact of hurricane David in the forests of Dominica. *Canadian Journal of Forest Research,* **13**, 201–11

McAlpine, J.R., Keig, G. and Short, K. (1975) *Climatic Tables for Papua New Guinea.* Division of Land Use Research Technical Paper No. 37, Commonwealth Scientific and Industrial Research Organisation, Australia.

McClure, H.E. and Hussein bin Othman (1965) Avian bionomics of Malaya. 2. The effect of forest destruction in a local population. *Bird Banding,* **36**, 242–69

248

McColl, J. (1978) Ionic composition of forest soil solutions and effects of clear cutting. *Soil Science Society of America Journal*, **42**, 358–63

McDonnell, M. and Stiles, E.W. (1983) The structural complexity of old field vegetation and the recruitment of bird dispersed plant species. *Oecologia*, **56**, 109–16

McIntosh, D.H. (1974) Progress Report 1966–72 by the Department of Forests of Papua New Guinea. Prepared for the Tenth Commonwealth Forestry Conference 1974.

McSwain, R. (1977) *The Past and Future People: Tradition and Change on a New Guinea Island.* (Oxford University Press: Melbourne)

Marshall, A.G. (1985) Old world phytophagous bats (*Megachiroptera*) and their food plants: a survey. *Zoology Journal of the Linnean Society*, **83**, 351–69.

Mazuera, H. (1985) Composition and growth of four to fifteen year old natural regeneration in the Bajo Calima concession, In *Carton de Colombia, Forest Research in the Bajo Calima Concession*, Ninth Annual Report, pp. 145–165. (Cali: Colombia)

Meijer, W. (1970) Regeneration of tropical lowland forest at Sabah, Malaysia forty years after logging. *Malayan Forester*, **33**, 204–29

Ministry of Forests (1979) Revised National Forest Policy: White Paper. Government of Papua New Guinea, Port Moresby, 60 pp.

Morauta, L. (1973) Traditional policy in Madang. *Oceania*, XLIV; 127–55

Morauta, L. (1974) *Beyond the Village. Local Politics in Madang, Papua New Guinea.* (Athlone Press: London)

Morris, P. (1978) Small mammals in the forests of the Gogol Valley, In *Background Papers*, Gogol Valley Project, Man and Biosphere Workshop, Madang, 17–20 March 1978. pp. 27–33.

Myers, N. (1983) *A Wealth of Wild Species.* Westview Press, Boulder, Colorado.

Nagle, G.S. (1976) *Adviser on forest environment management, Papua New Guinea.* Project findings and recommendations. Terminal report FO:DP/PNG/74/033. United Nations Development Programme and Food and Agriculture Organization of the United Nations. Rome.

Neil, P.E. (1984) Climber problems in Solomon Island Forestry. *Commonwealth Forestry Review*, **63**, 27–34

Niall, H. (1968) Target Dates. *New Guinea*, **3**(1), 8–11

Nicholson, D.I. (1979) *The effects of logging and treatment on the mixed Dipterocarp forests of South East Asia.* FO: MISC/79/8 (Draft), FAO, Rome.

Noah, J. (1980) Forest Officer Madang Province, personal communication, December 1980.

Noah, J. (1986) Personal communication, February.

Nye, P.H. and Greenland, D.J. (1960) *The soil under shifting cultivation.* Technical Communication No. 51, Commonwealth Bureau of Soils.

Office of Forests (1979) *Compendium of Statistics.* Office of Forests, Department of Primary Industry, Port Moresby, Papua New Guinea.

Orken, M.B. (1974) 'They fight for fun', In Sack, P. (ed.) *Problem of Choice. Land in Papua New Guinea's Future.* pp. 141–150. (Australian National University Press: Canberra)

Overseas Development Group (1973) *A Report on Development Strategies for Papua New Guinea.* University of East Anglia.

Paglau, M. (1982) Conservation of soil water and forest, In Morauta, L., Pernetta, J. and Heaney, W. (eds), *Traditional Conservation in Papua New Guinea: Implications for Today.* Monograph 16, pp. 115–120. Institute of Applied Social and Economic Research, Pt. Moresby.

Paijman, K. (1976) (ed.) *New Guinea Vegetation.* (Australian National University Press: Canberra)

Pain, C.F. and Bowler, J. (1973) Denudation following the November 1972 earthquake at Madang, Papua New Guinea. *Zeitschuft für Geomorphologie* Suppl. Bd., **18**, 92–104

Palin, D. (1980) *Management of development forestry: a cooperative study of public forestry administrations in the Asia-Pacific Region.* GCP/RAS (SWE), FAO, Rome.

Paliwala, A. (1982) Law and order in the village: the village courts, In Weisbrot, D., Paliwala, A. and Sawyer, A. (eds), *Law and Social Change in Papua New Guinea.* pp. 191–217. (Butterworths: Sydney)

Patric, J.H. (1980) Effect of wood products harvest on forest soil and water relations. *Journal of Environmental Quality*, **9**, 73–80

Petr, T. (1976) Some chemical features of two Papuan fresh waters (Papua New Guinea). *Australian Journal of Marine and Freshwater Research*, **27**, 467–74

Pippett, J.R. (1974) *Report on the faunal survey of the Gogol Area of the Madang timber area, Madang Province.* Unpublished report, Wildlife Section, Department of Agriculture, Stock and Fisheries, Port Moresby.

Powell, J.M. (1976) Ethnobotany, In Paijman, K. (ed.) *New Guinea Vegetation.* pp. 106–183. (Australian National University Press: Canberra)

Powell, J.M. (1982) Traditional management and conservation of vegetation in Papua New Guinea, In Morauta, L., Pernetta, J., Heaney, W. (eds) *Traditional Conservation in Papua New Guinea: Implications for Today.* Monograph 16, pp. 121–134. Institute of Applied Social and Economic Research, Port Moresby.

Powell, J. and Hope, G. (1976) Vegetation history, In Paijman, K. (ed.) *New Guinea Vegetation.* pp. 101–104. (Australian National University Press: Canberra)

Queensland Department of Forestry (1983) Rain forest research in North Queensland. Queensland Department of Forestry, Brisbane.

Raich, J.W. (1980) Fine roots regrow rapidly after forest felling. *Biotropica*, **12**(3), 231–32

Rand, M.C., Greenberg, A.E., Taras, M.J. (eds) (1976) *Standard Methods for the Examination of Water and Waste Water.* American Public Health Association, American Water Works Association, Water Pollution Control Federation, Washington.

Reiner, E. and Mabbut, J.A. (1976) Geomorphology, In Robbins, R.G. (ed.) *Lands of the Ramu-Madang area, Papua New Guinea.* Land Research Series No. 37, pp. 71–78. Commonwealth Scientific and Industrial Research Organisation, Australia.

Richards, P.W. (1979) *The Tropical Rain forest.* (Cambridge University Press)

Richardson, D. (1981) *The progress of Jant – no profit no tax*; *1100 per cent asset increase.* The Times of Papua New Guinea, 13 August 1981.

Richardson, D. (1981) Forestry and the environment in the South Pacific. Topic Review 8. In *Topic Reviews 1981*, South Pacific Regional Environment Programme, South Pacific Commission, Noumea.

Richardson, D. (1977) A faustian dilemma. *Unasylva*, **29**(117), 9–11

Riley, I.D. (1983) Population change and distribution in Papua New Guinea: an epidemiological approach. *Journal of Human Evolution*, **12**, 125–32

Riswan, S., Kenworthy, J. and Kartawinata, K. (1985) The estimation of temporal processes in tropical rain forest: a study of primary mixed dipterocarp forest in Indonesia. *Journal of Tropical Ecology*, **1**, 171–82

Robbins, R.G., Saunders, J.C., Pullen, R. (1976) Vegetation and ecology, In Robbins, R.G. (ed.) *Lands of the Ramu-Madang area, Papua New Guinea.* Land Research Series No. 37, pp. 96–109. Commonwealth Scientific and Industrial Research Organisation, Australia.

Ross, A. (1986) Economics Branch, Department of forests, personal communication. Port Moresby.

Sack, P. (1974) *Problem of Choice: Land in Papua New Guinea's Future.* (Australian National University Press: Canberra)

Saldarriaga, J.G. and West, D.C. (1986) Holocene fires in the northern Amazon basin. *Quarternary Research*, **26**, 358–66

Salo, J., Kalliola, R., Häkkinen, I., Makinen, Y., Niemala, P., Puhakka, M. and Coley, K. (1986) River dynamics and the diversity of the Amazon lowland forest. *Nature*, **322**, 254–58

Sato, J. (1976) Two year 'minus growth' makes industry men pessimistic about quick recovery, In *Industrial Review of Japan* 1976, The Japan Economic Journal, pp. 110–111. Tokyo.

Satoh, K. (1980) General manager of Jant Pty. Ltd., personal communication, 12 December 1980 at Madang.

Saulei, S. (1985) *The recovery of tropical lowland rain forest after clear-fell logging in the Gogol Valley, Papua New Guinea.* Ph.D. thesis, University of Aberdeen.

Saulei, S. (1984) Natural regeneration following clear-fell logging operations in the Gogol Valley, Papua New Guinea. *Ambio*, **13**, 351–54

Saunders, J. (1976) Forest resources, In *Lands of the Ramu-Madang area, Papua New Guinea.* Land Research Series No. 37, pp. 110–125. Commonwealth Scientific and Industrial Research Organisation, Australia.

Seddon, G. (1984) Logging in the Gogol Valley, Papua New Guinea. *Ambio*, **13**, 345–50

250

References

Serjeantsoan, S. (1978) *Preliminary report of health status in the Gogol Valley,* In Background papers, Gogol Valley Project, Man and Biosphere Workshop, pp. 46–51. Madang, 17–20 March 1978.

Seubert, C.E., Sanchez, P.A., Valverde, C. (1977) Effects of land clearing methods on soil properties of an ultisol and crop performance in the Amazon jungle of Peru. *Tropical Agric. (Trinidad),* **54**, 307–21

Shimokawa, E. (1977) Japan's dependence upon woodchips for pulp. *Unasylva,* **29**(115), 26–7

Short, K. (1976) Climate, In Robbins, R.G. (ed.) *Lands of the Ramu-Madang area, Papua New Guinea.* Land Research Series No. 37, pp. 58–70. Commonwealth Scientific and Industrial Research Organisation, Australia.

Simberlorf, D. (1982) Big advantages of small refuges. *Natural History,* **91**(4), 6–14

Sinclair, J. (1981) *Kiap.* (Pacific Publication: Sydney)

Sioli, H. (1968) Hydrochemistry and geology in the Brazilian Amazon region. *Amazonia,* **1**, 267–77

Skelton, D. (1981) *Reforestation in Papua New Guinea.* Paper presented to PNG Office of Forests – CSIRO Pulp and Paper Seminar, Port Moresby, June 1981.

Skelton, D. (1986) Research Officer, Department of Forests, personal communication.

Sopper, W.E. (1975) Effects of timber harvesting and related management practices on water quality in forested watersheds. *Journal of Environmental Quality,* **4**, 24–9

Spencer, M. (1976) Ecological and epidemiological consequences of logging in the Gogol Timber Rights purchase area, In *Ecological Effects of Increasing Human Activities on Tropical and Subtropical Forest Ecosystem.* Australian Unesco Committee for Man and the Biosphere, Publication No. 3. pp. 207–209. (Australian Government Publishing Service: Canberra)

Sricharatchanya, P. (1987) Going against the grain. *Far Eastern Economic Review,* **137**(38), 86–7

Sterba, J.P. (1987) *Malaysian tribe battles to save forest.* Asian Wall Street Journal, 5 August 1987.

Stocker, G.C. (1981) Regeneration of a North Queensland rain forest following felling and burning. *Biotropica,* **13**, 86–92

Symington, C.F. (1933) The study of secondary growth on rain forest sites in Malaya. *Malayan Forester,* **2**, 107–17

Takeuchi, K. (1974) Tropical Hardwood Trade in the Asia Pacific Region. World Bank Staff Occasional Paper No. 17, New York.

Taylor, B.W. (1957) Plant succession on recent volcanoes in Papua. *Journal of Ecology,* **45**, 233–43

Territory of Papua and New Guinea (1968) Programmes and Policies for the Economic Development of Papua and New Guinea. Port Moresby.

Toky, O.P. and Ramakrishan, P.S. (1983) Secondary succession following slash and burn agriculture in north eastern India. II. Nutrient cycling. *Journal of Ecology,* **71**, 747–57

Tua Kaima, Sam (1986) *The failed missions of Yali Singina.* Times of Papua New Guinea, 15 March 1986, p. 9.

Turner, J. and Lambert, M.J. (1986) Effects of forest harvesting nutrient removals on soil nutrient reserves. *Oecologia (Berlin),* **70**, 140–48

Uhl, C. (1982) Recovery following disturbances of different intensities in the Amazon rain forest of Venezuela. *Interciencia,* **7**, 19–24

Uhl, C., Jordan, C., Clark, K., Clark, H., Herrera, R. (1982) Ecosystem recovery in Amazon caatinga forest after cutting, cutting and burning and bulldozer clearing treatments. *Oikos,* **38**, 313–20

Unesco/UNEP/FAO (1978) *Tropical forest ecosystems: a state of knowledge report.* Unesco, Paris.

Van Balgooy (1976) Phytogeography, In Paijman, K. (ed.) *New Guinea Vegetation.* pp. 1–22. (Australian National University Press: Canberra)

Van der Weert, R. and Lenselink, K.J. (1972) The influence of mechanical clearing of forest or some physical and chemical soil properties. *Surinam Agriculture,* **20**, 2–14

Van der Weert, R. (1974) Influence of mechanical forest clearing on soil conditions and the resulting effects on root growth. *Tropical Agriculture (Trinidad),* **51**, 325–31

Vergara, N. (1979) *Soil compaction*. Paper presented at Man and Biosphere Workshop, 17–20 March, Madang, 1978.

Viner, A.B. (1975) The supply of minerals to tropical rivers and lakes (Uganda), In Hasler, A.D. (ed.) *Coupling of Land and Water Systems*. pp. 227–262. (Springer Verlag: Heidelberg)

Viner, A.B. (1979) *The status and transport of nutrients through the Purari River (Papua New Guinea)*. Purari River (Wabo) Hydro Electric Scheme Environmental Studies No. 9, Office of Environment and Conservation and Department of Minerals and Energy, Papua New Guinea.

Vitousek, P.M. and Reiners, W.A. (1975) Ecosystem succession and nutrient retention: a hypothesis. *Bioscience*, **25**, 376–81

Waiko, J. (1977) The people of Papua New Guinea, their forests and their aspirations, In Winslow, J. (ed.) *The Melanesian Environment*. pp. 407–427. (Australian National University Press: Canberra)

Webb, L.C. (1960) Political review. *Australian Quarterly*, **32**, 95–101

Webb, L.J. (1958) Cyclones as an ecological factor in tropical lowland rain forest, north Queensland. *Australian Journal of Botany*, **6**, 220–28

Webb, L.J. (1977) *Ecological considerations and safeguards in the modern use of the tropical lowland rain forests as a source of pulpwood: example, the Madang Area PNG*. Office of Environment and Conservation, Department Natural Resources, Papua New Guinea.

Webb, L.J., Tracey, J.G. and Williams, W.T. (1972) Regeneration and pattern in the subtropical rain forest. *Journal of Ecology*, **60**, 675–95

Weinstein, F.B. (1976) Multinational corporations and the third world: the case of Japan and South East Asia. *International Organisation*, **30**, 373–404

Westman, W. (1985) *Ecology, Impact Assessment and Environmental Planning*. (John Wiley and Sons: New York)

Westoby, M. (1984) *Constructive ecology: how to build and repair ecosystems*. AES Working paper 1/84, Griffith University, Brisbane, Australia.

Whelan, B.R. (1977) *Nutrient levels in the Walsh and Barron Rivers draining agricultural catchments in North Queensland*. Hydrology Symposium, Institution of Engineers, Brisbane, 28–30 June, 1977.

White, A.E. (1975) *Notes on reforestation cost estimates for Eucalyptus deglupta in Papua New Guinea*. Tropical Forest Research Note 23, Department of Forests, Port Moresby.

White, K.J. (1975) *The effect of natural phenomena on the forest environment*. Presidential address to the Papua New Guinea Scientific Society, Department of Forests, Papua New Guinea.

White, K.J. (1976a) *Australian forest policy in the Territory of Papua and New Guinea*. Presidential address to Papua New Guinea Scientific Society, Port Moresby.

White, K.J. (1976b) *Notes on enrichment planting in lowland rainforests of Papua New Guinea*. Tropical Forest Research Note 31, Office of Forests, Papua New Guinea.

White, K.J. (1976c) *Lowland rain forest regeneration in Papua New Guinea with reference to the Vanimo sub-province*. Tropical Forest Research Note 32, Office of Forests, Papua New Guinea.

Whitmore, T.C. (1975, 1984) *Tropical Forests of the Far East*. (Clarendon Press: Oxford)

Whitmore, T.C. (1974) *Changes with time and the role of cyclones in tropical rain forest on Kolombangara, Solomon Islands*. Commonwealth Forestry Institute, Paper 46.

Whyte, I.N. (1975) *Land classification and mapping for reforestation planning in the Gogol Valley Timber Area*, Papua New Guinea. Unpublished manuscript, Department of Forests, Papua New Guinea.

Whyte, I.N. (1977) *Results of a regeneration survey in the Gogol*. Presented at PNG Botanical Society meeting, Bulolo, May 1977.

Williams, J. and Hamilton, L.S. (1982) *Watershed forest influences in the tropics and subtropics: a selected annotated bibliography*. East-West Environment and Policy Institute, East West Center, Hawaii.

Wilson, W.L. and Wilson, C.C. (1975) The influence of selective logging on primates and some other animals in East Kalimantan. *Folia Primatologica*, **23**, 245–74

Wirawan, Nengah (1984) *Good forest within the burned forest area in East Kalimantan*. World Wildlife Fund Report, WWF Project 1687, Bogor, Indonesia.

Womersley, J. (1983) Former Director, PNG Herbarium, Lae, personal communication.

World Bank (1976) *Papua New Guinea: its economic situation and prospects for development.* World Bank, Washington.

Wright, J. (1987) *Why Levers walked out of the forest.* Pacific Islands Monthly pp. 25–27, January 1987.

Wyatt-Smith, J. (1954) Storm forest in Kelantan. *Malayan Forester,* **17**, 5–11

Yauieb, A. (1978) *Complete integrated utilization of tropical forests – Papua New Guinea's experience.* FID II/20-2, Eighth World Forestry Congress, Jakarta, October 1978.

Z'graggen, J.A. (1975) *Languages of the Madang District, Papua New Guinea.* Pacific Linguistics, Series B No. 41, Australian National University, Canberra.

INDEX

ecological research programme, 27
ecological theory, 143
economic,
    changes, 64
    resource loss, 181
economy, 5
ecosystem response forecast, 143
Eight Aims, 190
employment, 167–169
    managerial, 169
    preferential, 168
    statistics, 168
enrichment planting, 91
environmental, conditions, 218–219
    control, 102–104
    damage, 26
    erosion, 50, 102
    impact assessment, 144
    logging patterns, 102–104
    protection, 76
Eucalyptus, 35, 91, 118, 141, 172, 216, 217
Europeans, 60
events, summary of, 227–230

Far North Coast Block, 88
fast growing species, 35, 73
field operations, 102–104
fires, 20, 50
Five Year Plan, 28–30, 227
floristic recovery, 157
flow-on payments, 165
forest area, 22, 23, 28
    classification, 28
    commercial use, 26–31
    development, 29
    exploitation, 31
    industry, 193
    policy, 27, 30, 205–208
    resources, 22–23, 215–218
    traditional use, 23–26
    types, 47–48
Forestry Department, 26

gardening, 62, 160
geography, 2–6
Gogol Reforestation Company, 94, 195
Gogol Timber Project, 41, 69
Gogol Timber Rights purchase areas, 43
Gogol Valley,
    background, 41
    climate, 41
    geology, 45–46
    geomorphology, 45–46
    topographic classes, 46
Government,
    objectives, 194, 195
    payments, 191
    view, 189–196

health, 61–62, 180
Honshu Paper Co. Ltd., 69
    economics, 199
    sales and earnings, 200
human inhabitants, 56–62
hydrological research, 129

imports, 11
Indonesia, 30, 228
information, 177–179
infrastructure, 37, 72
integrated industry, 72
investment, 16–17
    Australian, 16
    Japanese, 16
    guidelines, 239–242

Jant, 69, 74, 229
    accumulated losses, 192
    and Wewak, initial activities, 76–80
    balance sheet, 198
    construction programme, 78–79
    operating profit, 192
    operation status, 79
    patrol, 178
    project view, 197–201
    public image, 179
    reforestation delay, 199
Japanese consortium, 69
    investment, 16, 38, 197–199
    pulp and paper industry, 199
    Wewak agreement, 70

land, 15–16
Land Bills, 76, 228
land disputes, 7
    leader, 59
    leasing, 76, 216
land ownership, 3, 34, 56, 75, 84, 95, 165,
    215, 217
    and Government, 177, 178
    project views, 197
land suitability matrix, 82
land-use, 80–96
    actual pattern, 90
    cattle, 90
    enrichment planting, 91
    final plan, 86
    plantation, 84, 91–92
    post-logging, 87
    reserves, 90
languages, 57
learning experience, 87
log,
    optimum use, 72
    production, 31
    volume, 32
logging,

reforestation, 75, 89–95, 216
  planning, 81
regeneration,
  modes, 111, 114
  natural, 33–34, 116 (*see also* under
    regrowth)
  of secondary species, 111, 114
  of species richness, 112, 116
  processes, 144, 152
regrowth, number of plant species,
  111–113
regrowth observations, 155
  secondary species, 111
  studies, 109
  survey, 110–111
  tree density, 112, 115
religion, 59
research, cover crops, 93
  plantation species, 93
  trials, 93
reserves, 83, 86, 88, 90, 96, 160
resource degradation, 25
  surveys, 27
  use, 62–63
  value, 72
road construction, 78–79
  development, 169, 196, 213
  system, 64, 71, 229
rock types, 46
root systems, 141
royalties, 164–169, 212
royalty payments, 167, 168, 196

salvage logging, 173–174
secondary tree species, 22, 111, 114
seed dispersal modes, 146, 235–238
  by birds and bats, 147, 150
  by frugivores, 150
  by other animals, 152
  by wind, 147, 149
seedling pool, 145
self-government, 10–12, 229
silvicultural problems, 31–35
  systems, 32
social diversity, 184
  impacts, 163
  structure, 58
  unrest, 12–15
    Bougainville, 13
    Gazelle Peninsula, 14
    Papua, 14
socio-economics, 212–215
soil, 52–55
  compaction, 142
soil moisture storage, 45
  nutrient concentrations in, 54
  physical properties, 142–143
  seed store, 145

watertable, 142
species diversity, 36
  richness, 113, 116, 123
spiritual beliefs, 59
squatters, 159
stores, 175
streamwater chemistry, 135
  nutrient concentrations, 137
subsistence agriculture, 24
  base, 23
sub-tropical rain forest, 158

timber,
  estimated standing volume, 52
  production, 30
  project, agreement, 72–76
    negotiations, 69–72
  resources, 51–52
  rights purchase (TRP), 27, 30, 34, 41, 42,
    52, 64, 227–230
  royalties, 168
  survey, 22, 51
time for recovery, 154, 159
Tolai, 14, 227
topographic features, 2
tractor use, 87–88
traditional resource use, 23–26, 62–63
training programmes, 78
Trans-Gogol Local Government Council,
  184, 230
transport, 175
trapping animals, 118, 119
tree farm, 36, 171–173
  Eucalyptus, 172
  genera composition, 53

understorey birds, 124–128
utilization problems, 35–37

vegetation, 5, 47–49
  distribution, 48
  initial effects of logging, 108–116
vegetation, total species complement,
  111–113
vegetative regrowth, 146
veneer, 30, 72, 89
village court, 182
  incomes, 180
  life, 179–181
  reserves, 90
volcanoes, 4, 49, 50
  disturbance by, 157
  successional development after, 157
volume of closed broadleaved forests, 36

water balance model, 43
  peak discharge changes, 130
  quality, 131